# THE REALMS OF GOLD

ALSO BY RAY VICKER

*The Kingdom of Oil*
*Those Swiss Money Men*

# THE
# REALMS
# OF
# GOLD

*Ray Vicker*

**CHARLES SCRIBNER'S SONS** • *New York*

Library of Congress Cataloging in Publication Data

Vicker, Ray.
   The realms of gold.

   1. Gold—History. I. Title.
HG289.V52     553′.41     75–2364
ISBN 0–684–14269–4

1 3 5 7 9 11 13 15 17 19 H/C 20 18 16 14 12 10 8 6 4 2

Printed in the United States of America

# CONTENTS

# THE REALMS OF GOLD

# CHAPTER I

# The Royal Metal

On Tuesday, July 1, 1969, two hundred fifty thousand people jammed narrow streets of Caernarvon, Wales, a British town surrounded by a corset of medieval walls. People gaped expectantly at Caernarvon Castle's square towers and crenelated battlements as they good-naturedly jostled for positions on streets or perched on rooftops with binoculars. Within the film-set grounds of that castle a prince was to be crowned with all the golden appurtenances of office.

Gold and royalty are mated in the halls of regalia, partners in that kingly task of dazzling multitudes for the good of the crown and the subservience of peoples. Since the dawn of time, gold has awed commoners as they beheld it on royalty, the metal gleaming and shining as if sovereigns possessed some inner heavenly glow which occasionally betrayed its radiance. Today, the British monarchy well understands the public and personal relations value of golden pageantry to maintain the crown and all of its appurtenances in the United Kingdom.

On this day, the crowd overwhelmingly wished long life for the queen. But wishing is not enough in this violent age when bloody political protests are sometimes viewed as a natural right, as if the majority had no rights of its own. Police helicopters hovered overhead, blades thrashing. Blue uniforms mingled with the throng. Welsh nationalists had threatened to disrupt ceremonies. Police meant to accept no nonsense.

Four thousand guests had been invited within the stout walls of the castle to witness the investiture of Prince Charles as Prince of Wales. A new specially designed gold crown waited under guard with other gold artifacts for the ceremony. So careful is the watch over Britain's crown jewels that these valuables aren't even insured.

The British monarch has three gold crowns to wear at appropriate occasions: the Crown of St. Edward, which is the official coronation crown, the Imperial State Crown, made for Queen Victoria in 1838, and the Imperial Crown of India. The latter crown was made for George V when he was crowned emperor of India in 1911 in Delhi.

All the crowns, when not in use, are kept in the Tower of London, that grim one-time palace and prison which sits beside the Thames in east London. Here you can see them and a brilliant assortment of other crown jewels almost any day of the week, though in summer you may have to wait for two hours in a long queue before reaching the strongroom, where the jewels are displayed behind thick glass.

On this investiture day, the queen wasn't wearing any crown, for the occasion didn't call for it. This didn't lessen the eagerness of the crowd for a glimpse of her.

Shortly after 2:00 P.M., cheers of the two hundred fifty thousand people in the town warned that the queen was approaching. Visitors could tell her location by the way the cheers rippled through the narrow streets, as if the sound were riding on a track with the queen's open landau. An escort of mounted cavalry led the way, cuirasses glistening in the sun which was again peeking between dark clouds. Liveried footmen walked beside the vehicle, stiff and formal, as only British lackeys can be when royalty secretes some of its authority onto servitors.

A blast of trumpets preceded the queen's entrance into the castle. Then, the walls resounded to "God Save the Queen" as she stood stiffly beside her throne. On this particular day, the queen of England would follow an ancient custom of placing a gold crown upon a royal head to signify a regal transition. Always gold, for this is the royal metal.

An audible sigh escaped from the assembled guests when the queen seated herself on her throne. A thousand years ago, on Whitsunday in 973, Edgar was crowned first king of all England in the Saxon abbey of Bath. This slender woman on the throne of England represented that millennium for nearly everyone here. She was more than a person; she was a symbol.

The prince marched onto the stage at the queen's royal summons. He bowed three times to her, knelt on a cushion before the throne. The queen girted him with a sword, placed a gold coronet on his head, slipped a gold ring onto his finger, then delivered a gold rod into his hands.

For all the thousands of kings who have ruled big and little kingdoms through history, only a comparative handful of royal crowns now remain. England's King Edward II possessed ten crowns. Not one is known to exist today. If a king lost power, his crown was soon melted down, either to mint coins or bars, or to make a new crown for the successor.

Often kings hocked crowns to raise money for various wars or adventures. .England's Henry IV had an expensive crown made which he lovingly called "The Great Harry." His son, Henry V, pawned it to raise money for his wars with France. King Edward III obtained a loan of twenty-five hundred pounds sterling from merchants of Cologne, the Rhine River port, giving the queen's crown as security. History—that narrator of incomplete fact and fiction—doesn't say what the queen thought about that, though she must have had the affection of her people in her bareheaded state. When the king couldn't repay the debt, his subjects redeemed the crown by shipping thirty thousand packs of wool to Cologne.

Obviously, gold in any form provides good security for a loan, especially where a kingly promise is involved. But pawned crowns had short lives, which reminds us that a useless life is an early death. A merchant had little use for a crown as a crown. He might have many uses for the gold it contained. Thus, gold has a way of returning to its bullion state, as if magnetic forces are continually pressing upon the artifacts created from it.

And, of course, accidents took their toll of crown jewels, too. It was in 1216 that King John was on the march across the sand flats beside The Wash, the bay which divides Lincolnshire from Norfolk. The tide was out when the king's party started across, accompanied by the royal baggage train, which carried the king's crown and his personal jewelry. The group had tarried too long. Before high ground could be reached, a tidal wave swept the train away.

The king escaped, but he lost his crowns, his gold bullion, and his precious stones. Ever since, treasure hunters have searched the bay area, hoping for clues which might lead to the location of this kingly wealth.

Buried treasure is almost synonymous with gold, whether the treasure is buried by the sea or under tons of earth. Every society has its tale of great wealth in the form of Spanish gold doubloons, of lost crown jewels, or of a lost, superrich gold mine.

The gold of royalty sometimes figures in finds of buried treasure, too. Such luck favored the peasants who paused for a rest near Toledo, Spain, in 1858. One of them caught the gleam of metal beneath the grass beside the road. Idly he turned over a clod of dirt, found himself staring at several gold crowns.

The peasants sold the lot to a merchant who smuggled the find to Paris. This Treasure of Guarrazar, as it is called, was sold to the Museum de Cluny. It consists of eleven crowns of pure gold, some set with precious stones. One is lettered with the name of its one-time owner, King Suinthila, 621–631 A.D.

During the Dark Ages, that period which followed the Fall of Rome, kings hung votive crowns before altars of coronation churches. When Toledo, the Spanish city, fell to the Moors in the eighth century, twenty-five kingly diadems hung before the high altar of the cathedral. Arabic documents say these were: "beautifully ornamented with jewels, one crown for each of the kings who had ruled over the country."

Arabic records do not say what happened to those crowns. The Treasure of Guarrazar came from that cathedral, perhaps stolen by some hapless Spanish priest who was trying to rescue the hoard from the Moslems. In any case, less than half of the treasure has been found. Perhaps other crowns still lie under Spanish soil waiting for finders. Perhaps, too, those crowns were melted long ago.

One of the oldest crowns in existence is that of the Lombards who once ruled in northern Italy. Last to wear this crown was Queen Theodelinda, who died in 627. This ancient relic now is in the Cathedral of Monza in the town of that name near Milan. It is a simple crown of sheet gold laid on each side of a ring of iron. Legend says that this iron was from a nail in the True Cross of Christ. Whether true or not, the band of iron does emphasize how Christian kings aligned their thrones with Christianity and stressed the Divine Right of Kings. Kings were kings by grace of God, this doctrine claimed, and common men risked the wrath of God by opposing the will of a king.

Once a king died his golden wealth seldom remained undisturbed for very long. After his death in the ninth century, the Emperor Charlemagne was buried like a pharaoh of old Egypt with his golden artifacts. His body was embalmed and seated on a throne of gold, clothed in imperial robes, a sword at his side with hilt and scabbard of gold. A sceptre and shield of gold hung on the tomb wall. A gold chain to which was fastened an alleged relic of the True Cross was wound around his head.

Those treasures are long gone, melted down to provide cash for men who could see more uses for gold in the world of the living than in a tomb of the dead. Today, only the crown of Charlemagne remains, the same crown used at his coronation on the feast of the Nativity in 800 A.D. It rests in a museum in Vienna, Austria.

While the first trinkets and amulets of gold probably were hammered into shapes from original nuggets, the crown the Prince of Wales wears today was created by electroforming. This is a process by which the gold is suspended in an acid solution and made to "grow" into a mold. This comparatively new process permits designers to create bulky pieces with little weight. Prince Charles' crown weighs only three pounds versus nine or more pounds for a conventionally made crown.

Such a reduction of weight is important. Gold is a heavy metal, too heavy to rest comfortably upon anyone's head as a crown. If there is a single ailment identified with royalty, it is the simple headache. If a crown doesn't fit the head, it may rest on the forehead, and that is enough to give anyone a headache in minutes.

The coronation crown of British monarchs weighs 5 pounds, 2¼ ounces. But when Queen Elizabeth wore it in 1953 for her coronation, the crown had an inner, adjustable lining like that in a crash helmet, spreading the weight smoothly over her head. In the old days, crown makers weren't so ingenious. Many a kingly rage might have been due only to the headache resulting from a poorly fitting, heavy crown.

No matter how gold is manufactured, it remains a treasured metal, prized by kings, sought by adventurers, and held by wealthy folk who distrust paper currencies. In recent years, gold has been more prized than ever simply because some of those paper currencies, including the United States dollar, have been losing value steadily due to the eroding effects of inflation. As the dollar's value has declined, gold's value has risen.

An ounce of gold that was worth $35 in 1968 was worth $198 in December, 1974. Today, many people think that gold or gold equity shares are better to hold than dollars as a store of value. They know that gold held worth long before the dollar appeared on the scene and that the yellow metal probably will be around long after the dollar has been superceded by something else.

Gold is the first metal mentioned in the Bible. The land next to Eden is "Havilah, where there is gold," says that book. Numerous other references to gold are found in the Holy Book. The Book of Genesis says that Abraham was very rich not only in cattle but in silver and gold. In the Book of Exodus, the sacred vessels of the Jewish tabernacle are listed: the ark, or reliquary made to hold the sacred commandments, the altar, the rod of Aaron, and the seven-branched candlestick which contained a talent of pure gold.

At present prices for gold, that candlestick would be worth $150,000 for its metal content alone. The biblical goldsmiths Bezaleel and Oholiab allegedly fashioned this candlestick under the direction of Moses, who followed a pattern he had seen in a vision. We know what that candlestick looked like, for when the Romans destroyed the Temple of Jerusalem, they seized all the treasures in it, including that candlestick. When Titus, the conquering general and later emperor of Rome, erected his arch in the capital to commemorate his victories, his stonemasons sculptured a reproduction of that candlestick on the inside of the structure. The arch still stands in the old Roman Forum at the head of the Sacred Way beneath the bluff of Palatine Hill in Rome.

The candlestick itself probably reposed in one of the pagan temples of Rome for centuries. One story says the Emperor Maxentius (306–312 A.D.) carried it away with other loot when fleeing the city from his enemies. When he found himself too weighted down for flight, he tossed the candlestick and other gold objects into the Tiber at the Molle bridge. There it still reposes, according to this tale, and since gold is indestructible its beauty is unchanged.

But Gibbon, the historian, has a different story. He says that somehow the candlestick found its way to Carthage in North Africa. It was part of the loot seized by the Byzantine emperor Belisarius when his forces added North Africa to the empire in 534 A.D. He deposited it in a Christian church in Jerusalem where it served for nearly two centuries. Then, in the year 614, Jerusalem was captured and sacked by the Persian king Chosroes. Nothing has been heard of that candlestick since, so it probably was melted down long ago.

Gold has always been desired by men and women, and desire often outruns capacity to earn. No other metal awakens quite the same response in the human mind: an emotion which verges upon the irrational when desire is allowed to feed upon itself. Men kill for gold. They cheat and lie for it.

Pygmalion, the king of Thrace, murdered his brother-in-law for gold. The daughter of Spurius Tarpeius, the Roman nobleman, was bribed with gold to admit the Sabines into the citadel of Rome. Marcus Crassus (115–53 B.C.), the Roman general, invaded Parthia to seize its golden treasure. His army of eleven legions was overwhelmed and Crassus fell. The victorious Parthian king ordered some gold to be melted immediately, and the molten metal was poured down the throat of the Roman general.

"Thou has thirsted for gold, therefore drink gold," the Parthian commander said as he stood over Crassus.

Today, antigold lobbyists point to such tales and claim that gold is inherently evil. Actually, gold is merely a beautiful metal, neither deeply evil, nor especially saintly. It is man, not metal, which sins or merits heaven. The commodities which men cherish are merely the reflections of human personalities, lifeless materials which acquire value through the desire focused upon them. If man and his markets had not ennobled gold, then some other metal or commodity might have been selected to play the same role, lumps of coal if such were scarce, or cowrie shells, as indeed was the case early in man's history.

"I marry one with gold and treasure," goes a line in a Danish ballad of medieval times. A Danish chronicle reports that "a dowry of 100,000 Rhine guilders" was not unusual in the foremost marriages of the sixteenth century.

In Renaissance times, even poor maidens sometimes found themselves in need of gold. In Denmark, for instance, it became the custom to adorn a bride with great splendor on her wedding day. Girls who could not afford purchase of such adornments had to rent them. And a gold bridal brooch was considered the most necessary part of the bride's trousseau.

In 1557, Queen Dorothea came to the rescue of the poor girls of Copenhagen. She had a special brooch, six inches long, made as a gift to the females of her land. This was kept in the town hall and loaned to brides who couldn't afford such a piece on wedding days.

Herbert C. Hoover, America's thirty-first president, must have also been intrigued by the way men pine for gold. Not only was he a mining engineer in early life, but he also was somewhat of a scholar. It was he who translated a sixteenth-century text about gold from the original Latin. The translation, published in a slender volume in 1912, was of the treatise *De Re Metallica*, written by Agricola, a noted metallurgist of his time. He had assembled numerous quotes and reports about gold from ancient writings, providing us with glimpses of how the ancients viewed this monetary metal. For instance, there is Aristodemus, the Spartan, revealing too much about his character when he says: "Money makes the man; no one who is poor is either good or honored."

Almost the same view came from Timocles, another Greek

philosopher, who said: "Money is the life and soul of mortal men. He who has not heaped up riches for himself wanders like a dead man amongst the living." In the Greek world, money usually was in the form of gold and silver.

Propertius, another Greek writer, wrote: "This is indeed the golden age. The greatest rewards come from gold. By gold, love is won; by gold, faith is destroyed; by gold, justice is bought."

The lust for gold led Pizarro to the empire of the Incas in what is now Peru. His prospects looked bleak when he landed on the beaches of Tumbez in 1531 with two hundred foot soldiers and a hundred horsemen. The mighty Andes barred his way to the Inca capital. Atahualpa, the Inca ruler who had just seized power in a bloody civil war, had an army of thirty thousand to fifty thousand men.

But Spaniards knew that the Incas possessed gold, gold in quantities undreamed of in old Castile. Pizarro dazzled his men with visions of all that gold lying in the Inca cities waiting to be seized by brave and hardy men. Untold wealth soon would be theirs, he assured anyone who seemed to be faltering.

The Spaniards seemed to be entering a trap when the party, armor clanking, banners raised, marched into the city of Cajamarca. Mountains ringed the plain on which the city sat; a mighty Incan army camped beyond the ramparts. The city itself was deserted, as if it might be the jaws of the trap.

Pizarro placed his handful of men in defensive positions, then boldly dispatched messengers, seeking a meeting with the Inca ruler. An unsuspecting Atahualpa entered the city with several thousand warriors in bright cotton tunics. Slaves with brooms of thatch swept pavements in advance of the Sun King's gaily feathered litter. A hundred musicians played pipes and drums. Dancing girls cavorted beside the procession. At a signal, a canon boomed. Spaniards leveled muskets, fired at point-blank range. Inca warriors fell right and left. Few even tried to fight against these strange white men who could persuade the gods to hurl lightning through their sticks. In the wild melee, two thousand Inca warriors died, while only one Spaniard was wounded. Atahualpa, the mighty Sun King, was taken prisoner, told that he would regain his freedom if he filled a room with gold.

The Sun King bowed his head in acceptance.

So the word went around the empire, carried by the *chaskis* from Quito to the shores of Lake Titicaca: bring gold to Cajamarca. Trains of porters and of llamas converged on the town carrying gold vases, bowls, votive figures, plate, artifacts. Perhaps never in history was so much of the goldsmith's art gathered together in one place. But Pizarro, a crude soldier, saw only gold, not the exquisite workmanship of the pieces which jammed the collection room.

Indian workmen were drafted to build clay furnaces. Then the gold was melted down into gleaming bars, in one of the greatest rapes of artistic treasures ever perpetrated anywhere. More than six tons of gold artifacts, representing centuries of Incan culture, were destroyed. At present prices the gold content alone would be worth around $40 million. As intact treasures for sale to museums those artistic pieces probably would be worth hundreds of millions. Yet this was only the start of the loot waiting for the Spaniards.

Atahualpa had kept his side of the bargain—a roomful of gold for his life. But after Spaniards had melted down the treasure, they callously forgot about that deal. The Sun King was strangled in a public execution in the town square of Cajamarca. The demands of honor and the lust for gold often conflict and lie in precarious balance on the scales of human conduct.

Englishmen, too, had that lust for gold. Britain's first "foreign investment" was the outfitting of an expedition in Queen Elizabeth I's reign to seize part of the gold fleet of Spain on the high seas.

Sir Francis Drake had the blessing of the queen when he raised funds from the public and sailed on *The Golden Hind* for the Spanish Main. He sailed for the glory of England. He returned a hero, holds laden with gold and treasures estimated at that time as worth between £300,000 to £1,500,000. Shareholders received a dividend of 4,700 percent on their investments. John Maynard Keynes, the British economist who helped shape the Bretton Woods monetary agreement in 1944, wryly wrote that Drake's voyage "may fairly be considered the fountain and origin of British foreign investment."

There is irony, too, in the fact that gold assisted the Russian revolution of 1917. Lenin, the apostle of that revolution, had shown contempt for gold in his writings. He predicted that when communism established its socialistic utopia gold would become so worthless that it would be used in lavatories.

It didn't take long after the revolution started for him to become convinced that gold still had a part to play. The civil war between the Red government and the White armies of anticommunists dragged on, and the government's paper currencies depreciated.

However, the Red government had seized gold reserves of about 164 million ounces in the Russian State Bank. No lavatories were built with those reserves. Instead, the government carefully managed that gold to purchase vital supplies and ammunition.

For safety's sake, the gold was loaded into thirteen boxcars and transported to Kazan, on the Volga River east of Moscow. In August, 1918, Admiral Kolchak, one of the White leaders, swept into Kazan in a sudden thrust, capturing the trainload of gold. The victory at first seemed to be a mortal blow to the Red Army. By peculiar quirks of fate defeat is sometimes transformed into victory; and so it was insofar as Reds were concerned.

The gold became a useless weight to the White Army. Russia was a land of few roads, with limitless forests and steppes stretching to the horizons. A mounted army could drive across fields, with cavalry making its own paths. Trucks heavily laden with gold could not. So, as the White Army departed from Kazan it had a choice to make, stick to the railroad line with the gold, or abandon the gold to achieve greater mobility.

Admiral Kolchak decided that the gold was too valuable to abandon. He stuck to the railroad and lost all flexibility of movement. The line across Siberia ran eastward into hostile territory. Doggedly, he held to the rail line, protecting his trainload of gold. Communist forces used their greater mobility to whittle away at the White Army, finally trapping the Kolchak corps on the frozen wastes of Siberia. The Admiral was captured and executed. The gold-train was recaptured, two-thirds of its valuable cargo still intact.

Some historians aver that the history of the Soviet Union might have been much different had not Admiral Kolchak succumbed to the lure of gold at a time when he should have been more concerned about the position and mobility of his forces.

Yet, despite all evidence of gold's ability to excite passions and ruin judgment, I was once pleased to discover a small corner of the earth where men seemed able to live with an awesome collection of golden treasure without detriment to their values, their perspective, or their sense of humor.

I visited the crown jewels of Ethiopia, which is quite a contrast to visiting those on display in London, Vienna, or Moscow. Ethiopia, of course, has a long imperial history. In fact, the ex-Emperor Haile Selassie claimed direct descent from the Queen of Sheba, that same queen who paid an amorous visit to the biblical King Solomon in Jerusalem. As her good-will offering, she presented him with one hundred and twenty talents of gold, two hundred shields containing six hundred shekels of gold and three hundred shields of silver, enough to turn the head of even a rich king.

There seems to be an element of exaggeration here which should be noted, then marked "believe it or not." A few years ago when gold was selling at $35 an ounce, some historians estimated that a biblical talent of gold would be worth nearly $30,000, provided that it were twenty-four carats fine gold. But to put that in today's perspective, consider that the free market price of gold has climbed by five times since that estimate was made. So she brings him 120 talents in gold as a gift! That would be about $18 million worth of the most liquid commodity known, enough to stamp King Solomon as one of the most successful gigolos of all time.

The king might have been pardoned for asking her what her intentions were. Solomon, no quibbler over details, simply responded by inviting her to bed. And this is how the imperial Ethiopian line was established, or so said Ethiopian court legend.

In any case, Ethiopia, or Abyssinia as it sometimes was known, was so remote from the tides of history that for most of its existence Europeans and Moslems have left it alone. It was Christianized very early by missionaries of the Coptic Church and it existed as a kingdom almost untouched by the drift and flow of western civilization. To Europeans during the Middle Ages, it was the mythical kingdom of Prester John, where streets were paved with gold and where a dusky people practiced Christianity in high mountain retreats while surrounded by lowland heathens.

A few years ago I met the Emperor Haile Selassie in his Addis Ababa office in the Menelik Palace, which is more a cluster of buildings within a compound than the typical western idea of a palace. During the course of the interview I expressed interest in Ethiopia's history and in the crown jewels, which I had heard were kept in Axum, the holy city of the Ethiopian Coptic Church in the mountain fastness to the north.

"You must visit Axum," he said, graciously, "and you must see the crowns of my ancestors."

So, Margaret, my wife, and I found ourselves in Axum, with its curious obelisks, its thatch-hut *tukuls*, or houses, around which goats forage, and its resplendent Coptic churches where some colorful service is likely to be underway on almost any given day. Legend says this was the Queen of Sheba's capital, that she returned here after her tryst with King Solomon to give birth to a son who became King Menelik I.

Between the copper-domed New Cathedral and the old Church of St. Mary's is a small, green-domed chapel which sits by itself on the grounds of the two much grander churches. Entry is via the gate to the Church of St. Mary's. The ground is considered so holy that no woman is allowed to enter the fenced-in compound which surrounds the Church.

Our guide held up a hand, stopping Margaret when she sought to follow me through that gate. "No women," he said.

Through signs and a few words of English, he let us know that she had to walk completely around the fenced-in area to the back of the church and its satellite chapel. He nodded his head vigorously and said: "You see crowns. Many crowns."

Rather dubiously, Margaret departed by herself to find the rear of the church via the rutted and dusty roadway. I entered the compound with the government official, a young man with a tuft of beard, jodhpurs, and a fly whisk, which he used to flail the air briskly every few moments. Fortunately, the flies liked him better than me, so he had need of the whisk.

The crown jewels are kept in a dusty room of the small chapel in glass cases akin to those you might have found in a country store of three decades ago. Crown after crown in pure gold, decorated with jewels, were casually scattered in those cases as if they might have been paper helmets and caps offered for sale just before New Years'. A bearded, black-robed monk with a flat hat sat on a three legged stool in a corner, reading aloud from a prayer book, his head nodding in cadence with the rhythmic chant of the prayer.

The crowns were more like helmets than like the metal rings which Europeans know as royal diadems. Each crown was a lacework of gold filigree, woven into intricate shapes, with spangles and tiny bells hanging like earrings at various places. Unpolished rubies, sapphires, emeralds, and diamonds attracted the little light which filtered into the room.

The crown collection was started by King Fasilas (crowned 1632), and allegedly contains the crown of every king and emperor since, including that of Haile Selassie. With scarcely a glance at the monk-guard, my guide opened one of the cases, and removed a magnificent crown which seemed to be sheathed in diamonds set in gold. "This," said he, "is the crown of Haile Selassie. It is worth two million dollars."

He passed it across the glass counter to me, and I almost dropped it through the glass case, for my hand wasn't prepared for the weight of it. I held the crown in my hands for a few moments, turned it around to study several of the stones and the intricate gold work. I had never held two million dollars in my hands before in any shape or form.

Then I thought of Margaret, forlornly standing outside somewhere. "What of Madam?" I asked. "How can she see these?"

My guide said something to the black-robed monk. He arose, disappeared through a back door which led into a sunlit court where green grass flourished. A barred fence enclosed the court and I could see Margaret standing there, face pressed against the bars, probably thinking that I had forgotten her. With the monk's help, my guide and I moved a long table into the bright sunlight directly in front of the fence. The monk spread a red velvet cloth onto that table. Then, he and the guide started carrying crowns one at a time from the chapel "strongroom" to the table, placing them literally under Margaret's nose.

The crowns might have been dime-store jewelry, for the careless manner in which they were handled. Another monk appeared from somewhere to watch the exercise, and he made a humorous attempt to put the crown of King Teodor onto my head.

Light conditions, of course, were perfect for color pictures. I had a 16-millimeter movie camera with me and the monks graciously held and turned various crowns as I took pictures, Margaret straining her neck in the background.

"Very valuable," one of the monks said to me, and I agreed until I gathered that he was referring to my Bell & Howell 70D movie camera.

CHAPTER II

# Gold's Characteristics

The National Museum of Iraq in Baghdad is housed in a neo-Babylonian structure which looks like a Sumerian palace set beside a busy traffic circle. Inside, one expects to find a record of Sumerian history, but one finds something else, too: exhibits of Stone Age cultures which existed in Mesopotamia long before the Iron Age or the Bronze Age.

In one exhibit several bracelets and necklaces gleam in golden magnificence among the static collection of flint and obsidian tools which record backwardness by the standards of our smug technological age. Stone Age men with gold? Yes, before any other metal was known, for gold is the first metal which man saw, the first that he learned how to fashion. It is a metal which may be hammered into ornamental shapes in its natural state, without remelting. Even Stone Age man could fashion bracelets to signify rank, and necklaces which might contain amulets to ward off evil.

Gold is a scarce metal. There never seems to be enough to go around, always more seekers than finders. Scarcity guarantees that the demand keeps the price high. If you gathered together all of the gold that has been mined since the dawn of time, you would have about eighty thousand metric tons of it. Piled in gold bricks, this would make a cube with sides of a little over fifty feet square, and that cube would fit easily within lines of a baseball diamond.

The metal is virtually indestructible, a quality which must have impressed ancient man at a time when life seemed very fragile. Gold is almost impervious to acids, to corrosion, and to the calamities which affect other materials. Thus, nearly every ounce which was ever found or mined still is around somewhere. Some of it may be at the bottom of the sea, in shipwrecks of long ago. It lies there, waiting to be found again, unaffected by the salt water.

Obviously much gold has been melted over and over again through the centuries. So if you have a gold ring, watch, or brooch, reflect that the gold in it may have been part of the death mask of a pharaoh eons ago. That mask might have gone into the melting pot of a tomb robber to appear again as coins at the court of King Solomon, only to be remelted to become the drinking cup of a Roman. And who knows? The gold in that ring may again be in the crown of a king two thousand years from now, if kings still are around.

Gold is forever.

Even the granite temples of Karnak in Egypt are so weathered by time after four thousand years that imagination is necessary to recreate them in minds of beholders. Not so with the mask of Tutankhamen, the boy pharaoh, which was found across the broad Nile from Karnak with other gold artifacts in a tomb of the Valley of the Kings. After being buried for over thirty-three hundred years, that gold mask and other gold ornaments gleam as brightly as they did on the distant day when King Tut was laid to rest with his gold shrine, his sandals, his calcite drinking cup, his jewelry, and his furnishings, all guarded by the doglike form of Anubis, the guardian of the necropolis.

Because of its durability and the worth packed into a small size, gold makes a convenient monetary metal. Over the centuries, more than 160 substances, animal, mineral and vegetable, have been used for money. None performed the function as well as gold through most of recorded history. Legend says the first gold coins were struck by King Croesus of Lydia about 550 B.C. Archaeological studies indicate that King Gyges of Lydia actually may have preceded King Croesus as a minter of coins by over a 100 years. In any case, the ancient world liked the convenience of gold coins.

Gold remains in monetary use as a store of value in reserves to this day, though many nations, including the United States, no longer mint coins. In fact, the United States didn't even allow its citizens to hold gold from January, 1934 until January 1, 1975. Gold's role in coinage has been steadily reduced because there isn't enough gold in this world for it.

The future role of gold in the monetary system must be determined by international monetary experts who are seeking to revamp the monetary system. The high free-market price, however, indicates that a lot of people in this world believe that gold still has a role to play in the monetary sphere, and at a much higher price than the $42.22 which the United States established on February 10, 1973.

Gold's characteristics, of course, have much to do with the position it occupies in the affairs of men. It is one of the heaviest of metals, 19.32 times the weight of its own volume of water. Its chemical symbol is Au, atomic number 79, and atomic weight, 197.2. Its melting point is 1,063 degrees centigrade or 1,945 degrees Fahrenheit. It is found in its native state as nuggets, spangles, grains, and streaks.

Pick up a gold bar or a piece of gold of any size, and the first impression you get is one of weight. Gold is heavy, very heavy. Rub your finger nail along it and you may mark its surface. Gold is that soft. Because of this softness, skilled artisans find it easy to shape the yellow metal into exquisite forms.

An ounce of gold, which in its pure form would be about the size of an American half dollar, could be hammered into a thin sheet which would cover 100 square feet. That also would cover a good many phonograph records, should you have that in mind. As you perhaps know, when a record sells a million copies or more, the custom is for the grateful company to give the entertainer a golden disc as a souvenir. It sounds very extravagant. But the gold on that disc is so thin that a little over a dime's worth will cover the record.

Gold is so ductile that an ounce can be drawn into a fine wire fifty miles long. The same amount could plate a thousand-mile strand of copper wire. Obviously, with gold, a little bit goes a long way.

When these properties are allied with its attractive color, and its ability to reflect light, it is evident why gold has always been the favorite of jewelers. Moreover, since it does not rust, jewelry of gold retains its glitter and lustre forever, or at least as close to it as the word can apply to the things of man.

For most people gold means jewelry and behind the jewelry industry is a complex of refiners of metal, of fabricators who produce castings, sheet, strip, plate, and bars in endless shapes for customers, and of craftsmen who work on the edge of artistry, sometimes sliding across that borderline to become true creators in metallic art forms. Louis Osman, designer and creator of the gold crown of the Prince of Wales, was a successful architect in Britain before he turned a goldsmithing hobby into a new career as an artist-craftsman.

In that gold complex, too, are plants which produce gold reflectors for spacecraft, gold-tipped contacts for electrical circuits, frost-proof gold-impregnated glass for cabin windshields of jet aircraft, and hundreds of other products for industry.

In all these applications, the term "carat" is a measure of quality. This weight-measure, first developed for gems, came from the pearl trade of the Orient. In early times, small units of weight were invariably seeds. Pearl dealers noted that the dry seeds of the locust-pod tree were remarkably uniform in weight. So this seed was adopted as the unit of measure for pearls and precious stones. Each seed is close to a fifth of a gram, the weight now fixed on the metric carat.

With gold, however, the carat has nothing to do with weight. Pure gold is defined as twenty-four carats gold. Thus, twenty carats gold is 20/24th pure gold; eighteen carats gold is 18/24th, or 3/4th, pure gold, etc. Because gold is so soft, one seldom encounters ultrapure gold except in the form of gold bars as they might arrive at a jewelry manufacturing concern or perhaps be sold at a Swiss bank. Gold is usually alloyed with copper, nickel, silver or other metals because these latter add to the hardness of the material without detracting from its beauty. Ultrapure gold would scratch easily, and might show signs of wear after a period of time. With only a small quantity of alloy, the gold develops a much harder finish.

The quality of gold is also rated in parts per thousand. Thus 995 gold means that the gold is 99.5 percent pure, while 999 means that it is of a still higher quality, 99.9 percent pure. Most of the gold which enters the market from South Africa is over 995 purity. To obtain even purer gold, it must be refined through the electrolytic process. The Soviet Union, which is a poor second in the new-gold production stakes, refines all its gold this way for 999 quality.

Gold bars are stamped with numbers which designate its quality. With acids, a skilled assayer can determine the true quality of any gold sample in minutes. In the world of gold, every shipment is checked and checked again, for the tales of robbery and fraud having to do with gold fill police files around the globe.

Gold is plentiful on the planet even though it is scarce to man and nonexistent on the moon. It occurs even in sea water, but only in a relationship of one part to about six hundred million parts of water. Nobody knows how to separate the gold from the water commercially, so that gold is effectively locked in the sea until some future marine-mining engineer appears with technology not now in existence.

Within the earth there is far more gold. Writing in a 1949 scientific report, Dr. Harrison Brown of the University of Chicago Institute for Nuclear Studies expressed the view that precious metals, especially gold and platinum, are heavily concentrated in the iron-nickel core of the earth. He estimated that, if it were possible to sink a hole fifteen hundred to two thousand miles deep, man could obtain enough gold to plate the surface of the earth several yards thick.

But man is lucky to get two and a quarter miles down in his mines today. Some of the deep gold mines in South Africa reach a depth of twelve thousand feet. At this depth, the pressure of all that weight above is so great that rock-bursts sometimes occur. Part of a tunnel wall may explode as if by TNT, spraying deadly particles around. Mining engineers at those depths try to relieve stresses by shifting weights to other areas through timbering and hydraulic jacks. Still, it is evident that it will be a long time, if ever, before man reaches depths of fifteen hundred to two thousand miles into the earth.

Native gold is seldom found in a pure state. Usually it is alloyed with silver and frequently with other metals such as copper and those of the platinum group. It also occurs combined with tellurium, and small quantities are found in pyrites and other minerals. It often occurs as ore streaks in quartz rock.

Today, South Africa is the largest gold producer, accounting for three-fourths of the Free World's production. This is where the modern gold trail starts, the place from whence comes the gold going into most jewelry, into industrial applications, or into fresh hoards of bars. This is where the golden streaks imbedded deep in quartz rock prompt men to burrow like animals through thousands of miles of tunnels.

At the 6,500-foot level in the Vaal Reefs Mine in the Transvaal Province of South Africa, the gold-bearing reef looks like gray asphalt, in a streak eighteen inches wide. White stones are scattered through the vein like nuts in a fruit cake.

"There it is—the cause of it all." Gypsy Vermeulen, the white Afrikaner shift-boss shouts above the staccato roar of an air drill handled by two blacks. As he talks, he places a finger on the rock "banket," as the reef is called in South Africa. The stope, or working tunnel, is only three feet high and one must crawl about thirty yards from the main tunnel to reach the point of the action.

It would take an expert to recognize the reef as being gold-bearing, for there isn't even a glint of yellow metal in that gray substance. I broke off a piece as a souvenir, and have yet to meet a person who can recognize that reef chip for what it is.

"Sometimes some of us work for years in a mine and never see gold as such," confides one engineer at Vaal Reefs. Then he adds: "But of course we know banket when we see it."

Gold nuggets are something else. These may occur in a pure, or nearly pure state. Usually they are found in alluvial streams, amid the gravel which may have washed down from prehistoric mountains that might be now nearly worn away. That gold probably was lifted from deep within the earth into high mountain ranges by some prehistoric shift in the rock mantle of this planet. Over eons of time the mountains wore away and the gold washed into alluvial basins. Sometimes that gold was waiting close to the surface for man to find. Other times new debris and sediment of wearing mountains settled over the alluvial gold, trapping it within what was also to become rock as more and more sediment collected atop it. The biggest gold nugget ever found was the Welcome Stranger, a 2,280-ounce chunk of near-pure gold which was found in 1869 near Moliagul in Victoria province of Australia. An even bigger chunk of quartz and gold, the Holterman Reef, was found in New South Wales, Australia, in 1872. It weighed 10,080 ounces with gold representing 7,560 ounces of it. This latter rock specimen, however, was not a true nugget, though the finder did not spurn it for that reason.

CHAPTER III

# Treasures of Kings

Egypt was the original producer of gold, and it was here that mining first developed as an industry and that goldsmithing became an art. Some of the finest examples of this high art survive in the tomb of Tutankhamen. It is a modest affair, with a short gallery, a storeroom, an anteroom, and a burial chamber of twenty by fourteen feet, hardly large enough for the sarcophagus. Fluorescent lights illuminate paintings on the wall which portray the king's funeral. Tutankhamen still lies serenely in his gold coffin, body encased in gold contoured to his limbs and features. His face mask is of beaten, solid gold inlaid with semiprecious stones.

King Tut was only a minor figure in Egyptian history. He died at eighteen, too young to have accomplished much, though he had held the throne for nine years. Yet he is the best known of all the pharaohs thanks to the golden treasures discovered in his tomb by archaeologist Howard Carter in November, 1922, after five years of apparently fruitless digging. It took Carter ten years of patient work to photograph and catalogue all of the thousands of items found. Included among the major items were four shrines covered with gold leaf, with smaller shrines set within larger, three coffins of gold, again with smaller in larger, a golden fly whisk with a warrior charioteer on its face, a bed of gold, bracelets, necklaces, diadems, daggers, pendants, sandals, pectorals, all of gold.

Because gold is forever, it was the metal of many of the artifacts which a pharaoh took with him into the next life. Yet, that gold attracted grave-robbers who violated tombs, sometimes only a short time after the original burial. And those tomb violations could upset the peaceful eternal life envisioned by the pharaohs, for Egyptians believed that the quality of their hereafter depended upon the tomb itself, and the undisturbed mummy. Iron artifacts might have discouraged the graverobbers. But iron rusts, and pharaohs did not care to risk having their possessions withering to dust during their eternal lives. So they stuck to gold like sepulchral lemmings, as if inviting their own spiritual assassinations.

Broken seals and evidences of disarray in King Tut's tomb indicated that robbers had penetrated the tomb long ago. But something frightened them at the crucial moment and they fled, never to return. So King Tut's tomb remained undisturbed.

Yet he was just a minor ruler. What treasures must have been buried with some of the powerful pharaohs of the Old, the Middle, and the New Empires, rulers like Seti I, or Cheops or Rameses II. Through ancient Egypt's history about ninety pharaohs were laid to rest, most of them with golden treasures which might have made those of King Tut seem picayune. Nearly everything has been lost to the greed of men for gold.

This country's gold mining industry already was old when King Tut appeared on the scene. Perhaps as early as 4000 B.C., Egyptians living at El-Gerza, a little south of modern Cairo, were fashioning necklaces, ear rings, and bracelets of alluvial gold. By the time the Pharaoh Narmer joined river settlements into one kingdom, gold-working had reached an advanced stage. Narmer may have been the legendary Menes, whose name comes down to us from Greek manuscripts.

After he had established his new kingdom, he minted gold bars to a standard fourteen-gram size, stamped with his name. These, then, could be used as money. Moreover, he fixed a ratio of 2½ to 1 for silver, in relationship to gold. At that time, and for nearly three thousand years, Egypt must have been the world's leading gold producer. Its gold came from two areas, from the plateau between the Nile and the Red Sea and from Nubia. (*Nub* was the Egyptian word for gold.)

The Nubian gold was found in the sands of the Nile. The first plateau gold was found on the surface, but, later, extensive underground operations developed. Today, the remains of some of these old mines still may be seen in the desert east of Edfu. At Wadi Hamish, underground tunnels and passages stretch for miles, most with entrances blocked by desert sand.

"It is not safe below," one young Egyptian, who had appointed himself as our guide, said when I peered into one cavelike tunnel.

A perusal of old records shows that those ancient mines probably never were safe. They were worked with slave labor, with no regard for the health or lives of laborers. Shafts would be driven down to 300 feet deep. Tunnels would be bored horizontally from them to follow gold-bearing reefs in the quartz rock. The pick was the basic tool, first of bronze then of iron. Where the rock was especially hard, particularly in the bronze age, it would be heated, then cooled quickly to crack it.

In 240 B.C., Theophrastus, a Greek writer, gave a description of work in one of these mines. Said he: "Those who dig in the mines cannot stand upright at their work, but are obliged to lie down, either on their back or on their side, for the vein of earth they dig runs lengthwise and is only the depth of two feet, though considerably more in breadth, and it is enclosed on every side with hard rock, from which the ore is obtained."

This was written long after the golden era of those mines. But mining had changed little in its first several thousand years. So the description is just as apt for Egypt of 2000 B.C. as it is for the country in 240 B.C.

Not only did gold-hunting Egyptians bore into the plateau rock, they also sailed across seas looking for more gold in distant lands.

The land of Punt may have been one of these gold-bearing lands, though this is only surmise since nobody knows exactly where Punt was. Some sources place it where Somalia is today. Others say it may have been in ancient Ethiopia. Then again there are those who say Punt really was in the lower Zambezi River valley.

The lower reaches of the Zambezi are wide and easily navigable for the shallow-draft ships such as those used by the Egyptians. One can proceed as far as the rapids of Cabora Bassa in Mozambique and it is beyond that point, in what is now Rhodesia, that a mysterious, almost-forgotten civilization once flourished, that of Zimbabwe.

Here, on lush African plain, a walled enclosure surrounds a stone temple at the base of a ridge atop which is an extensive and now-ruined Acropolis. It was over a hundred years ago, in 1868, that Adam Renders, hunting for ivory in thick bush, found himself in a huge, open-to-the-air stone enclosure built by some remote people.

Some of the gold jewelry found on the site is on exhibit in a small museum at Zimbabwe and at the National Museum in Salisbury. This jewelry, and the knowledge that this civilization had goldsmiths, prompts some historians to contend that Zimbabwe and Punt are the same.

But, in the little museum on the site, the Rhodesian caretaker laughed derisively when I mentioned the myths which have surrounded this lonesome cluster of stone in the heart of Africa. "I know," he said. "I've heard all the stories, about the Egyptians, the Phoenicians, and such. Well, the Historical Monuments Commission looked into this, using carbon dating to establish times."

He explained how findings indicated that Zimbabwe's ruins were built in the 1100–1600 A.D. period by the black Rozwi people, a tribe which certainly was the most civilized in the area. Were there other civilizations predating this one? Who knows?

It is certain, though, that Egyptian galleys did reach the land of Punt, wherever it was, for frescos exist to prove it. These are on a colonnaded wall of the Temple of Hatshepsut, a striking edifice located under a sheer cliff on the western side of the Nile, opposite Luxor. A foot trail over the mountain leads from the Valley of Kings to the temple. A Polish archaeological team is restoring the ruin with that infinite patience necessary for any lover of antiquity.

"The frescos? They are to the left of the main ramp," a young, blond girl who looked like a student told us as she pointed downward at the temple. We were high on a ridge overlooking the site and it seemed like a good place to pause and rest, while viewing the magnificent panorama of red-gold rock and white stone temple. It hadn't occurred to us that she was with the archaeological team until she said: "The frescos are in very good condition, considering that they have been there for 3,600 years. Our principal task now is to protect them rather than to restore them."

She was a brisk, no-nonsense person who spoke English with a slight lisp. Her khaki pants were frayed at the knees, as if she might have spent much time on them, hardly in prayer. When I told her I was interested in the ancient goldworkings of Egypt and had visited Wadi Hamish, she brightened. Egyptologists live avidly in the past no matter what their political ideology, and they eagerly share knowledge with anyone who shows interest.

"Of course, you know about the goldsmithing relief from the tomb of Mereruka at Saqqara?" she said. It was a statement more than a question.

"The tomb near the Step Pyramid?"

She nodded.

I had toured that site with one of the archaeologists who participated in the original dig at Saqqara in 1927. In 1973, I had spent a day with him as he explained each facet of the mastabas and tombs of that site, as if I were a pupil and he a professor. I didn't remember any goldsmithing relief.

"The mural shows the weighing of gold, refining, the pouring of molten metal, and the beating of gold into sheets," my new Polish friend said.

That particular wall-relief dates from 2300 B.C., which indicates the sophistication of Egyptian goldsmithing even in that long-ago time. Through records such as this, through exhibits in the Egyptian Museum in Cairo and through examples of goldwork preserved in the Louvre, in the British Museum in London, in the Metropolitan Museum of Art in New York and elsewhere, it is possible to piece together an extensive picture of the goldsmith's art in ancient Egypt.

Very early the Egyptians learned how to sheath wood and metal objects with gold foil, how to cast gold, and how to draw it into thin wire which then could be worked into delicate jewelry pieces. One example is the ethereal diadem of the Princess Khnumet, found in her tomb at Dashur and now in the Cairo Museum. Dozens of tiny gold flowers with carnelian centers and turquoise petals are soldered to thin strands of gold wire which form a frail circlet strengthened at six points by a cruciform ornament. The piece dates from 1875 B.C. yet would make a fit crown for any queen today.

Jewelers often decorated their work with gold granulation. Granules were very fine, probably made by cutting gold wire into tiny pieces which were then heated and rolled between two flat surfaces into minute balls. These could be soldered by the score or by the hundreds onto pieces of jewelry, and were often joined together to form minute patterns of glistening gold.

On the forehead of the King Tut funerary mask are solid gold insignias of the vulture goddess Nekhbet and that of the sacred cobra Buto. These probably were cast by the lost-wax process, a method in which wax is carefully shaped into the pattern of the object to be cast. A sand mold is packed around this wax pattern. Then it is heated and the molten wax is allowed to run out, leaving a vacant space in the shape of the pattern. When metal is poured into this mold, it settles into the shape of the now-lost pattern.

By 2000 B.C. goldsmiths were able to create cloisonné work, a technique whereby gold wire or strips form the ribs or skeleton of a piece of jewelry. Small pieces of glass, semiprecious stones, and faience fill in the spaces between the gold. A cementlike paste may help bind such work together, while metal may be used as solder.

Some Egyptian gold has a rose sheen on its surface. It appears that this color was deliberately produced in a manner which now is unknown. Tomb paintings show that gold was made into hollow rings for transport. These rings had a negotiable value, though all gold production was under royal command, and proceeds, generally, went into the pharaoh's treasury.

Perhaps it is fortunate that it was King Tut's tomb which was left intact for us, for Egyptian goldsmithing and the production of gold reached its heights in the period from 1500 to 1300 B.C., which included the short reign of King Tut. At the time, Egypt supplied gold to that other great civilization, Mesopotamia, of the Fertile Crescent. Confirmation of this comes from one of the most remarkable letters to come down to us, a dunning letter from Burnaburiash, king of Karaduniash, to King Tut. Few letters matches this one for sheer gall. Burnaburiash wrote:

> To Tutankhamen [Niphuria in Babylonian]:
> All goes well for me. All hail to thee, thy house, thy wives, thy children, thy country, thy nobles, thy horses and thy chariots.
> When my fathers and thy fathers established between themselves friendly relations they exchanged rich presents and never refused each other, the one to the other, whatever beautiful thing they desired.
> Now my brother has sent me as a gift but two minas of gold. If now gold is abundant with thee, send me as much as thy fathers did, but if it is scarce, send me at least half as much. Why didst thou send me only two minas of gold? . . . Send me much gold.

The letter went on in that vein, as Burnaburiash showed that he didn't think two minas (about twenty-five ounces) of gold was enough for a pot to spit in. There is no record of how King Tut responded to the begging missive.

Little gold was produced in the Tigris and Euphrates valleys, scene of the great civilizations of Sumeria, Babylonia, and Assyria. But excavations at Ur and exhibits in the Iraqi National Museum in Baghdad show that these peoples had excellent goldsmiths at a very early date. Undoubtedly most of their gold came from Egypt through trade. Some may have come from Arabia, or even from distant India. In any case, as the city-states of the Euphrates grew in power and wealth, their holdings of gold increased, too.

Gold seems to flow like water in the direction of those nations which are the most prosperous in goods and chattels. No other commodity in human history has matched gold as a store of value for the wealth accumulated by man. Gold is packaged power, a financial fuel-cell which, properly handled, can stimulate endless forms of activity of benefit to holders. Yet, in itself, it is only a tool in monetary affairs, only a reflection of a nation's or a man's wealth. In the civilizations of the Fertile Crescent, the work of the goldsmith traces the rise of culture to its apogee as effectively as a line on a chart.

Evidently the skills developed by Egyptian artisans had spread to the Euphrates, and probably far beyond. Had those skills been devoted to any other metal than gold, the work would have degenerated long ago. Their goldwork shimmers and glitters with the brightness of the sun, as fresh as the day it was created, providing insights into the civilization of old Sumer. It reveals to us how deep is man's reverence for gold, a reverence which is founded upon six thousand years of respect, and perhaps of lust and avarice and envy. But these are qualities which are within men, not the gold itself.

Sometimes it is said that gold brings out the worst characteristics of man. The case is unproven, since, if gold were not in existence, man most likely would have focused his attention upon some other material for his cash standard of value. Too often gold is blamed for what really are the weaknesses of man.

There is far more evidence in concrete form that, at least insofar as the artist is concerned, gold brings forth the best in man. Perhaps nowhere is this more in evidence than in the goldwork left to us by the Minoans, those slim-waisted people whom the Egyptians called the Keftiu. By 3000 B.C. these peoples were established on the island of Crete, an adventurous, seafaring tribe which soon dominated the eastern end of the Mediterranean. They developed close trading relations with Egypt early, and undoubtedly drew on its culture. Knossos, their capital, located near modern Herakleion, became a great city, with lordly palaces, paved streets and a port crowded at all times with galleys from Ugarit, Sotira, Byblos, and other ports of the ancient world.

Since very little gold ever has been found on Crete, it's believed the Minoans drew gold from Egypt as the wealth and trading power of the island developed. By the year 2000 B.C. Minoan goldwork already had reached a high level of excellence. By the time the Minoan civilization reached its peak in the period from 1700 to 1400 B.C., its goldsmiths were among the finest to be found in the world.

Some of their work is in the museum in Herakleion. That collection includes pendants, necklaces, earrings, and belt ornaments of hammered gold. One necklace is composed of a golden string from which hang twenty-five small droplets or "tears" of gold. Earrings are simple loops of gold. A pendant has a golden woman holding a swan by the neck in each hand, her feet resting on a bed of lilies, with five coinlike golden "moons" hanging down. Every piece shows delicacy and refinement, as if the collection might have been made for a wealthy noblewoman to wear at the religious festivals of Minos.

Minoans knew all the techniques which early Egyptians had practiced, repoussé work, thin beating, granulation. They also were adept at combining gold with other metals, as an inlay on bronze, for instance. They knew how to work with gold of several colors to form color combinations in jewelry. They developed geometric patterns, long preceding those which were to become so popular in the Moslem world.

In one case in the archaeological museum in Herakleion there is a chryselephantine sword-handle, the ivory looking as if the worms of time had been at it, the gold still bright and shining. Chryselephantine is a combination of ivory and gold, usually with the ivory as a base with patterned niches carved out for insertion of gold. Sometimes a figurine may be of ivory, with golden strands for hair.

Other exhibits show how Minoans made bronze daggers and swords inlaid with gold in decorative patterns. One wall fresco taken from the palace of Knossos shows a man arranging a necklace around a woman's neck. Even in those days, a lady sometimes needed help from her husband before stepping out with all her finery. Note, too, that the man *is* helping the woman at her toilette. In many societies of the ancient world a woman was little more than a beast of burden to be allowed respites only for breeding purposes. Minoan women seemed to enjoy a freedom which was unusual for that day. They wore tight bodices and flaring skirts, their breasts bare and held so tightly by those bodices that nipples thrust forward as if daring their men to make something of it. One has the opinion that Minoan women didn't need any militant organization to have their way. They merely hitched their belts a little tighter when social sparring dictated, and literally thrust their defenses forward.

There's no sign of such women in modern Herakleion, of course. It sits beside the sea, mountains behind, a crowded, busy city with an Oriental-like bazaar and a Venetian fort which dominates the old harbor. The ruins of Knossos, three miles from town, and the museum on Eleftherias Square are the main attractions. Knossos is unique as an ancient city because it had no protective wall around it, which indicates that it must have been so powerful at its peak that citizens had no fear of attack. Legend has it that one of the Minoan kings established the first organized navy. That fleet kept invaders far from Crete's shores until one day, when catastrophe struck.

On a spring day about 1400 B.C., a mighty fleet dropped anchor off the coast and invaders poured ashore. They probably were of Greek origin—or possibly of that mysterious tribe known only as "the Sea Peoples" for want of a more specific name.

They overwhelmed the palace guard and put the building to the torch. It appears that the throne room may have been a sanctuary for the priest-kings of Minos, and that a ritual had been rudely ended by the invaders. Excavators found an overturned oil jar and various utensils which indicated that the last priest-king may have been exhorting his gods for some miracle that would save his kingdom from the invaders.

That plea was unanswered. Smoke-begrimed beams show that the life of the palace ended suddenly, in a great conflagration. The civilization of the ancient world was once again shifting its focus as it had done periodically since time began. The ancient world was moving into a period of flux, with the decline of old Egypt, the emergence of the seafaring Phoenicians, the growing power of the Assyrians and the appearance of Greek tribes on the mainland of Europe and in the western part of what is now Turkey.

Goldsmiths were there to record the story of the new civilizations in the crowns, diadems, necklaces, bracelets, and artifacts of the kings, queens, and nobles who were striding upon the platforms of history. By this time, gold no longer was solely the prerogative of royalty. Enough of it had been found for some of it to dribble down to lesser people in the form of signet rings, bracelets, and pieces of jewelry. The lust of later men for that gold provided the impetus for uncovering the histories of the earlier ages.

# CHAPTER IV

# Myths and Fact

At Troy, in Turkey, there is a little museum which owes its existence to the University of Cincinnati. Here are several excellent Greek pottery pieces of the fifth and sixth century B.C., but nothing to revive the glory of old Troy.

On a parapet of the ancient site, several men worked in a trench near what is left of the Temple of Athena under the direction of a young foreman in his twenties, a shirt-sleeved, breezy archaeological student from Istanbul. He had been to America as an exchange student and he obviously had affection for things American, and for wandering Americans.

"Have you found anything?" I asked.

He shook his head, smiling. "We are not excavating. We are straightening this trench after the rains." Then, he showed us how past excavations have revealed different layers of time back to 2700 B.C., speaking with the enthusiasm of the student who is still awed by the knowledge which has been unveiled to him.

He had little good to say for Heinrich Schliemann, the German merchant-archaeologist who was Turkey's first surveyor of ancient sites. Said he: "He stole our treasures, and now they probably are lost to us forever."

"But if he hadn't been so hungry for gold perhaps old Troy would never have been found," I said.

He nodded. "Yes, and the treasures would still be here for us to find. Gold! That is all Schliemann wanted."

It is what all treasure-hunters have craved. The first excavators at ancient sites were grave-robbers who searched for gold and precious stones, not caring much about their forms and shapes. Undoubtedly, grave-robbers destroyed far more than they sold intact for gain. Yet, today, museums of the world encourage pilferage of archaeological sites by paying huge prices for artifacts which might be smuggled to them. This I said now to my student acquaintance.

"But," he protested, "it isn't the intrinsic money value of gold which museums find so attractive. It is the fact that gold endures so well that it often tells a more complete story than does anything else."

"Exactly," I said. "The archaeologist sees something in gold just as does the miser, though each values different qualities in it."

The Boston Museum of Fine Arts gained some publicity in 1970 when it acquired 137 gold artifacts as a centenary gift from one of its trustees. The find had been purchased for a reported six-figure sum and the only thing said about origin was that it came from "an unknown site somewhere in the eastern Mediterranean." This, of course, sounded as if archaeological-site looters may have robbed pieces from some location and smuggled the artifacts from the country involved. Naci Temizer, director of the Archaeological Museum of Ankara, after studying pictures of the artifacts in the London *Times,* said he was sure the pieces originated in Anatolia.

Dr. Cornelius Vermeule, curator of the Boston Museum's classical department, defended the acquisition on the grounds that, if the Museum had not obtained the cache intact, this "homogeneous group" would have been broken up and sold separately, forever destroying the scientific value of a united trove. In his opinion, this consideration overrode the distaste for dealing in artifacts which had been greedily dug up without regard for the scientific value of classifying objects carefully.

"It would have been far more scandalous for this group to continue its peregrinations, . . . with private collectors wanting bracelets and hair-rings for their wives," said he.

The 137 gold pieces in the collection weighed twenty-two pounds. Included were necklaces, brooches, and other jewelry. The theory advanced by those who considered the hoard to be genuine was that it may have belonged to a princess who might have lived in any of several countries such as Turkey, Cyprus, Lebanon, Syria, or Greece. All of these countries have laws forbidding the export of archaeological finds without permits, which are granted only for inconsequential objects.

"There can be little doubt that the treasure comes from Turkey," said Peter Warren of the department of Classics at the University of Durham, in England, after viewing photographs of a brooch in the collection.

In a letter to the London *Times* he wrote:

> What are we to make of the museum's action? I feel that they must be condemned *in toto.* It will be argued that the treasure can now readily be admired and studied, and it will surely receive exemplary

publication. But this by no means offsets the loss of knowledge of its exact provenance and find circumstances, which would have provided primary evidence for the history of the area, particularly of its metallurgy.

The museum may say that by buying it from the antique market which it had already reached they have saved it for students and visitors. Certainly, museums in general are much less guilty in these respects than the vast private market. But by the very fact of having a large sum of money available for it, Boston is deliberately and explicitly encouraging robbery of this kind, of material which properly belongs to the country where it was found and which would have been at least as important for the evidence of its find-context as for its beauty.

The six-figure price reportedly paid for these artifacts illustrates how the archaeological value may add to gold's worth. Had this treasure trove been melted down by its discoverer, the gold content would have been worth about $10,000 at the free-market gold price pertaining at that time.

The bonanza prices are drawing forgers into the market, too. Gold, like jade and rock crystal, is one of the easiest materials for an archaeological forger to shape into fakes. Naturally, he would use gold of appropriate fineness, to enhance credibility.

Gold is practically indestructible, which means, also, that it does not "age" or undergo chemical changes when buried. A piece might lie beneath the soil for thousands of years, yet may glitter with its original brilliance when the earth is washed away. Moreover, carbon-dating is useless since there isn't any carbon involved. As long as a fake piece carefully follows the style of the intended period, it is difficult to detect the forgery.

Microscopic examination of an article's surfaces may reveal if modern tools have been used in manufacture. But skilled forgers try to avoid this trap. And the payoff may be substantial: a hundred times or more the value of the gold content, which, with the work involved, would be the forger's investment.

The Boston collection, itself, drew accusations of forgery after the controversy made world headlines. Among those challenging the authenticity of the articles was Professor Spyridon Marinatos, inspector-general of Greece's archaeological services.

Said he: "In the last generation, largely as a result of improved technical methods and, sad to say, of the advances of science, there has been such a profusion of forgeries in the world that archaeology as a science is in danger of becoming discredited."

The Boston Museum, of course, was convinced of the authenticity of the collection or it would not have exhibited it.

It is certain, though, that excellent replicas in gold may be manufactured with the gold-working techniques now available. In the Victoria and Albert Museum in London there are replicas of the Scythian treasures of the Hermitage Museum in Leningrad, done so skillfully that they might fool an expert. The British Museum likes to add originals from the British Isles to its collections, making flawless replicas for the nearest local museums adjacent to discoveries. But these and the Victoria and Albert replicas are listed as such, and there is no effort to dupe the public. A forger, however, finds monetary reasons for trying to sell replicas not as copies but as genuine pieces. South American Indian collections are riddled with fakes, claims one gold expert at Sotheby's, and these fakes are hard to detect, says she.

One of the most successful exhibitions ever held by the Metropolitan Museum of Art in New York was its Gold show of April through September, 1973. Attendance exceeded two hundred thirty thousand, one of the largest for any special exhibition ever to take place in the institution. The story of gold was told not only through jewels but also through imaginative pieces such as a golden rattle made for a colonial American baby and a Chinese rank badge in which peacock feathers were as important as the golden thread. Emphasis was on the beauty and craftsmanship of the artifacts rather than on intrinsic values.

In Bogota, Colombia, there is a museum which devotes all its exhibits to gold. A development of the country's Central Bank, this institution is aptly named the Museum of Gold. Colombia is the largest producer of gold in South America, and it once led the world in production. So Colombians are rightly proud of their gold-production heritage and of the Indian culture which first developed the country's mines during Incan and pre-Incan times.

The building is a three-story air-conditioned edifice with interior walls of mahogany, cedar, and marble. Designed by German Samper, a leading Colombian architect and pupil of Le Corbusier, the structure itself is a piece of art. You enter through two steel doors which are guarded by armed porters, with an attendant pressing a button to open doors only after the visitor has passed a hard-eyed inspection. In the museum are darkened rooms with lit showcases where some of 6,000 gold artifacts are on display. Headdresses, pectoral plates, bracelets, flutes, earrings, and other items in gold provide magnificent examples of Tairona, Quimbaya, and other tribal work.

In one room is an immense aerial photograph of Lake Guatavita, the holy lake of an ancient tribe, which inspired the El Dorado legend. This lake is high in the Andes, north of Bogota, a mysterious place which intrigued the early Spaniards.

Here in a tribal ceremony the chief of Guatavita would cover himself with gold dust until his dark body was a glistening yellow living sculpture. He was carried on a raft of reeds to the lake by high priests of the court and the craft was pushed from the shore. To the sound of chanting, the wail of flutes, and the pounding of drums, the raft slowly moved into deeper water. The chief would dive into the water, wash off the gold, and swim back to shore.

The Spaniards heard about El Dorado, the golden one, and searched futilely for his kingdom. In the nineteenth century, a British expedition found the lake, drained it, and uncovered some gold objects. But much of the gold of El Dorado may be waiting to be discovered.

When one reflects upon the search for El Dorado it is easier to understand alchemy. Alchemists helped expand man's knowledge of the sciences through their search for a cheap way to manufacture gold. Chemistry developed from this occult science.

The alchemists had a three-fold quest. They sought the philosopher's stone, the universal panacea, and the meaning of life. One of man's most notable characteristics is that he aspires for the stars even when his feet are planted firmly in mud. Alchemists contended that all metals came from the same source. But some metals are more mature than others. Gold, for instance, was regarded as the most perfect of metals, the ultimate on the scale except for the philosopher's stone, itself. Obviously, anyone who found the philosopher's stone would have great wealth. Discovery of that stone also would point the way to the universal panacea and to the meaning of life.

Hermes Trismegistus is the father of alchemy, a mythical father who never existed. Like the Good Fairy he is a creature of the imagination. His roots are in the ancient Egyptian god, Hermes. He was the source of all wisdom, the benevolent character responsible for all new discoveries.

While gold was the attraction which lured most men (and some women) into the practice of alchemy, their experiments with metals and other substances led to discoveries far removed from the transformation of lead or iron into gold. Even before the time of Christ, Egyptians knew how to weld metals, to test silver and gold, to dye textiles, to purify metals through cupellation, and to produce colored glass. (Cupellation is the refinement of gold, silver, or other metals in a hearth by exposure to high temperatures in a draft or blast of air. Lead, copper, and other unwanted minerals are oxidized and sink into the porous walls of the earth, leaving the pure metal in its liquid state.)

Cupellation of gold may have led to the discovery of glass. When sand rich in gold is melted with soda, the slag contains glittering crystals of glass. Those crystals may have caught the attention of some devotee of the god Hermes in ancient times. Then it would have been a small step to make glass as a separate operation.

If those very early alchemists failed to transform base metals into gold, they did learn diplosis, the art of increasing the weight of a precious metal by alloying it with base metals.

Some early Egyptian processes for gold-plating copper and other metals are described in ancient texts. And the claim is made that objects so treated "have the appearance of gold and the deception cannot be detected by the touchstone." The latter stone is a black siliceous stone similar to flint which may be used to test for gold. When real gold is rubbed along such a stone, a streak is left upon the stone's surface.

Alchemists failed to find the philosopher's stone, of course, or to transform ignoble metals into gold. But through history their work in pursuit of this quest provided the base for many of the sciences of today.

Sir John Cockcroft, speaking at the Empire Mining and Metallurgical Congress at Oxford in July, 1949, said: "We are often asked if we can produce gold artificially. We can in fact do so, but since we have to start from platinum, and the process is rather expensive we are not likely to put gold mines out of operation in the foreseeable future."

Ironically, though most men are always searching for their El Dorado, man has an ambivalence about gold. It seldom is refused when offered; yet sometimes it is viewed as something unclean. Olympic athletes, for instance, have long competed for those first-place gold medals which are the badge of excellence in sports. But those medals are not of solid gold. They are gold washed, or dipped, because Olympic ideals call for athletes to compete for the love of sport, not for anything of monetary value. Thus one of the medals may actually be worth only a few cents, despite its golden glitter.

Such ambiguity seldom was found among the Etruscans, a people who felt that gold personified the love of luxury which characterized their lives. Girls accumulated dowries of gold by working as prostitutes before marriage, valuing gold much more than they did chastity.

The Etruscans of old Italy still are a mystery, a people who are to us almost as airy and vague as the fairies of Ireland or as the Greek gods who occupied the heights of Mount Olympus. Archaeology at root is a mystery tale, with the hoped-for denouements, the rediscovery of peoples, hidden under blankets of time. Whole peoples have lived, left many clues to their existence, then faded from the scene. Yet we aren't clever enough to decipher those clues and to lift the mystery. So it is with the Etruscans, a people with a language which has never been deciphered, but with goldsmithing talents which do reveal many things to us through their jewelry, and through paintings on tombs.

They reached the peak of their power around 500 B.C. They never did form a unified state, but various cities grew wealthy, and goldcraftsmen had numerous opportunities to show skills. Etruscans employed nearly all the metalworking techniques known today, except for electroforming. This included engraving, embossing, hammering, repoussé, inlaying, and gold-leafing. They excelled in filigree, twisting fine gold wires into complex patterns and shapes. They also used granulation to provide a sparkling sheen to goldwork, with thousands of microscopic granules forming part of the pattern. For centuries, granulation was a lost art, as jewelers puzzled how to do it. But the best of modern goldsmiths have revived this ancient technique.

Today, the Tuscan hills which once were home to the Etruscans are as soft and gentle as in those days long before the time of Christ. Arezzo, which sits in terraces on a hill crowned by a citadel, once was one of the Etruscan cities. Now people come to see the fifteenth-century frescos in the Church of San Francesco or to visit the home of Petrarch. Others visit the plant of Gori & Zucchi, the largest gold-jewelry factory in the world.

Many of the workers of the Arezzo factory may be descendents of those same Etruscans who once occupied these hills.

"We like to think so," I was told by one of the plant executives, when I visited the factory. Then, he added: "Nearly everything that we can do with gold, today, they could do, and that was five hundred years before the time of Christ."

Man in his ego likes to believe that his own age is a wonder era which outstrips anything which has gone before. Sometimes future shock is replaced by a past shock when we look backward to see how well some ancient civilizations handled certain things. Every race has its own mythology, and perhaps ours is the belief that we are wonder-workers creating a utopia.

In ancient times mythology played a role in the everyday life of man, and often gold was written into the script. The legend of the Golden Goose exists in many languages. One of the feats performed by Hercules was the fetching of the Golden Apples from the Garden of the Hesperides. Jason, leader of the Argonauts, searched for and found the Golden Fleece, only to discover that it did not solve his problems.

Truth may lie behind some legends, too. Heinrich Schliemann followed the tales of Homer to assist him in his excavations of both Troy and Mycenae. He read the *Iliad,* noted how Homer placed Troy by the sea, and then used Homer's tale as if it were a literary treasure-hunter's map. His findings confirmed that Homer's apparent fairy tales were founded upon facts.

If Homer had been telling the truth, then perhaps other myths had a foundation of fact. Logic might be applied to tales to ascertain foundations. The Golden Goose? Perhaps in antiquity a goose may have pecked at small gold nuggets along an alluvial stream. Her owner may have found himself in possession of a gold-machine which fattened his purse every time he cleaned his pens. Time may have expanded nuggets into eggs in the oft-told tale.

The Golden Apples from the Garden of the Hesperides may have been smoothly worn, sizeable gold nuggets found by some long-forgotten expedition. If apple-sized nuggets aren't exactly plentiful, they are possible. Even Jason's search for the Golden Fleece may have been factual.

The legendary Grove of Ares may have been by the Black Sea, in the land of the Scythians or their neighbors. Herodotus visited Olbia, a Greek colony at the confluence of the Bug and Ingul rivers in what is now southern Russia. He observed the Scythians firsthand and wrote about their customs. From him and other writers, we know that the Scythians were master goldsmiths, with gold supplies which may have come from alluvial streams.

They may have worked the gravel of streams by using sheepskins to trap heavy particles of gold. Jason's Golden Fleece may have been truly golden, a sheepskin laden with a rich harvest of gold granules. When he sailed with his Argonauts to find that Golden Fleece, Jason may really have been starting a voyage of plunder, intending to sack gold-camps along shores of the Black Sea.

For centuries, the Scythians themselves were almost a part of mythology, the works of Herodotus and a few other writers being the only ties which modern men had to them. Thanks to golden treasures found in southern Russia and in the Altai Mountains, we now know much more about this tribe and the part that gold played in their lives.

The Scythians were a rough, hardy people who roamed Western Asia, finally settling around the Black Sea. Here they developed a civilization from the seventh to the third centuries B.C.

They absorbed enough of the civilization of Greece and Persia to develop an art of their own which had its best reflection in their goldwork. In addition to the gold they might have found in some of the streams in southern Russia, they also probably drew heavily from the Ural-Altai region of what is now the Soviet Union. This is a wild, lonely country of vast deserts, of broad steppes where collective wheat farms squeeze grain from the windblown soil, and of high mountains to the south and east. From the air, the land looks like arid stretches of Arizona, red and pink in an afternoon sun, golden at break of dawn, broken by rocky canyons and arroyos, with solitary buttes rising from plains. Snow crests of the Tien Shan range and its various spurs top a rock rampart which blocks the Ural-Altai from China's Sinkiang province. And those Tien Shans have been gold producers, too, for millenia.

In the summer of 1973, I visited this remote part of the country which is far off the usual tourist tracks. On the way, I stopped at Kiev in the Ukraine to see and hear about a new Scythian art treasure which had been found at Tolstaya Mogila on the Dnieper river. Ukranian archaeologist Boris Mozolovsky explained how a bulldozer, carving into the frozen ground of a hill, had turned up a few artifacts of an earlier civilization.

In the Middle East this might have resulted in the formation of a conspiracy of silence by the workingmen (from an ore-concentration plant in this case) as they looted the tomb to sell findings to eager buyers of the archaeological underground. In the Soviet Union, it is not so easy to sell such artifacts. Moreover, tomb looters face possible death penalties for robbing the state.

Workingmen notified authorities. Soon a team of trained archaeologists were at work, unearthing what proved to be a Scythian tomb mound.

Says Mozolovsky: "Work uncovered a young Scythian princess buried with all her clothing, dress, headdress, mantle and slippers, all decked with gold medallions. All her adornments were also of gold. Round her neck was a solid gold clasp with the design showing fourteen lions hunting deer."

The tomb dated from the fourth century B.C. and proved to be one of the richest ever found in that part of the Soviet Union.

Much of the gold of those Scythians probably came from central Asia from the Altai Mountains, the Oxus Valley, or perhaps even from the Kyzyl Kum sands of Uzbekestan, where modern Russians are squeezing gold from heat-shimmering desert sands. That red sand sparkles on the plain with a glare which hurts the eyes. On roads, it rises in rosy clouds behind wheels of giant trucks bearing gold-rich loads to a concentration plant.

At Zarafshan (which means "gold-bearing"), a pioneer town of wide streets, prefabricated eight-story apartment buildings and force-fed gardens form an oasis amid the desert. A seven-hundred-mile pipeline brings life-giving water from the distant Amu Darya river.

Soviets are ultrasecretive about their gold production. But the thousands of people living in the town, and the scope of the gold-works on the edge of the city, indicate a high yield: it would take a substantial production to sustain the economic life of such a community.

"Just say that we are processing millions of tons of gold-bearing ore," says one husky, blond engineer with shoulders nearly as broad as a door. Kremlinologists who follow economic developments in the Soviet Union believe that total annual production is about two hundred fifty metric tons, enough to give Russia the number-two position in world gold output but still just over a quarter of South Africa's total.

In Frunze, Kirghizia, I heard more about the gold-producing potential of this part of the world. "Our mountains have been producing gold since long before written history," I was told in an office of the republic's Academy of Sciences. Coushbeck Usenbekov, the republic's chief historian, is a thin-haired oriental who enjoys talking about the history of this Central Asian part of the Soviet Union.

Skilled Scythian goldsmiths hammered and fashioned golden combs for the long hair of chieftains, ornate gold cups for banquets, and various other items which feature the animal imagery that is the mark of these dwellers of the steppes.

Ever since 1830, archaeologists have been unearthing some of their tombs in southern Russia, or further east in central Asia. Collections have been assembled at the Hermitage Museum in Leningrad, that stellar museum which is housed in the old winter palace of the tsars.

As is often the case with museums in the Soviet Union, we found the wing containing the Scythian collection to be closed the day we visited the Hermitage. As is also often the case in the Soviet Union, we found that gates opened even on an off-day when the right strings were pulled. We were the only visitors in the gallery that particular day and we made a leisurely study of the collection with the assistance of one of the museum's curators.

She was an archaeologist who specialized in the Ural-Altai cultures of central Asia, a serious, efficient woman in her mid-thirties. Her long, straight blond hair formed a bun on the back of her head, and she wore a smock. She knew her history of the primitive civilizations of the Soviet Union well. Evidently she thought we were somebodies and we did not enlighten her. So she accepted her self-appointed guide-role with enthusiasm.

The collection is tastefully displayed in groupings and separate cases, aimed at providing even the casual viewer with an understanding of why the gold cups, vases, buckles, ornaments, combs, and other artifacts comprise a unique compilation.

"In one tomb alone sixteen kilos of gold ornaments and jewelry were found," said our guide. Then she explained some of the funerary customs of the Scythians. After a chieftain or king died, the kingdom went into mourning for forty days while the body was prepared for burial. At the end of that time, the dead man's wives, his cupbearer, his grooms, and his other servants were killed. Then all were buried in a mass grave.

"See!" Our friend sensed that her interpretation of the Scythians was being understood. She was one of those mousey persons who bottles speech as a defense against needless embarrassment, but who opens her vocal floodgates when facing responsive listeners. Now, she pointed to a sword sheath of gold from Kul Oba in southern Russia, explained how it had been found, where, the part it had played in a Scythian funeral.

It was a tribe related to the Scythians, the Cimmerians, that ended the career of the legendary King Midas, that character whose name has become synonymous with gold in Greek legend.

The legend of King Midas is a fairy tale concocted, like so many others, to emphasize a moral. King Midas had been given magical powers by the gods. Anything he touched, turned to gold. His food turned to gold when he tried to eat it, and when he caressed his daughter, she turned to gold under his touch. His great wealth attracted the attention of a warlike tribe which overwhelmed his capital. The King poisoned himself as the city's defenses collapsed. Why the poison didn't turn to gold hasn't been explained.

A legend. Yet there really was a King Midas, king of the Phrygians, a tribe which occupied central Anatolia for a time. There is gold in streams in this area, too, and in ancient times the amount must have been much greater than now. Undoubtedly, the Phrygians exploited this gold, and their king accumulated great wealth. And from this developed the legend.

You can see the tomb of Midas at Gordium on the Sakarya river about fifty miles west of Ankara, in Turkey. It was unearthed by a University of Pennsylvania team. But archaeologists found no gold in the tomb, though they did find the skeleton of a man who must have been a Phrygian king. Midas? Who knows?

As for Gordium, another legend had developed about it. In the fourth century B.C., the Acropolis, on a hill overlooking the city, contained a chariot which was supposed to have belonged to King Midas. The yoke was tied to the shaft of the chariot with an extremely complicated knot. An old oracle said that whoever could untie the knot would conquer all of Asia.

So, enter Alexander, the Greek warrior, in 333 B.C. He heard the story and was told that no one had ever yet solved the secret of the knot. Before a crowd of his soldiers, he looked at that knot, drew his sword, and cut the rope with one blow. Soldiers have their own way of solving problems. Alexander had his role to play, too, in the long and glittering history of gold. His conquests not only involved the defeat of armies, but the cornering of the world's gold and silver supply, too. Even in that distant time, smart people realized the value of dollar diplomacy, only it was drachma diplomacy then. But before this developed, somebody had to invent coinage. It took the Lydians to do that.

# CHAPTER V

# Minting of Coins

Two boys played along the banks of the fast-running stream at the foot of the stony hill. Both had the close-cropped hair favored by Turkish mothers, since it saves trips to the barber and reduces the area for lice. On the hill the temple ruin lay like decaying bones in bright sunlight, saying little about past glories, much about current poverty. A flock of goats nibbled on the greenery of the ridge which once was crested by the Acropolis of Sardis. One old nanny was udder-deep in poppies which formed great red patches along the valley slopes.

The goats probably were the responsibility of the boys, but they found the brook more interesting. Until they saw me. Both came running, hands outstretched, small coins in palms. They understood no English and I spoke no Turkish. Yet I could see they thought they could tempt me with some old coins at a price. The winds of tourism are blowing across Turkey, whipping cash into the air. Everyone who can stand is chasing that money, souvenirs clutched in hand ready for trade. One of the boys had a Roman aes which, if genuine, might have been minted in the age of Augustus.

I took it, noted how heavy it felt. Probably leaded, I thought, and a counterfeit. But the older of the boys, a sharp-eyed little fellow with the persistence of a bazaar trader, was asking only the equivalent of fifty cents for it. I offered him twenty-five and he grabbed my money so quickly that I knew his coin was counterfeit.

Still it made a good souvenir, coming from this Sardis where Herodotus tells us the first coins known to man were struck. These were of gold, not of the bronze used in the Roman aes. They were made by the Lydians, those people who had built the temple of Artemis where I stood. Their capital, Sardis, had stretched up the valley, a rich city known throughout the ancient world.

The Lydians were a people of legends as was King Midas, whose kingdom with its gold-bearing streams eventually fell to them. Sardis grew wealthy with that gold. Lydians were the first to realize, though, that raw gold and silver were poor media for the development of trade. So they invented the coin, a piece of gold or silver of standard weight with marks on both the obverse (head) and the reverse (tail) sides.

And as soon as the coin was invented there were counterfeiters forging crude copies, as if both coin and counterfeit were joined by some Hegelian concept of contradictions. Always with gold there seems to be this duality, the forces of darkness struggling with the hosts of light. Slaves would wrest the gold from the ground to make a holy cross for the high altar in a church. Gold bars in a national treasury may lend strength to a country even as other gold bars being smuggled out may weaken that nation, with the final result determined by the weight of the bars on each side of this monetary scale.

But the first coin had to be true or it would not have been worth copying. It is hard for people to realize, today, that for a good part of man's existence, he had no coins to stimulate trade (or counterfeiting). The first trade was through barter, a hunter exchanging a skin for a portion of wheat, for instance.

Homer in the Iliad tells us that:

> *From Lemnos Isle a numerous fleet had come,*
> *Freighted with wine.*
> *All the other Greeks*
> *Hastened to purchase, some with brass, and some*
> *With gleaming iron; some with hides, cattle, or slaves.*

This was a clumsy way of doing business, with every exchange overlaid with suspicion. Yet it worked because there was nothing else. Each man had an idea of the amount of labor which went into his products. Those hours provided a rough gauge for transactions, a cooking pot which took three days to make might be worth three receptacles which took a day each to complete.

As man domesticated animals, cattle assumed a certain monetary value. Other media of exchange included stones, sea shells, cocoa beans, rice, pieces of copper, and more than a hundred and sixty other commodities.

The Pharaoh Menes came close to inventing the coin when he ordered those fourteen-gram bars to be made. However, that unit was too valuable for ordinary commerce—$67.38 each at a gold price of $150 an ounce.

But gold and silver, as the two most valuable metals known, did become media of exchange before the coin was invented. Pieces of these metals were passed back and forth in trade, with each merchant possessing a scale for weighing the metals. In Babylonia, bits of gold weighing 8.34 grams each were known as shekels. In appearance, they look like small pieces of yellow dough which may have been formed by rolling between fingers. The Hebrew gold shekel weighed about 16.4 grams each, with a silver–gold relationship of 13.33 to 1.

Anyone who accepted a shekel gambled on its quality. The alluvial gold of the Mideast often really was electrum, a mixture of silver and gold. The purity of the gold varied from shekel to shekel. Buyer and seller had to haggle over the worth of the shekel as well as of the goods. It wasn't merely a case of buyer beware; both seller and buyer had to beware.

The Lydians changed that and in so doing they paved the way for trade between nations on a scale which ancient man could not have conceived no matter how wild his imagination. The tale is that Lydia reached its peak under the Mermnades dynasty, which acquired power through a strip-tease act that backfired.

King Candaules of Lydia had a beautiful queen, and he regarded her not as a wife but as a possession to exhibit to glorify himself, an object, militant women might charge. Her beauty merely bolstered his own conceit at having acquired such a prize.

One day the king invited Gyges, the commander of his armies, to hide in the royal chamber to catch a glimpse of the beautiful queen in the nude. This was the only way, said the king, to really appreciate the charms of the fair lady.

Gyges did as he was told. A king was a king in those days, and anyway most men don't need any encouragement when offered an opportunity to glimpse a nude woman. But the queen caught Gyges in his Peeping Tom role. She was furious at him for ogling her, and at her husband for permitting it. One of the men must die to retrieve her honor, she told Gyges.

"Well, it isn't going to be me," Gyges indicated. So he killed the King and seized both throne and queen.

He proved to be a good king, extended Lydian power over neighboring city-states, and added to the royal treasury. It may have been he who ordered the first gold coins to be minted near the end of the seventh century B.C. A successor, King Croesus (560–546 B.C.) carried this a step further, creating the first bimetallic system. He ordered the minting of one coin of pure gold, another of silver, and fixed the ratio between them at 13.33 silver coins to 1 of gold.

The coins were crude, more oblong than circular, with the head of a lion facing a bull stamped on one side. That stamp meant that coins had the support of a powerful Mediterranean kingdom, with Croesus guaranteeing their weight and purity. Whereas traders had questioned every shekel which passed into their hands, they accepted these coins without question. Gold had become a monetary metal, with silver as its junior partner.

It is difficult to overestimate the importance of this development, for man now had a medium of exchange which had eluded him for thousands of years. A voyage to distant lands could be made by a ship captain with only a bag of coins as his cargo, and he could return with a shipload of merchandise. A producer with a surplus of goods could sell that surplus for gold or silver coins, and those coins would serve as a store of value long after the merchandise might have deteriorated had it been kept.

Lydian kings realized the value of honesty in coinage, and they adhered to high purity standards when they minted their staters. So did the Persians with their darics, the Athenians with their owls, and Alexander the Great with his staters. Not so with many other of the city-states and kingdoms which flourished at that time, and definitely not so with many nations which followed.

Darius the Great, the Persian ruler who built a kingdom from the Mediterranean to the Indus River Valley, didn't need to fake the coins coming from his mint, for he had the wealth of the world at his fingertips. It was he who carried coinage a step further from those staters of the Lydians. He had his own portrait stamped on the coins minted in his kingdom. Thus, he was placing his own personal prestige upon them, though not as an ordinary human being. In those days, a king was viewed almost like a god, a figure meriting reverence. A coin with a representation of Darius on it, usually shown as a hunting bowman, indicated the presence of Darius in spirit if not in fact. So, every time a citizen handled one of these coins, he also had a reminder that he had better behave, lest the mighty Darius punish him.

Darius lived from 558 to 486 B.C., ruling from 522 to 486 B.C., and it was under him that the coin economy developed to the point where it became a force in everyday life. The bimetallic system of Croesus had been established around 560 B.C. In less than half a century, the system had spread throughout Asia Minor and into the kingdom of Persia. Just as the credit card swept through the western world in the post–World War II period, coinage rolled through the ancient world, spreading financial revolutions in its wake.

Coinage added a new dimension to taxation. Heretofore, taxes had been imposed in kind, with the ruler's warehouses collecting and holding grains, wines, and other products which might have been exacted from subject peoples. The Persians accepted coins for tax settlements, as well as products. From that day on, governments have had hands in pocketbooks of citizens, for better or worse.

The Persians may have been the first to recognize the political value of gold. Having decided that every politician has his price, they proceeded to buy. A stubborn vassal who revolted would find his rebellious army being bribed from under him. Greek cities were kept divided by Persian gold as well as by their own carefully cultivated jealousies. Persian gold helped purchase entry of the Persian army into the Greek city of Eretria in one of many wars. At the holy Isle of Delos, Persian gold proved even holier than the local shrine, winning a tenuous friendship for the eastern power. Herodotus, always an observant chronicler, even coined a word, "Medizing," to signify how Greeks could be purchased by Persians (Medes) with gold.

The payoff, indeed, goes back to the second coin, if not the first. Even today, the United States Central Intelligence Agency and others often use gold to pay off spies. Sometimes payments in gold have been cloaked in respectability, for the sake of the donor rather than the receiver. When the Roman Empire was threatened by barbarians, gold helped to contain those enemies at the tottering gates. Romans still had a shred of self-respect left, even in the final days when such shreds were flying in intemperate winds. So they developed ingenious ways to disguise their payoffs.

Emperors lavishly distributed medallions of gold for minimal services rendered by barbarian warriors. While ostensibly given as "honors" to friendly forces, these medallions really were bribes for good behavior. Even when the good behavior was not forthcoming, the Romans had little choice. They merely minted more gold medals for distribution.

The Persians had so much gold that disbursing it to divide enemies often seemed better than tackling the enemies in a bunch. In 525 B.C. when Persia added Egypt to its empire, it found itself in control of most of the gold-producing regions of the ancient world. Only Carthaginian-controlled Spain lay outside its sphere. Gold flowed into

Persian coffers from Egypt, Anatolia, India, Afghanistan, and central Asia. And trade developed on a scale unknown heretofore. Coins found in widely disbursed tomb sites provide evidence that commercial routes reached from deep within Asia to the cold shores of the Baltic Sea.

Today, of course, it is paper money rather than gold which tempts traders. That paper became acceptable only after men were trained to believe that it was "as good as gold." Such training became the task of the goldsmiths of the Middle Ages, who extended receipts to businessmen who left gold with them, with the receipts then becoming "as good as gold" when transferred to someone else.

That trust of paper as money has been deteriorating in recent times, which is why the United States dollar has been slipping in relationship to gold. Whereas in the summer of 1971, a U.S. dollar was reckoned to be worth 1/35th of an ounce of gold, in December, 1974, the dollar was rated at only 1/198th of an ounce. To put it in another way, it took $35 to buy an ounce of gold in 1971, $198 to buy the same amount in December, 1974.

Should trust in any currency disappear entirely, all trade stops where that currency is the medium of exchange. Nobody would accept Confederate money for his goods, for instance, for trust in it has long gone. Since the U.S. dollar's convertibility into gold was repudiated by the President Nixon government in August, 1971, some people have not wanted to hold dollars if they could help it, preferring gold or any other currency which might be linked to it. Through most of history, gold has been the medium which has been acceptable in international commerce no matter what convulsions might be shaking empires.

Man always has been willing to go far for gold, and when he finds it he wants to corner it all if possible. First to try that maneuver was Alexander the Great, a man with the morals of Jay Gould, the financier, who tried to corner all the gold in the United States in black September, 1869. Twenty-three centuries separated the fourth century B.C. from the nineteenth century A.D., but man's attitudes toward gold had little changed. Alexander the Great, however, came much closer to cornering the market than could Gould.

Alexander has had his sycophantic minstrels singing his praises all through history. The record shows him to have been a ruthless killer who murdered his favorite "boy friend," slaughtered populations of whole cities, and sought gold like a colossal brigand. Though Persians were masters of gold diplomacy, they were no match for Alexander, either at monetary diplomacy or at war.

Alexander valued gold so much that when he crossed into Asia in 334 B.C. with forty thousand men to attack the Persian empire, he had a skilled mining engineer with him. He meant to create a mining as well as a political empire. He didn't miss much of the available gold, either. Every time a city fell to his forces, Alexander seized the civic treasury, added it to his own. At Sidon, a Phoenician city, he appropriated all the gold coins in the town. To avoid the burdens of gold, with battles to be fought, he buried those staters at a secret site. Victory followed victory and wealth poured into Alexander's treasury. He collected so much gold and silver elsewhere that he forgot about his Sidon treasure, and he never returned to claim it.

Alexander wasn't one to put all his eggs in one basket, for he not only had all the eggs, he had all the baskets, too. He not only conquered the ancient world, he eventually owned it all.

In 1850, workingmen digging at a site uncovered two copper pots filled with the gold staters. Most of the coins disappeared into pockets of workers, but more than 2,000 of them were salvaged by the Turkish governor of the area, coins which eventually reached world coin markets. Numismatics owes a debt to people like Alexander who buried coins for safekeeping. Over the centuries, literally hundreds of such treasure-troves have been found at different times, replenishing stocks of coins for collectors.

Alexander may have left more treasure-troves buried along his routes of conquest. If so, they are still waiting for discovery, and the gold will be as bright as when buried long ago.

From Sidon the Greeks headed directly for the Jewish capital, in the Judean hills, marching in neat order, spears raised, banners flying. It is a winding road through arid hills where scattered pine trees grow. Today that road has wrecks of trucks and tanks shattered in the 1948 war of independence, and there is little to remind one of that time in 333 B.C. when the road served only for foot soldiers, donkey trains, and wooden-wheeled carts.

But Jerusalem on its hills must have caught the eye in that distant time as it does today, with its buildings perched atop a ridge to face the pass down to the Mediterranean on one side, the Jordan valley and the Dead Sea on the other. It is a city built for defense, where the heights often have forestalled invaders. This, however, was Alexander, the master soldier, with a fresh, undefeated army.

Jaddua, the Jewish high priest, begged God for aid, and received an answer in a vision. Welcome the Greek warrior. Show him the Temple. God would do the rest.

So gates were opened. Jaddua, dressed in white, walked out, arms upraised, *shalom*ing. Alexander ordered his archers to hold arrows, and swordsmen to sheath swords. Led by Jaddua, he strode to the Temple, was told there about the prophecies of Daniel which predicted the overthrow of Persians by a Greek warrior. Alexander, easily flattered, saw this as a favorable omen. He told the Jews that he had come as a friend, and promised them his protection.

He marched away with his army to seize control of most of the then-known world. Victory followed victory, and his wealth accumulated. At Susa, the Persian capital, he found a thousand tons of gold and silver ingots in the treasury, along with two hundred fifty tons of gold coins. Not only was he conquering the ancient world, he also was cornering the gold and silver supply.

So what do you do when you have much of the world's gold plus the army to defend it? If you are like Alexander you start believing you are a god, and nothing destroys human relationships as fast as playing god among friends. It is one sure way of losing friends, even though, with enough gold, you may influence people.

And Alexander did use gold to influence events. Persians had coined money conservatively, preferring to hold surpluses in bar form in treasuries. Alexander reversed monetary policy. He ordered gold and silver bars to be minted as coins, then lavishly distributed the wealth to court favorites. He created a professional army of paid soldiers, rewarding them handsomely for more victories. He built new cities, poured money into the economy of the world.

But he minted money faster than goods could be produced to match. So he created the first monetary inflation known. Prices skyrocketed. Dissension was being planted in his empire even as he put it together. He died at thirty-two, a disappointed and lonely man, still calling himself a god even as, like King Midas, he was drowning in his own gold.

He did leave gold and silver legacies which survived long after his iron sword had rusted with him in his grave. The drachmas and staters he minted became the first world-wide currency, coins used from the Nile to the Indus and from the Black Sea to the Indian Ocean. Long after Alexander's death, those coins still circulated throughout this area, fostering a trade which saw the silks of India reaching the villas of Rome while the woolens of Thrace found markets in Anatolia.

As trade florished, merchants in Tyre, Athens, Babylon, Ecbatana, and other cities grew wealthy. They bought gold signet rings for themselves, gold jewelry for wives and girl friends. The art of the goldsmith bloomed as never before, with the goldsmith working not in the service of a king but as an individual entrepreneur producing works of craftsmanship for wealthy customers.

The path of gold moved westward after Alexander. Carthage, in North Africa, created a western Mediterranean empire which contained the rich gold mines of Spain. Strabo, the Roman writer, says that at peak forty thousand slaves dug gold and silver from those mines. This enriched Carthage and consumed slaves, as if humans were being sacrificed to the god Mammon, pounds of flesh for ounces of gold.

Most of man's gold up to the nineteenth century was mined by slaves or serfs. Sadly, no matter how much wealth gold represented, its industrial relations usually were based upon the cheapest possible labor. Even today, the gold mines of South Africa adhere to this centuries-old policy.

Rome never was a state to worry about industrial relations. It started as a gold-poor nation and it watched enviously as Carthage worked the rich mines of Spain. Control of those mines became one of the prizes in the bitter Punic Wars, fought between 264 and 146 B.C. Carthage's gold purchased a mercenary army comprised of a half-dozen nationalities. Rome's soldiers had a kinship which bound them together. In the final analysis, mercenary warriors could not match Rome's nationalistic spirit.

Arnold Hermann Ludwig Heeren, the German historian, wrote: "Rome trusted to itself and its sword, Carthage to its gold and its mercenaries. The greatness of Rome was founded upon a rock, that of Carthage upon sand and gold dust."

Gold is forever, but not the men who trust in it. Spain became another Roman province and Carthage was destroyed. That Spanish gold helped create the Roman Empire. By the Christian era, Spanish mines were yielding as much as twenty thousand pounds of gold annually.

Romans could do many things; they couldn't control their money, and this may have played a part in their downfall. Almost from the first coin, of course, there were rulers who needed more cash than could be provided by the gold and silver in the royal mint. So it sometimes seemed advisable to add copper or zinc or some other ignoble metal to the gold or silver, as one might water milk to obtain more glasses of it from a given supply.

The ancient Greeks, however, had been believers in sound money. They believed that a money standard should be fixed so that the lender receives the same amount of money back when repaid by the debtor. This basic money concept has collided time and again with the easy-money philosophy advanced by the Romans. They believed that money should be only a medium of exchange, with the standard of value changed at the convenience of the state. Since the state usually had less money than it wanted to spend, rather than a surplus, this meant that the currency should be debased.

Thus, the Roman emperors thought nothing of adding more and more copper or lead to their gold and silver coins as a way to increase the number in circulation. This, of course, didn't add any more real wealth to the empire. It merely created a continual inflation as prices rose to compensate for the currency loss being experienced through addition of dross metals to the coinage.

The Roman philosophy about money closely matches that of many present-day monetary authorities, people who still preach that money should be the tool of the state rather than of the citizens who have earned the wealth. So the supply of paper money is ever increased as the printing presses roll. But no new wealth is created in this fashion, so prices rise up and up as the watered currency chases the supply of goods available on the market.

George Finlay, a Scottish historian, writes of Roman monetary policy:

> In reviewing the causes which contributed to the decline of the wealth and the diminution of the population of the Roman Empire, it is necessary to take into account the depreciation of the coinage, which frequently robbed large classes of the industrious citizens of a great part of their wealth, reduced the value of property, produced confusion in legal contracts, and anarchy in prices in the public markets. The evils which have resulted from the enormous depreciation of the Roman coinage at several periods can only be understood by a chronological record of the principal changes, and by remembering that each issue of a depreciated coinage was an act of bankruptcy on the part of a reigning emperor.

With Rome's decline, the westward march of history faltered for a time. Constantinople became the new capital of the world, the empire of Byzantium rising from the ashes of Roman civilization. It was the Emperor Constantine who established the city on the Bosporus in 325 A.D. In the same year, he reformed the imperial currency, creating a new gold piece, the solidus or bezant. This unit, which contained sixty-five grains of gold, became the key currency of Byzantium.

Just as the dollar became a world currency in the twentieth century, the bezant was used by merchants from China to Ethiopia and from the steppes of Russia to the walled cities of the Adriatic. It became the epitome of sound money, a currency which retained its worth for nearly eight hundred years. No other currency in all history, certainly not the dollar, can match that record.

Finally, in the twelfth century, the bezant was "watered" with a twenty-five percent addition of base metal. The decline of empire had begun. Was it the weakening of the currency which started that decline, or was that money malaise merely a surface reflection of basic cracks in the government structure that were becoming apparent? It probably was the latter. The Turks were knocking at the gates of Byzantium with the hilt-ends of their swords, and they weren't the kind of people who could be dissuaded from conquest by gold medals hastily minted and distributed with a few fawning remarks.

As the power of Byzantium receded, that of the city-states of Italy and countries of Western Europe increased, a situation reflected in the gold coinage. Florence, in 1252, introduced gold coinage to Western Europe, followed by France in 1254, England in 1257, and Venice in 1284.

Some monarchs followed the Roman practice of debasing the currency. England's Henry VIII did away with the Henry VII gold penny with its twenty-three carats and three and one-half grains of fine gold. Instead, he introduced a lower-quality coin called a crown, which was composed of twenty-two carats gold and the rest alloy. He found himself still spending more than he was earning, so he lowered the gold content to twenty carats.

In all eras individual counterfeiters thrived—at least for a while, though the death penalty often applied to those caught minting their own coins. Counterfeiters learned early how to gild gold and how to plant a lead core within a silver or gold coin. In a cave near Alexandria, Egypt, archaeologists discovered a small furnace and other counterfeiting tools which dated to the time of the Ptolemies. The entrepreneurial spirit always has been strong in the world of gold, often for ill-gotten gain, sometimes for honorable ends.

With the development of numismatics, counterfeiters also learned how to mint fake coins created so accurately as to defy detection by many an expert. During the Renaissance, expert forgers developed such skills that their fakes now have worth in numismatic collections as old, clever forgeries. Fakes of old Roman coins made in fifteenth-century Padua, Italy, are especially prized.

These fakes are even called Paduans by coin collectors, who value them for their craftsmanship. Giovanni Cavino and Alessandro Bassiano were two of the best of the counterfeiters. All of Cavino's forged pieces are now listed and published in catalogs, and there is brisk demand for his work among collectors around the world. His Roman sestertii and other coins of the empire are masterpieces of the engraving art, models to inspire any crook who believes in perfection in his illicit trades.

A German forger of the nineteenth century, Karl Becker, deserves a place in the Counterfeiters' Hall of Fame, too. He produced more than six hundred fakes, running the gamut from ancient Greek and Roman coins to medieval and Renaissance pieces. Like Cavino, he too has his fans among collectors.

"His most successful dies were those which he cut for a series of Roman denarii, where the style and the 'feeling' of Roman portraiture were beautifully captured," says George Taylor, a professor at the American University of Beirut in Lebanon, and a Fellow of the Royal Numismatic Society.

False ancient coins are so numerous that the great museums of the world keep trays of forgeries, or casts of them, for reference. The major museums maintain laboratories equipped with electronic gadgets and devices which closely check coins and the metals in them. An expert eye is a great help in locating fakes, too, for not all forgers have worked with the skill of a Cavino or of a Becker.

A few years ago, the South Shields Museum, in County Durham, England, displayed a coin which was thought to be a sesterce from the reign of Hadrian Augustus, minted between 135 and 138 A.D. A nine-year-old girl who had grown interested in her father's coin collection studied the coin and declared it to be a fake. Moreover, she recognized the fake as a copper replica given away by a soft-drink company in exchange for bottle caps.

The red-faced museum director took another look and decided the little girl was right. The replica had been found by some small boys near a Roman ruin, and museum authorities had jumped to some quick conclusions without knowing much about numismatics, or what neighborhood kids were doing, either. None of the museum's officials were collecting pop-bottle caps to garner prizes. And one museum official embarrassedly said: "In the future, we shall view any coin which is brought in to us with the gravest suspicion."

But nobody lost any money because of that coin, which is more than can be said of many of the fakes which reach the market.

Prices being paid for coins by numismatists provide much inspiration for the counterfeiter. In November, 1972, a collection of 347 Roman gold coins auctioned in Geneva by Sotheby's, the London-headquartered auction house, brought a world record price of $2.2 million. The coins were offered by the Metropolitan Museum of Art, New York City. Sotheby's had expected the sale to bring in a third of that total. One coin alone, a rare Roman piece dating from around 280 A.D. and bearing the head of the Emperor Saturninus, fetched $55,200.

A counterfeiter might try to make such a coin with less than $50 worth of gold plus his engraving skill, which indicates his scope for profit provided he could find a well-heeled, ignorant buyer.

Occasionally, a counterfeiter is caught by the law, and his story makes it appear as if enforcement authorities are hawkishly protecting the coins of the realm. Any numismatics expert knows that forgeries are his greatest problem, not only those which might be of recent manufacture, but fakes which might have been made years and even centuries ago.

The ease with which a counterfeiter may operate in the coin field is startling. In London, in 1969, police apprehended one Anthony Dennington, a part-time film extra and occasionally a street salesman, who had established his own mini-mint in the Chelsea section of the city. His tools of trade were rather simple, a $14 electric kiln, a small oxygen acetylene burner and some false-tooth powder.

He started in business by purchasing several replicas of old coins sold in base metals by the British Museum before that institution realized how such copies might be used or misused by forgers. Dennington employed the false-tooth powder to form molds about the replicas. He purchased a few old gold rings, watch cases, and spoons, melted them down, then carefully poured them into his molds. With a little polishing, the resulting products were sold to coin collectors as the real thing. Since prices in the numismatics field may range from a few times to several hundred times the metal content (and even more with the rare coin), he had found a very profitable way to transform his investments of a few hundred dollars into several thousand dollars in short order.

Once he had his operation started, he could extend the range of his minting. Perhaps he might have gotten away with it if he had not become too greedy and enlarged his operation a little too quickly. Somebody who had been rooked by one of his coins complained to the police. Soon Scotland Yard, in the person of Detective Sergeant James Driscoll, launched an investigation. Dennington's three-room flat was raided.

Police found 2,000 coins, 500 moulds, and forgeries of 38 different types of coins issued during the reigns of fifteen British monarchs. Among them were four perfect reproductions of the Henry III gold penny of 1257. Only seven originals of this particular coin are known in the world.

"Sure, I was making coins," Dennington admitted when arrested. "There is nothing wrong in that. I made copies of old coins, not current ones. There's no law against that."

The court at Old Bailey had other ideas. Dennington was found guilty of six charges of "causing people to pay money by falsely pretending" they were buying antique coins. He was given a sentence of two years.

Dennington was casting his coins. Most coins today are made from strip gold which is rolled to the desired thickness of the coin. Blanks to the appropriate size are stamped by a punch press. Then the blank is hydraulically pressed in a die to produce the finished coin.

In a small shop in Milan, Italy, I once watched a goldsmith as he bent over a die to place a flat disc of gold into it. The hydraulic machine over the die squeaked and groaned, then slammed hard against the die under the touch of the smith's hand on a lever. A United States $10 gold piece lay under the hammer, a perfect specimen which he passed to me for inspection. It was hot from the enormous pressure exerted by the hammer upon it and I held it on an asbestos glove while I studied the design.

Only an expert could have identified the coin as a replica. It couldn't be termed a fake unless passed as the real thing, for it did contain the 15.05 grams of 900-parts-per-thousand gold, exactly as the

United States Mint used to make them. But the U.S. Mint hasn't made any since 1933. So such a piece can't be called genuine.

Unfortunately for coin collectors, many of these gold pieces do appear in the numismatics market, not as replicas but as genuine coins of the era marked on faces. This particular goldsmith insisted that his coins were going to gold-hoarders as replicas, not into the numismatics market as fakes. Maybe so. But with premiums of 2,000 and 3,000 percent on rare coins and of 500 percent on easy-to-pass big-circulation coins, the temptation is strong for any holder of a replica to sell it as the real thing.

In Beirut, Lebanon, at another small goldsmithing shop, I watched a second "mint" produce several dozen British gold sovereigns, each of the prescribed gold content and size, each looking to me as good as an original. Again, I was assured that there was no law in Lebanon against manufacturing replicas of this type. As long as buyers were willing to pay a premium for them, this goldsmith was ready to manufacture them. And what if those buyers resold the pieces as genuine British-made sovereigns? This goldsmith, a moustached Syrian with a jolly, well-fed appearance, shrugged. This wasn't his affair, he assured me. If laws were broken in some distant country, then it was up to that country to solve its own problems.

Gold always has been popular in the Middle East as a means of settlement and a store of value. In the late 1930's and during the World War II period, Saudi Arabian oil revenues had to be paid in gold sovereigns. Subsequently, the dollar became the standard of value and contracts were closed in this currency. But individual sheikhs and wealthy merchants retain faith in the gold sovereign (a broad term which often covers any gold coin in the Mideast, though genuine British sovereigns also are common). When King Saud of Saudi Arabia went into exile in 1964, he cashed a private hoard believed to have numbered two million gold coins. The vast majority of all the gold coins in circulation in the area are forgeries, products of goldsmithing shops in Lebanon and in Syria.

The most common coin dies noticed in Lebanon are for the following coins:

*Sovereigns.* This is probably the most common of all, for this particular coin is extremely popular in the Sudan and in North Africa. When Egypt's Nasser was waging his war in Yemen, gold sovereigns were used by both sides to bribe and persuade tribes. At peak of the fighting, Lebanon was exporting as many as 1,750,000 gold sovereigns per annum to the Yemen. Arabs are conservative and like coins with heads of rulers they have heard about. Almost all forgeries are in coins of Edward VII and George V. King George VI made less of an impression upon peoples of the Arab world, and his coins are not liked. Coins of Elizabeth II, generally, are shunned. She is a woman, and Arabs don't like representations of females on coins.

*Queen Victoria Jubilee £5 (1887).* Oddly, the prejudice against women does not apply to this particular coin. Britain in the Victorian period was such a power that it made an impression upon the world, including the Mideast. Queen Victoria is recognized as a powerful figure, too, and her coins are treated with respect. These particular coins contain 39.94 grams of fine gold each and often are placed in simple frames to be worn as pendants.

*Turkish reshad.* This is an early twentieth-century coin of 7.217 grams fine gold. Most of these go to Anatolia.

*Mexican 50 peso.* These are manufactured for the Latin American market, with distribution focusing on Curaçao. Argentines are particularly heavy buyers of this coin.

*U.S. $20 double eagle.* This coin has world-wide distribution. It is popular with gold-hoarders who save the coins for the gold content rather than for the numismatics value. However, many of these fakes do work into the numismatic collections of individuals. With gold coins, it definitely is a case of let the buyer beware.

*Russian 10 or 20 ruble.* There is a small demand for these, especially in Iran.

*French napoleon.* This is a coin which is very popular in France and in the French-speaking world. It, too, is well liked by gold-hoarders who are saving for that rainy day when the heavens open wide and all paper currencies are swept away.

Sometimes unscrupulous goldsmiths will shave the gold content of the pieces manufactured. Usually, the replica-makers closely follow weights and purities of the genuine coins. Many of the shops are looking for repeat business, and the premium on their coins is enough to guarantee a steady and easily-made profit. Thus, truth pays, and their "honestly made" replicas are extremely difficult for anyone but a coin expert to identify.

The coin is only one product found on the gold trail which lay along the Mediterranean for much of man's history. The voyage of Columbus and subsequent explorers shifted that trail to the New World, but the route remained a rough and rocky road until Africa again entered the gold picture.

It was a chance discovery on the lonely veldt of the Transvaal in South Africa which changed the geography of the gold trail. Admittedly, today there is some unhappiness in certain quarters concerning that shift. Some take this almost as a personal affront, and transfer their distaste for South Africa onto all of its products, including gold.

No one can say that this metal is good, that one bad, this element a boon, that one a burden. Even uranium, the substance of atomic bombs, may also be a fuel for man-harnessed power. Morals have as little to do with gold as piety has to do with the materials which go into a church. Still there will always be people who will search for material scapegoats, when they should be looking into men's hearts and minds.

It is a fact that the modern gold trail has its feeder inlet in South Africa, a nation which has established apartheid as its racial policy. One must go to South Africa if one wants to start today's gold trail and ride it to the jewelry shops of New York, Paris, London, and elsewhere.

CHAPTER VI

# The Gold Trail

In February, 1886, George Harrison and George Walker were hired to build a stone shack for the widow Oosthuizen's farm, in Langlaagte, a few miles west of where the city of Johannesburg, South Africa, now stands. This was a land of wide, open spaces, of prairie and rolling hills where herds of springbok, wildebeest, and impala roamed on grasslands. Pretoria, the Boer capital of the Transvaal Republic, lay a long days' ride away. It was a provincial town of farmers who were determined that this land would continue to be a farming country for Afrikaans people.

Harrison was an itinerant laborer who liked his liquor when he could get it, a rough, tough drifter who had prospected in the gold fields of Australia before being attracted to the Transvaal. While working with a pick to pry rocks for the stone hut, he uncovered a piece of quartz with some fine-grained streaks along its face. Could it be?

He stopped work, located a sledge hammer in the farm's tool shed. He broke the rock with the sledge, borrowed a frying pan from the kitchen to rock the pebbles around. Sure enough. Gleaming yellow particles much heavier in weight than the rock settled into the bottom of the pan.

"I think I have found gold," he said to his working partner, maybe not in those exact words, but to the same effect.

Both men staked claims, not sure that they had found much of anything, unaware that they had struck the Witwatersrand Reef, the richest gold-bearing reef ever to be found anywhere.

Word of the claim reached Pretoria, and Harrison was asked to make an affidavit concerning his find. What he wrote is preserved in the City Museum of Johannesburg amid the artifacts of what overnight became one of the busiest mining camps in the world. Said Harrison: "My name is George Harrison and I come from the newly discovered gold fields Kliprivier especially from a farm owned by a certain Gert Oosthuizen. I have a long experience as an Australian gold digger and I think it a payable gold field." The affidavit was addressed to Stephanus Johannes Paul Kruger, the doughty, chin-whiskered president of the republic, who later was to see his beloved country torn apart by British troops.

Kruger knew what the discovery of gold would mean. His was a small, rural republic without the resources to defend itself against determined men driven by the lust for gold. He knew what had happened in California and in Australia after discoveries of gold. Men had poured into the gold fields from around the world, eager for sudden wealth, ready to fight for real or imagined rights, unwilling to bend very far to legal authority. Kruger dispatched two commissioners, C. Johannes Joubert and Johann Rissik, to the new mining camp to establish some form of control.

As for Harrison, the cause of it all? He sold his claim for £10 and disappeared from the pages of history. One report says he was killed and eaten by lions in the eastern Transvaal. The gold trail has many tragedies like that, of wealth dangled before someone's eyes only to fade, or of immense deposits discovered by someone who gains nothing from the bonanza.

Men did pour into the Transvaal, just as Kruger had feared, gruff adventurers, polished card sharps, experienced miners, fast-talking promoters, speculative businessmen, daring investors.

The gold trail, wherever it lay, has always been filled with extraordinary characters. Southern Africa had its own monumental heroes, men like Cecil Rhodes, the nineteenth-century tycoon who had a dream of empire rather than of wealth. He used diamonds and gold as a means to this end, knowing that if he discovered one or the other he would not have to colonize that part of Africa. Man's greed for those precious minerals would attract people in a mad rush, and the land would be settled overnight.

Historians don't give enough credit to greed as a motivator for actions which in retrospect are clothed in more acceptable garments. Even those people who score wealth as an evil which should be controlled often spend their lives chasing financial rainbows, and if they are successful in finding a golden pot at the base of one of those figurative arches, the proceeds probably will go into a numbered Swiss bank account. Rhodes understood this with that cold appreciation for logic sometimes found in a man who looks after himself first.

Physically, Rhodes was a big man, tall, broad-shouldered, blond, one to stand out in any crowd and to dominate it with a few crisp, sharp orders. Giving orders was his forte, each issued with a cutting edge which left no doubt as to who was the boss. Wherever he happened to be, he liked to take charge, and there usually were enough sycophants to oblige him. At one time, Rhodes controlled much of the mining industry in southern Africa, and a word from him could start a new railroad a-building, or a new colony developing. He helped to chart the gold trail upon the route it now follows from the mines to the markets of the world. Gold for him was only a commodity for building an empire that never materialized. The gold trail remains, for gold has always proved more durable than empires.

This I reflected as I sat on a boulder atop the Matopos, a jumble of granite hills south of Bulawayo in Rhodesia. This country bears Rhodes' name, of course, and Rhodes' grave is atop those Matopos. His tomb was hollowed from the rock, then covered with a simple slab of copper. Huge boulders fringe the grave like some prehistoric mound paying honors to a tribal chieftain. From the heights the country around is visible for miles, a panorama which Rhodes named "the World View."

Rhodes played his part in the development of Africa, and he had a role in something else, too, the shift of gold mining's focus from the northern to the southern hemisphere. Today, one single South African mine, the Vaal Reefs mine, produces more gold than do all the mines in Canada combined. America's total gold production is only five percent of South Africa's.

The latter's forty-five producing gold mines are employing over a quarter of a million men in workings which probe more than two miles into the earth. All of their efforts produce only 24,500,000 fine ounces of gold annually, or about 762 metric tons of the stuff.

To get that gold, the miners must hoist more than 80 million tons of rock to the surface. Their year's gold output would fit into the back end of a medium-sized truck. Such a load would flatten the truck, though, for gold is one of the heaviest of metals and the truck hasn't been built yet which will carry 762 tons at a crack.

World gold production statistics indicate the lead which South Africa has over the rest of the world. The following figures come from P. D. Fells, chief researcher with the Consolidated Gold Fields Group in London, an astute bullion expert who prepared the tabulation from preliminary data. Fells can account for just about every ton of production and where it goes. Figures are in thousand fine ounces.

| | |
|---|---:|
| Republic of South Africa | 24,5000 |
| Canada | 1,704 |
| United States | 1,125 |
| Ghana | 887 |
| Philippines | 578 |
| Rhodesia | 514 |
| Australia | 466 |
| Japan | 354 |
| Colombia | 161 |
| Mexico | 129 |
| India | 106 |
| Nicaragua | 96 |
| Zaire | 84 |
| Elsewhere | 2,153 |
| | 32,857 |

Those figures show that in 1974, South Africa accounted for 74.6 percent of the free world's gold production. The Communist Bloc's output can only be estimated. However, in 1974 the Bloc sold 7.2 million fine ounces. This means that a total of 40,000,000 fine ounces moved onto world markets.

Researcher Fells estimates that 23,726,700 ounces of that gold went into fabrication, which includes watches, spectacles, jewelry, dental fillings, medals, and all the other uses to which gold is put.

Meanwhile, only a negligible amount filtered into the monetary reserves of various countries to back up the money in circulation.

The soaring gold price is accounting for a sharp fall in the amount of new gold going into fabrication. Gold's demand is, indeed, a factor of price where industrial uses of the yellow metal are concerned, evidence indicates.

An estimated 16,460,000 ounces went into caches of gold-hoarders and speculators. More will be said about them later. Suffice it to say here that a huge amount of gold is in the hands of people around the world who are worried about currencies, the threat of trouble, or about confiscatory taxes. Some of these people may literally have some gold buried in their backyards for rainy days. In India and other parts of Asia, the hoarded gold may be collected as jewelry. The French, avid hoarders, like to collect gold coins as well as small bars of gold. Germans prefer coins. In Switzerland, children may find small gold bars in their Christmas stockings, or in gift packages on birthdays. The total volume of gold in the hands of hoarders may only be estimated. Some sources aver the total exceeds 600 million ounces, which at current prices would be valued at around $100 billion.

Other people holding gold may be shrewd speculators who are gambling that the future price of gold will be much higher. In any case, in 1972, gold fabricators and others were able to draw more than four million ounces of gold from speculators and hoarders.

Another source of gold should be mentioned, too. This is in sweeps, the scrap and reclaimed gold which comes from the stampings, the filings, the cuttings, and even from the dust on a plant floor.

Gold is a valuable commodity and the crysophobe case against it has never reached the shop floor no matter how often some antigold folk may deride the metal as a "barbarous relic." Every tiny sliver cut from an article by a craftsman is collected for reuse.

When one goldsmith shop in Milan renovated its building, an old wooden floor was carefully torn up, then burned on a concrete base. More than $10,000 worth of gold was sifted from the ashes, enough to more than pay for the bonfire. At Gori & Zucchi's modern plant in Arrezo, Italy, workers depart from the plant over a series of vibrating grates. These shake loose any minute specks of gold which might be sticking to shoes.

"We pick up several thousand dollars worth of gold a year this way," said one security guard, explaining the operation.

Naturally, security is superstrong in gold shops, too. Modern plants have Big Brother gold-detecting devices which trigger alarms when any worker steals even tiny bits of gold. Big Brother loves Little Brother, but only when the latter behaves. Perhaps the temptations of Little Brother are no greater when working with gold than with brass; but the suspicions of the gold-shop owner are much greater than are those of his brass-shop counterpart. A rise in crime rates may reflect only the increased surveillance in the gold shop. Most shops require workers to wear overalls sans pockets, and plants handle the laundry, a bit of paternalism which has nothing to do with employee welfare. The gold collected in the laundry water far more than compensates for the cost of the service.

Every year, too, a certain amount of gold comes from reclaimed articles: an old athletic trophy, watchcases from defunct watches. Gold is used over and over again. Sometimes there may be disappointments in reclamations, too. The American winner of the 1907 Kaiser Wilhelm Yacht Race in Germany was given a gold loving cup.

In 1918, in a wave of patriotism, that American donated the cup to a fund drive, believing its gold content represented a substantial sum. The cup proved to be of pewter coated with a thin layer of gold worth only $25. Kaiser Wilhelm probably had been duped by a goldsmith who gambled that a wealthy yachtsman hardly would be melting down his winner's cup.

In South Africa, mines pour their gold into 1,000-ounce bricks, which usually are around eighty-eight percent pure gold. This would be 880 gold under the usual system of measuring quality in the industry, meaning that there are 880 parts of pure gold in every 1,000 parts of brick or bar. Normally, too, nine percent of the metal in those 1,000 ounces bricks will be silver, the other three percent other metals. Those "other metals," moreover, may be very valuable indeed, including such metals as platinum and palladium, which are more valuable than gold.

All of South Africa's gold is refined at the Rand Refinery in Germiston, a suburb of Johannesburg. The refinery sits in parklike surroundings, protected by a high, wire screen fence with cold-eyed guards at the gate. Nearly $5 billion worth of gold passes in and out of the main gate every year, enough to prompt supersecurity measures.

"Nobody has gotten away with anything yet from us," said W. W. Bath, the big, wavy-haired general manager of the refinery. He is a hearty, friendly man who bubbles with enthusiasm where gold is concerned, one who obviously relishes his job. The refinery is owned by the South African Chamber of Mines, the association of South Africa's mining industry. Bath assumed administration of the operation in 1964 and has modernized the entire facility. The only remaining relic of another day is the headquarters office, which is housed in a gracious Cape Dutch–styled building with red roof and walls of white stucco.

The refinery not only has sharp guards on duty, it also is rigged with electronic devices which trigger alarms. Even a draft of wind or a mouse sometimes sets them to ringing. Each department takes responsibility for every bar which enters its area, and the surveillance of bars is almost morbid. Twice a month, security measures are checked in about the same manner as fire-prevention systems might be checked in other buildings or plants.

Interpol, the international police agency, circulates information to the gold-mining industry about robberies, new tricks tried by thieves, and various frauds tried or perpetrated.

"There is a pattern among thieves," explains Bath. "If one trick succeeds, you can be sure that others will attempt the same thing again, sometime, somewhere. We note every trick that is tried and we react to it."

A tour through the Rand Refinery is like a visit to Golconda, or perhaps like something that Francisco Vasquez de Coronado expected to find in 1540, when he led his expedition into the American Southwest looking for the legendary seven golden cities of Cibola. El Dorado at the foot of the rainbow!

A truckload of bars from the West Rand Consolidated mine had just arrived in an armored van. The vehicle was parked under an overhanging cement canopy. Several brown-uniformed guards watched intently as a crew of workers unloaded the ingots onto a roller platform. Workers shoved the golden bricks through an opening in the side of the building into the receiving room. There, each bar was checked by a smock-clad supervisor who noted the numbers stamped on the surface.

"That's a million-dollars worth of gold there," Bath said, casually. It all seemed so ordinary, that the bars might have been iron or some equally unimportant metal. But the glittering yellow surfaces held the eye. A bar of gold is something like a bold nude woman who suddenly appears among an assembly of men. The men might be church elders discussing sacred business, yet the woman is likely to attract all attention. And even after the initial shock, men will steal glances in her direction.

I watched as each bar was weighed, marked, then passed to the melt house for sample. Soon bars were fiery red molten metal, throwing heat around the shop. A white workman dipped what looked like a long soup ladle into a molten kettle, withdrew it, and plunged it into water. He lifted out a horsepill-sized oval of gold, dropped it into my hand. This would be tested and assayed to determine the exact mineral content of the mine bars. The assay would determine how much the mine would have coming for that particular shipment. Meanwhile, the melted gold was being poured into 12.5 kilogram bars on a casting wheel, a device which moved molds around as if they were sitting on a slow merry-go-round.

From here the bars went to the refining department where further melting would eliminate more of their impurities. Gold melts at 1,945 degrees fahrenheit. The refining process used at the Rand Refinery is the chlorine process devised by F. B. Miller in Sydney, Australia in about 1868.

The process consists of passing chlorine gas through molten gold bullion in a suitable retort. In the process, approximately 500 kilograms (1,100 pounds) of bullion are melted in a clay-lined graphite crucible. Then, a pair of ceramic pipestems are inserted into the molten charge and chlorine gas is passed through the bullion.

The gas converts silver and base metals into chlorides which rise to the surface. These are skimmed off as if one were removing the foam from a beer glass.

Some statistics of the refinery's operations indicate how important scrap and waste retrieval may be in a facility such as this. It is estimated, for instance, that a loss of only .01 percent amounts to 500,000 rands annually, or about $750,000.

Rand Refining functions on a four-day cycle from arrival of the rough bars to departure of the refined product at 996 purity for most of the finished gold, and at 999 purity for a small percentage which is refined to an ultra-high level through an electrolytic process. Gold is so valuable that even a short delay could be costly, since gold draws no interest. Thus, the money tied up in a refinery's inventory could be drawing interest in a bank under other circumstances. So any extension of the gold time cycle by one day means a loss of over 800,000 rands or about $1.2 million for Rand Refinery.

Few products are timed to work-schedules as closely as is gold when it moves through the channels of industry. It simply is much too expensive to allow gold to lie around idle, so processors use stop-watch precision in speeding products and shipments to customers. Some commodities are so valuable that one must pay a price merely to hold them, and gold is one of them. "It might have been" is a sad phrase indeed when applied on a giant scale to interest.

The 400-ounce bars are packed three together in a plastic box bound with wire strapping which cannot be cut except by breaking a seal on each binding. The gold goes to the South African Reserve Bank in Pretoria, which sells all of the country's production.

Usually, that transfer is only a paper transaction. The Bank orders the Refinery to forward specific shipments to destinations in Europe or elsewhere rather than to its vaults in Pretoria. London and Zurich are the two gold-marketing centers which draw most of South Africa's gold.

The shipments to Britain go by sea in vessels of the Union Castle line; those to Zurich are trucked in armored vans to the nearby Jan Smuts Airport, just outside Johannesburg, where bars are loaded onto South African Airways passenger jets for the 6,300 miles air haul.

The London Gold Market is conducted in a comparatively small meeting room at headquarters of N. M. Rothschild & Sons, Ltd., the merchant-banking concern which is the English arm of the Rothschild empire. Robert Guy, a Rothschild executive, is chairman of the gold price-fixing committee which sets the gold price to open the market every workday morning at 10:30 A.M. It has been the custom for a Rothschild man to be the fixing chairman since the first fixing in 1919, when the firm was deputized to act as the Bank of England's agent in gold dealings.

The mahogany-paneled room has that air of quiet luxury which is associated with the Rothschild clan. It has been a long time since anyone could accuse the Rothschilds of looking shabby or in need of a loan. A pendulum clock of eighteenth-century vintage ticks on a side table. On walls hang portraits of nineteenth-century royal personages who obtained loans from the Rothschilds at various times. Eventually, money purchased aristocracy for the Rothschilds, too, which may be just. One might conclude that true aristocracy lies with the lender rather than with the borrower when most other things are equal.

In addition to Rothschild, bullion dealers who are market members are: Mocatta & Goldsmid, which is part of the Warburg Banking Group; Sharps, Pixley & Company, Ltd., an associate of merchant bank Kleinwort Benson; Samuel Montagu & Company, Ltd.; and Johnson, Matthey (Bankers) Ltd.

Mocatta & Goldsmid was founded in 1684, ten years before the Bank of England. Sharps and Wilkins began business about 1750, trading under this name until 1957, when the firm merged with Pixley & Abell to form Sharps, Pixley. Rothschild was formed in 1804 as a private partnership and remains such to this day. Johnson Matthey & Company, Ltd., a metallurgical firm established in 1817, transferred its bullion-trading activities to a new subsidiary, Johnson, Matthey (Bankers) Ltd., in 1965. The most recently formed member is Samuel Montagu, which began business as a partnership in 1853.

At the fixings, one in the morning and a second in the afternoon, each dealer is in touch with his office through an open telephone line. He knows the spread his own firm is quoting for gold, as well as what is on offer and what is bid. The eventual fixing-price reflects a balance between the bids and offers which each member of the exchange has on its books. Each dealer has a small Union Jack before him, which normally lies on its side. A dealer stands this upright or waves it if he wishes to halt trading, perhaps to discuss the market with his office. When all the flags are down again, the five representatives proceed with the fixing.

After the market closes, there is nothing to stop late trading outside that market.

The London market deals in standard bars with a minimum gold content of 350 fine ounces and a maximum of 430 fine ounces. Quality is a minimum 995-parts-per-1,000 fine gold, the so-called "good delivery" bars of the trade.

In order that gold bars may be accepted as good delivery on the London market, an applicant must obtain recognition of his bars as good delivery from the central bank of the country of origin. He also must obtain sponsorship from one of the members of the market. That member assays the gold bars, charging a fee for this service.

Prior to 1968, the London Gold Market dominated the field, with most new gold going through the hands of one of the five bullion dealers there. This was primarily a wholesale market, with hundreds of banks and dealers around the world handling the retailing end of the business. Creation of the two-tier gold market in March, 1968, with one monetary price and a second free-market price for gold, ended London's leadership. The three big Swiss banks, Swiss Bank Corporation, Swiss Credit Bank and Union Bank of Switzerland, formed a gold pool of their own, made overtures to the South African Reserve Bank for supplies, then established their own market in Zurich. Today, this market claims eighty percent of the business of selling the new gold which comes onto the world market.

Switzerland does offer numerous advantages to anyone in the business of marketing gold. Unlike Britain and numerous nations, Switzerland allows its citizens to buy, sell, or hold gold without question. Banks freely display gold bars of all sizes in windows, along with trays of gold coins. A prospective buyer may purchase anything from a postage-stamp-sized bar to a lot of fifty tons. While statesmen in many countries glibly orate about liberty, freedom, and other democratic privileges as if these grow lushly on home soil, Switzerland does more than talk about them. It extends such rights to the pocketbook, a freedom which even the United States did not dare to grant for forty-one years.

The Big Three banks have refineries. Union Bank of Switzerland owns the Argor refinery at Chiasso, near the Italian border. Swiss Credit Bank has its subsidiary, Valcambi, another refinery in the same town. Swiss Bank Corporation has a subsidiary, Métaux Précieux SA, which has refineries at Neuchatel, Switzerland, and in Paris.

Credit facilities are available at the banks. Their telex and cable communications link key cities around the world. The banks have portfolio customers who sometimes deal in gold. Switzerland's currency convertibility allows buyers to pay in almost any kind of currency. There are no taxes on bullion gold. Storage facilities are available.

This all adds up to the fact that Swiss banks are the supermarkets of gold, ready to buy, sell, or store gold, to cast it in any desired shape, to deal in gold coins, or to handle transactions in gold futures. Atop this, the Big Three now have access to their gold pool, which means that Swiss banks are equipped to handle almost any sort of demand within reason. Let the gold market go wild in a currency crisis and Swiss banks probably will have enough gold on hand to meet all reasonable demand.

Swiss banks are ultra-secretive about the size of that pool which they have established. Some people in the gold trade aver that it is on the order of three hundred tons; Swiss bankers only smile when such a figure is mentioned. But Swiss Bank Corporation does claim to be the biggest gold dealer of the Big Three banks, which would make it the biggest gold dealer in the world.

Headquarters for Swiss Bank Corporation's gold operations is on Paradeplatz in the heart of Zurich. This is an old town, with smart shops which advertise the prosperity of this Germanic community. People in Zurich have money, and there never is any doubt of it, though they don't throw it around. The bank building reflects the character of the town, a substantial structure which probably could survive an atom bomb, yet one with no showy frills which might lead customers to believe that money is being thrown away on noninterest-bearing decorations.

Walter Frey, the manager of the bank's gold department, is built as solidly as a gold brick, a tall, positive banker who has spent twenty of his thirty seven years with the bank in the gold department. One might say that Frey is a man who knows where all the gold bricks are buried, and it isn't surprising to find that he has more than a nodding acquaintance with finance ministers, central bankers, and other monetary authorities. If one of these parties is making a swing through Europe to ascertain trends in finance and gold, chances are that he will have Frey on his agenda.

But Frey laughs embarrassedly when it is suggested that, if he heads the gold operations of the world's biggest merchandiser of gold, then he must be the leading individual dealer. Swiss bankers aren't used to calling much attention to themselves.

Like most Swiss bankers he has a healthy respect for gold as a monetary metal to give strength to the paper currencies which may be floating about. Thus he is a prime advocate of a return to convertibility of the United States dollar, meaning convertibility into gold, of course. That would necessitate a higher monetary gold price than the $42.22 pertaining in 1974 and also would require absorption of a considerable amount of the $100 billion worth of United States dollars which float in international markets.

Though Swiss bankers respect gold for its monetary worth, generally, they like a return on their money too much to feel that gold is a good investment except in the most troubled of times. If ever you note that a Swiss banker is buying gold for himself, that will be the time to become ultra-conservative with your own investments. In fact, you should cancel your vacation, start growing vegetables in your backyard if you have one, sell all your stocks except for the gold shares, and prepare for a depression.

Across the street from Swiss Bank Corporation on Paradaplatz, one finds the headquarters of Swiss Credit Bank, another of the Big Three banks in the gold pool. The last time I called there, Ernest Bigler was the chief gold trader, a sandy-haired, slender banker of youthful appearance who occupied a desk which was nearly enshrouded by a huge breadfruit tree that long ago had outgrown its adolescent pot. Nothing seemed to fluster him. Even when a money crisis brewed, he remained cool and calm, as if a stream of orders for up to a ton of gold at a going price of over $3 million was in the same category as the purchase of a dozen tulip bulbs.

Paul Zubler, the tall, iron-gray gold chief at Union Bank of Switzerland, a short distance along Bahnhofstrasse from Paradeplatz, is handsome enough to pass for a successful actor approaching middle age. But he has none of the actor's inclination to seize the stage wherever it happens to be for a demonstration of his histrionic power. Speak softly. Be discreet. Let others do the shouting. That is the Zubler way. Yet an interview with him can be revealing for, like all Swiss bankers in the gold trade, he is thoroughly informed about all developments which might affect the gold business in any way.

He converses easily about Russian gold sales, the troubles of the United States dollar, influences of Watergate upon monetary affairs, and the pace of South African Reserve Bank gold sales. As he mentions South Africa, he glances at a running chart he maintains showing the Reserve Bank's weekly withdrawals of its own reserves. Such withdrawals mean that less gold would be arriving from the Bank onto world markets. In times of heavy demand, any pinch on supplies often triggers an upward movement of prices.

The gold trader must be an extremely astute merchandiser, for his saleable product may fluctuate violently in price. Shrewdness is especially necessary in Switzerland for Swiss banks charge no commission on gold. London bullion dealers charge a commission of 0.25 percent on all transactions; so they earn a profit no matter how the price reacts. Swiss banks take profits from the spread between buyer's and seller's prices. Of course, if a bank always has a buyer to match a seller there should always be a profit, with no possibility of loss. But it doesn't work that way. Potential buyers exceed sellers in some markets and vice versa. Moreover, Swiss banks operate with a gold pool which provides a tremendous supply cushion.

There may be short periods when banks are purchasing more than they are selling and other times when they are selling more than they are buying. Market prices must be advanced or reduced to assure that these market swings don't catch the banks selling high-priced gold at a little lower price. Obviously, such mental nimbleness is a function of all good merchandisers, no matter what the product. But the gold merchandiser is not able to utilize any tricks of the trade to get a better price for his product, i.e., place all the ripened fruit on the first layer of the box with the green ones on the bottom, or stage sales to stimulate business. One properly assayed gold bar is exactly the same as another of the same assay, so there's no point in trotting down the street to a competing merchant if prices are the same. Under the pool arrangement, all Swiss banks charge pool prices, which are set by the market, so at any particular moment all prices will be the same for idential qualities and amounts of gold.

There is one minor exception to this rule of product uniformity in the gold business. Gold bars of Johnson, Matthey, the British company, are especially liked in the Middle East because of the sheen on their surfaces. The sheen comes from flame-polishing of newly cast fine gold bars through placing cooling ingots under the flame of a burning gas jet. This gives bars a bright, smooth, and shiny surface when the metal cools.

Any refiner can give its bars the same treatment, and chances are nobody could tell the difference between the product of one refiner and another. Nevertheless, an industrial myth has developed about the Johnson, Matthey bar in the area between the Mediterranean and India. This myth may be akin to that of the father who thinks that his kids are smarter than all the others in town, but it has much broader circulation than any father ever could expect.

Zurich and London tower so far above all other markets in gold that those others are relatively unimportant. This includes the Paris Gold Market. When Charles De Gaulle was in power in France, he dreamt of making Paris into a gold center which would rival London. Then, perhaps Paris rather than the United States dollar would have determined the price of gold. His dream didn't materialize.

Today, there is a small gold market in Paris which caters to the gold-hoarding instincts of French citizens. The Paris gold market has none of the internationality of the two big markets. It has a provincial flavor which may be galling to the Parisienne, but is a fact of life like gravity, high taxes, and the declining quality of the French cuisine.

Kingpin of the Paris gold market is Jean-Claud Martini, chief gold trader at Compagnie Parisienne des Réescomptes. He is a diminutive, hard-driving man who acts as if he might be much bigger, with nothing to fear but his own strength. While the Paris market handles only a fraction of the world's gold, about seventy percent of that passes through the hands of Martini or one of his aides.

America, with its small production, is no longer a factor in gold, so it has little influence except as a big purchaser of the metal. Producers of new gold in the United States returned to a free market on January 1, 1975. They sell to processors such as Engelhard Mining and Chemical Company and Handy & Harman. Since then, numerous banks, several brokerage houses, and other firms have entered the gold market to cater to retail demand for the metal. Prior to that date, annual gold production for the United States was about forty-five tons, while consumption amounted to two hundred fifteen tons. Some U.S. imports came from Canada, which produces about sixty-seven tons annually while consuming only eight tons a year.

Buyers of gold are monetary agencies, hoarders, speculators, and fabricators. Central banks acquire gold as reserves to back currencies, or much less frequently in these days, to manufacture coins. Hoarders buy gold because they believe that this is the best way to protect savings. Speculators purchase gold hoping to make a profit on a price rise. Fabricators turn gold into finished products, perhaps first refining it still further either in their own furnaces or in facilities of processors.

Gold processing is a big industry which deals with small things that may have considerable human import, a wedding ring, a watch for a girl friend, a filling for an aching tooth, a gold bar to provide some hoarder with an illusion of security. (It is no wonder that gold has always occupied such an important place in man's scheme of things. Gold is a metal which may touch nerves as well as heart strings.)

# CHAPTER VII

# *Melters of Gold*

Ian Fleming, the creator of James Bond, built his character Mister Goldfinger around the late Charles Engelhard, the flamboyant head of Engelhard Industries, according to some of the gossip one hears in London. Engelhard Industries was, and the successor company still is, America's largest precious metals company.

Engelhard was a breezy, extroverted character who loved race horses, good living, and the excitement of international deals involving gold. His standing order to his employees was to "always travel first class," for he realized that a man and his company may benefit not only from prosperity but also from exuding wealth. Money gravitates to money just as good service often gravitates to the richest man in the restaurant. Engelhard never let anyone doubt that he had it.

He operated internationally, constantly pushing his companies to find new uses for precious metals. His companies produced sheet gold for buildings, showed how gold could be used as heat reflectors in spacecraft, and assisted electronics companies to develop better electrical contact devices with gold as a raw material.

Among other things, he made it easy for Americans to invest in South African gold mining shares through the American South African Investment Company (ASA Ltd.). This is a South African–based mutual fund which he established as a vehicle for gold-mining investments.

Once when in Johannesburg, I received an invitation to spend a weekend at Kruger Park with Engelhard. The park is one of Africa's best game reserves, a place to see and photograph lions, elephant, various kinds of buck, and numerous other animals which roam what is left of the African veldt. Engelhard divided his time between his New Jersey headquarters, Europe, where he had substantial interests, and South Africa. Despite the latter's racial problems, he regarded it as a nation with an unlimited future. South Africa certainly was a country which fitted his swashbuckling concepts of business and of how life should be lived.

I knew that he maintained a luxurious mansion in an exclusive suburb of Johannesburg. Walls were decorated with paintings done by an American artist whom he had flown to South Africa for the express purpose of providing an artistic theme for the house. I wasn't aware at the time, however, of what it meant to catch up with Engelhard to spend a weekend with him at a game park.

A limousine whisked me to the Johannesburg Airport where a private ten-passenger Heron awaited me. An hour's flight took me to Leydenburg, where another limousine awaited near the end of the airstrip, as if I might have been somebody. Porters ran forward to transfer baggage. A chauffeur introduced himself respectfully, and I climbed onto the back seat of what may not have been a Rolls, but so it seems in retrospect.

This automobile transported me to the edge of the game park and to a thatch-roofed lodge which, at first glance, looked like a princely version of Ann Hathaway's cottage at Stratford-on-Avon, England. But, Mbula, named after the giant tree in the patio, around which the house had been built, was far more than a cottage.

The slate which formed the living room floor extended into the patio. Glass panels along one wall slid into a concealed nook to make the living room and the patio one in nice weather, which is most of the time on the edge of Kruger Park. African wood carvings rested on tables. A half dozen Congolese spears were spread in a half-moon pattern over the fireplace. A tall wooden giraffe stretched its neck to reach the mantlepiece. Obsequious servants always seemed to have drinks ready.

With Engelhard everything was done with a flourish, as if the man were living in a baroque world. Seeing game wasn't a haphazard matter of trusting to luck alone. Aides had checked with park rangers concerning the probable location of lions, elephants, and various other animals in the park. Information had been relayed to the chauffeur of the station wagon which transported us through the myriad of lanes and roads. Animals, like men, follow definite patterns. A businessman ascertains the patterns of humans through his market surveys, and he acts accordingly. The successful game-viewer analyzes the patterns of animals, and he may see far more in the bush than does the casual tourist. Engelhard made a success of everything including game-viewing because he worked hard at it.

On this day, animals had their cues. They appeared on schedule, waited long enough to be photographed, then trotted into the bush. They might have left notes on the vegetation saying that the next show would be at 5:00 P.M. We returned to the lodge, with Engelhard in a jolly mood.

"Next time you are in the Gaspé, let me know," he said over a sundowner, speaking as casually as if I might be spending one week-end in South Africa, another in Quebec. Then he added: "We have a fishing lodge there, you know. Come try the fishing."

South Africa. The Gaspé Peninsula. Boca Grande, Florida. Rome. They were part of Engelhard's beat, within easy reach of his private plane. Wherever he happened to be, numerous aides assured many more comforts than most people find at home.

Engelhard appeared bigger than life when alive, even bigger in retrospect. Yet he was operating in an area about which the general public knows very little. Few people even know the difference be-tween yellow, red, white, or pink gold, or what a carat means. To most people gold comes from the mines, is refined into bars, then appears as wedding rings, watchbands, bracelets, and such.

Actually, a giant processing industry lies between gold mines and sellers of finished products. It involves melting, alloying, casting, rolling, drawing, and cladding to produce metallic forms, and the processing of gold into salts and compounds. Gold wire, sheet, tub-ing, and alloys are cast, stamped, drawn, or rolled into watchcases, watchbands, fountain-pen points, dental fittings, and semifinished jewelry such as ring blanks, settings, shanks, and findings.

There is liquid gold, which is a solution of gold chloride added to oil. It is used for painting or printing on a glazed surface, for touching up cheap jewelry, for instance, or for gold lettering in a signboard.

There is rolled gold, which is copper with a gold cladding. This is the sort of gold (if you can use the word) which is apt to be used for making that gold spectacle frame or for more of that cheap jewelry. Many watchbands are of rolled gold, which is far-removed from an eighteen-carat gold band. The copper, of course, stretches the gold content so that a little bit will go a long way. There is nothing wrong with that, as long as the buyer realizes that rolled gold may contain very little real gold. Unfortunately, the term is apt to be employed so smoothly by a merchandiser that the buyer sometimes is led to believe he is purchasing the real thing, and at a bargain price, too. All is not gold under that glitter.

In rolled gold, the amount of gold in the alloy weighs less than one-twentieth of the total weight of the metal. If the gold amounts to one-twentieth or more of the total weight, the alloy may be rated as "gold fill," though the caratage must be a minimum of ten for this rating.

Laminated gold is what its name implies, gold which has been laminated onto a less valuable metal, nickel, for instance. This is a combination which is popular with some watchmakers. Gold may be desired in literally hundreds of different combinations by customers. Certain alloys may improve the machinability of the product. Others may change electrical properties of the native gold. Amounts and types of alloys may affect color.

In its pure state, gold is a bright yellow with a glittering surface. But pure gold is soft and it scratches easily. Alloys harden the metal. Thus, eighteen carats gold is better wearing than is twenty-two carats gold. However, as alloys are added to create a harder finish, the melter must realize that those alloys will also change the gold's color. So the alloying task is a precision technological job which is handled according to the specifications of the customer.

Green gold has silver plus cadmium and zinc as alloying agents. White gold may be created by using nickel and zinc as alloys, though silver or palladium also may serve. The latter metal, however, is much more expensive than gold, another factor to be considered in the mixing of these gold witch's brews. Red gold is obtained by adding copper as an alloy. Blue gold, a color which has little popularity in modern times, contains iron as an alloy.

The demand for colored gold changes with the fashions, and to a certain extent with the temperament of the peoples of different countries. South America has always liked reds in its gold. Central Europe prefers paler hues. White golds are liked as settings for diamonds because white gold does not compete with the stones as might highly polished yellow gold.

"In order to get good white gold in any carat, the whitening agent must be nickel," says Michael Roberts, managing director of the Niagara Falls Casting (UK) Ltd., in Warwick, England. "Palladium produces a muddy color, and silver, which can only be used for nine carats white, produces an unattractive, yellowish soft gold."

There are endless combinations, and the good jewelry designer draws upon these possibilities to enhance his work. Shades of red and green gold, for instance, have their value in composite floral design.

Melters, of course, must be thoroughly familiar with results obtained from different combinations. Additions of zinc to the alloy tends to mellow the harshness of the reds. When used with silver, the zinc provides a greenish tint. But zinc reduces the melting point of the metal, which sometimes is a disadvantage. While nickel may be a whitener, it also is a hardener. This may be an adverse factor if gold is to undergo considerable complex working.

The caratage of a gold helps determine the possibilities which are open to the melter. Nine-carat gold has only 37.5 percent pure gold, providing wide latitude for different combinations. But this gold contains so much base metal that it may tarnish, perhaps not as easily as brass, but enough to displease some customers. In costume jewelry, however, the life of the style may be shorter than the nine carats' life. So the gold quality may not matter.

Fourteen-carat gold has a wide variety of combinations. Most of the alloys in this quality of gold are hard and more difficult to work than eighteen-carat gold. Hence most goldsmiths prefer the eighteen to the fourteen. There are specific applications where fourteen-carat gold is superior, in pins and spring applications, for instance.

Eighteen-carat gold still has enough latitude in alloying to produce a wide range of colors and hardnesses. All colors from reds through greens to yellow and white are produced with alloys mentioned. Twenty-two carat gold leaves only 8.3 percent alloy, which restricts the color ranges. The natural rich yellow color of gold predominates.

During my visit to the Rand Refinery in Johannesburg, South Africa, W. W. Bath, the general manager, illustrated how alloying may produce different colors in gold. When South Africa designed its Krugerrand, a one-ounce gold piece, Bath selected the gold melt for the coin.

"Look." He extended a small jewelry box which contained six different-colored rand pieces in a row. Above them were two coins of reddish tint placed to show the obverse and the reverse sides of what proved to be the coin finally selected. The coins glistered in the fluorescent light. Colors of the six in the row ranged from a bright yellow on the left to a red then to a white coin at the far right.

The coin to the far left was of nearly pure gold, 99.9 percent. It had been produced merely to assist in judging the color, for such a coin would be too soft for issue. The coin at the far right was twenty-two carats gold with the remainder in silver. This produced a yellowish white gold. The four coins between had copper and silver combinations, with copper increasing the redness of the coin. The second coin in the row, for instance, had an orange glitter. The center one, which had the most copper, had a bright, reddish glow. That color faded into a pink-red in the next coin.

"These are the only six such coins in the world," explained Bath. "We weren't sure of the exact color we wanted, so I tried the six different combinations, made the blanks and coins were stamped out." He rolled the case in his hands, then added: "I selected this one."

He pointed to the coin which contained twenty-two carats gold and the remainder in copper. It had a red-gold color which I would have selected myself had anyone asked me for my opinion.

I noted when talking to him that South Africa has swung over to the metric system of designating weights and measures in its gold industry. The troy ounce still remains the most popular way of designating the price of gold. But grams rather than grains or pennyweight have been adopted by nearly every country except the United States. The pennyweight was originally the weight of an English silver penny, or 1/240th of a Tower pound. One troy ounce contains twenty pennyweight or 480 grains.

Troy ounces. Grams. Grains. Pennyweight. This can be confusing in the world of gold. The grain goes back to the days when man was reaching hard for something to use as a weight measure. In olden times, merchants noticed that grains of wheat near the center of a wheat ear always seemed to have a uniform size, even though the ear itself might be scrawny or fat depending upon the weather factors in a particular year. So they adopted these grains as a measure of weight when weighing coins, gold nuggets, and such. The particular weight remained in use in Britain until that nation adopted the metric system of the European Common Market. In colonial days, it was introduced into America. One grain is equal to .0648 grams, or to put it another way, 15.432356 grains equal one gram.

Mining magnates in gold knew their weights all right. But up to 1967–68 they paid little attention to the vast market which had been developing for their end product. That market had grown without any effort on the industry's part. Gold was gold. Every properly assayed bar was alike after allowing for purity and weight differences. Every bar could be sold easily at the price of $35 an ounce plus handling charges and insurance (usually about ten cents an ounce). This price pertained from January, 1934, until March 17, 1968, when major industrial nations established the two-tier gold market, with one monetary price and another set by the free market. Creation of the two-tier system flashed warning signals for gold-mining companies.

Antigold forces alleged that the free price might slide well below the $35 monetary level. This would create selling and financial problems for gold mines. If central banks then refused to buy new gold, mine after mine might be forced to close.

In retrospect, it seems surprising that such views were held at all. The United States dollar was in trouble at that time, a problem which worsened as time passed. And when people become worried about a major currency such as the dollar, many turn to gold as a hedge. Thus, predictions of a collapse of the gold market were based only on wishful thinking, not upon any deep assessment of the facts. Some United States congressmen and senators were among the miscalculators.

One Wisconsin representative with a generally good record in the monetary field, for instance, was predicting that the free-market price might fall to as low as $10 an ounce. In 1974, the free price actually hit $198 an ounce: a quite dramatic contrast between prediction and fact. Undoubtedly, a political writer might draw some conclusion about the wisdom of congressmen from this, but we are not writing a political tome.

Gold-mining executives were not among the pessimists, yet they did have to consider the possibilities of a buyers' market. Marketing and merchandising techniques applicable to other industries seemed in order.

Consolidated Gold Fields, Ltd., London, a world-wide mining group with major interests in South African gold mines, already had made a market survey prior to March, 1968. The work by economist D. O. Lloyd-Jacob presented for the first time a detailed picture of demand factors for gold. This study has been updated twice since, the last time in the company's *Gold 1972* report, prepared by P. D. Fells, of Consolidated's research staff.

The original work stressed a factor which nobody else had emphasized up to that time. Industrial demand for gold was soaring. As inflation persisted year after year, the price of gold was falling in real terms. More and more people were being added to the jewelry customer potential.

"Gold may eventually become another silver, with industrial use entirely replacing monetary demand, with stocks built up for monetary purposes being consumed for industry, and with a subsequent free-market period when supply and demand have to get into balance on their own," said this report.

It was a prescient statement. Any investor who paid any attention to the implications of this report must have made a fortune.

Meanwhile, a very comprehensive market survey was completed separately by Charter Consolidated Ltd., London, a mining-company affilate of Oppenheimer's Anglo American Group. L. L. C. Smets, chief economist for Charter, headed an eight-man research team which conducted over five hundred interviews in twenty-three countries to complete a voluminous study which is perhaps the most detailed ever made in this area.

In an introduction, Smets wrote: "The non-monetary market for gold is a subject which has long deserved much more detailed and comprehensive study than it has ever received, a gap in our knowledge all the more paradoxical because of the mountainous literature surrounding gold in its monetary role. The introduction of the two-tier system in March, 1968, made it imperative for more comprehensive information to be obtained and this study originated from that need."

He added: "We hope that parts of the report will be found interesting or amusing to non-experts, since gold is really the most romantic of research topics and deserves better than to be considered purely in statistical terms."

Statistics of industry sources show that in 1974 world gold fabrication by end use was as follows:

|  | METRIC TONS | PERCENT |
|---|---|---|
| Jewelry | 270 | 33.9 |
| Dentistry | 65 | 8.2 |
| Electronics | 95 | 11.9 |
| Other Industrial | 60 | 7.5 |
| Coins, medals, medallions | 306 | 38.5 |
| TOTAL | 796 | 100.0 |

Often, in gold-industry language, all of those fabricating areas are lumped together as "industrial uses" for gold. As the above figures show, jewelry is the largest category in this industrial tabulation, though few outside the business think of jewelry as part of "industry."

Contact with the expert goldsmith does reveal him (or her) as more than a glorified factory hand. He is an artist as well as a technician, an expert at handling gems and all precious metals, not just gold, and he sees himself as an artist creating individual pieces to satisfy himself even when working for a client.

"You have to be completely tyrannical. I once did a piece of work trying to please someone, and it was disastrous," says Charlotte de Syllas, a restless twenty-eight-year-old Londoner who is reckoned to be one of Britain's most outstanding and original young jewelers.

She sometimes spends eight months and longer making a single piece of jewelry, focusing all attention upon the project rather than on the profit angle connected with it. She is a restless girl with long, dark hair, a face free of makeup, and an independent spirit which abhors mass production, at least when applied to her work. In 1973, when the *Observer,* a London newspaper, sponsored an exhibition of jewelry which visited several British cities, Miss de Syllas had her life's work on display, all seventeen pieces. For such a person, jewelry-making is not an industry but an art in itself.

Yet much of the world's jewelry is machine-made, coming from such plants as J. R. Wood and Sons in the United States (rings), Gori & Zucchi at Arezzo, Italy, which is by far the largest manufacturer of gold jewelry in the world, or from some of the nine hundred small manufacturing jewelers in the town of Pforzheim, West Germany. Observing some of the machines at work in the plant of Ballestra in Bassano del Grappa, Italy, is about like watching gold spaghetti dough pouring from a whole battery of dough shapers.

Ballestra concentrates on the manufacture of gold chains of eight to eighteen carats, which may be cut by jewelers into appropriate sizes for necklaces or chain bracelets. Five hundred chain-making machines stand row on row, each capable of ingesting from two to fifteen pounds of fine gold daily, depending upon the weight and size of the chain. Rolls of gold wire feed humming machines that look like the innards of oversized adding machines of the old-fashioned, mechanical type. Out come chains, glittering and golden, into collection pails, an apparently endless stream.

This, of course, isn't art. It is industry at its best, creating quickly and efficiently products which are in heavy demand around the world. Of course, watching that outpouring of gold one can reflect that such a sight might arouse conscience pangs in some souls. Perhaps sermons can be preached concerning the purchases of gold jewelry at a time when millions of people are undernourished. Before preaching, consider that India, a country which knows more hunger than most, is also one of the world's greatest hoarders of gold. Gold is the store of value by which peasants save their money for the nonrainy days, which are the days of hunger in the subcontinent. India wouldn't produce one more bushel of wheat if gold were removed from the scene and the peasant's money went into the paper money which is being steadily depreciated by government bureaucrats. As for the peasant, he probably would be a whole lot worse off.

Blaming the gold-jewelry purchaser for the ills of mankind is like kicking the wall because the television set doesn't work. After the kick, the set still won't work. If a women craves a necklace, she is only expressing a natural human sentiment for something beautiful to brighten her life. She probably will not be served by a lecture on vanity and materialism, least of all if it comes from the same person who may be passing the collection plate on Sunday.

Such were my reflections while watching that stream of gold chain pouring from that line of machines. Gold is like that. It makes you think, hopefully not of murder, though it does just that to some people. Other people may think of economic laws and how gold fits into them. Some may be reminded of early peoples, the Greeks, the Romans, the Egyptians, and how gold was venerated by them. One man may claim that gold is the metal of romance. Another may express a distaste for it, though few people abhor the comforts which gold may bring. To the Italian, gold is a symbol of love or affection. To the Frenchman, it means security. To the Hindu, gold represents status.

My thoughts were running in that vein one day, too, when I watched a load of South African gold being unloaded at Zurich's airport after the long haul from Johannesburg. An armored car waited on the tarmac, doors open for the incoming shipment. Several armed policemen stood warily to one side, dividing glances between the crew of men piling boxes of gold onto the ground and at passers-by in the area.

The international rule is that gold must meet certain minimum standards if it is to be handled by reputable agencies. This was "good delivery" gold, certified by the South African Reserve Bank and the Rand Refinery, and rated at 99.6 to 99.7 percent purity.

This quality is not fine enough for jewelry and certain other applications. Even when a jeweler-manufacturer intends to add alloys to gold, he wants to start with that gold as close to 100 percent purity as possible. This gives the fabricator full control over the manufacturing operation. Osmium, for instance, is an impurity which is especially disliked, even when in minute quantities within gold. Osmium is a very hard element of the platinum group which is used for compass bearings and the tips of gold fountain-pens. If in a jeweler's gold alloy, however, a tiny speck might streak the highly polished surface of a fine piece of work.

Thus, in Zurich, after gold is delivered to one or other of the Big

Three banks, it may go to a refinery rather than a bank vault. Large manufacturers have their own refining facilities. Smaller concerns prefer to buy their gold as semifinished items from refiners.

"The watchmaking and jewelry industries and the dental profession are our best customers," says Elie Gueissaz, managing director of Métaux Précieux SA, the Swiss Bank Corporation's refining subsidiary at Neuchatel, Switzerland. The plant sits near the shores of the lake of the same name as the town, with the Jura Mountains in the background. Gueissaz is a stylishly dressed, energetic executive with high forehead and round features who looks more like the model for a clothing firm than a refiner of gold. Gold is a product which seems to arouse sartorial instincts in men who handle it. One seldom encounters a slovenly dressed character in the realms of gold.

Switzerland's watchmaking industry is centered in the Jura Mountains area, Dominique Bonhote, the commercial manager of Métaux Précieux explains. He reports that Switzerland's watch and jewelry industry purchases about fifty tons of gold annually but consumes only about fifteen tons. The rest is returned as scrap to refiners, for remelting and reforming into items which will again fit watchmaking and jewelry needs.

Bonhote is a mine of information about the merchandising of gold, one of those diligent salesmen who studies a market avidly for his own edification as well as for hope of sales. He is trim, with an athletic build, prematurely gray hair—a man with élan.

Executives explained that the company sells more than five hundred different alloys tailored to applications. Jewelers and watchmakers follow sales trends, note popularities of different types of gold, and design products to fit moods of customers. One gold wire utilized in the electronic industry is made from metal refined to 99999 or five-nines purity before drawing that metal into wire finer than a human hair. That wire sells for SF, 25,000 a kilogram, or about $10,000 for 2.2 pounds.

Métaux Précieux, which also has an affiliated refinery in Paris, processes about one hundred sixty tons of gold annually. It advertises that in gold it offers: "recognized standard alloys—18, 14 and 9 carats —in standard coloring or other shades, or alloys of gold with palladium or nickel." Metal is offered in the form of "special casting alloys, sheets, strips, round and profile wires and tubes."

Security is a fetish at the plant, as it is everywhere else where gold is the product. Emphasis is on individual responsibility rather than people-control. Every worker on the production line assumes responsibility for the raw material which is presented to him when an operation starts. He is relieved of that responsibility only when the work passes to the next employee, with the metal content weighed to the gram.

At the end of the day, any worker holding gold carefully collects the unfinished pieces at his machine, plus each tiny scrap around the machine. The total is weighed. A worker is presented with a receipt, and the gold goes into a vault which would do credit to a central bank. Next day, the worker will collect the gold, again resume responsibility, and proceed with his work.

Accidents may happen, though. In May, 1973, a platinum-cobalt ingot of three kilos (about 6.6 pounds) disappeared. The bar was worth $15,000, certainly nothing to ignore. After an exhaustive and futile search, plant officials pieced together the story of what may have happened. Platinum-cobalt looks very much like steel. One of the workmen probably mistook the bar for a section of scrap steel. The bar was tossed into a scrap pile, trucked away to be melted, and lost in some foundry cupola.

Later that same month something else occurred which was not an accident. The plant had ordered a shipment of fifty-one one-kilo bars of platinum from a reputable refinery in Germany. The bars arrived, but didn't look right to the inspector who checks incoming precious metals. Immediately, the shipment was called to the attention of the State Controller of Precious Metals in Berne, Switzerland's capital.

An assay showed that, instead of being pure platinum, the bars were half platinum and half gold. At the time, platinum was selling for about $155 an ounce. Gold was selling for $120 an ounce. The shipment represented a unique situation. *Bars had been watered down with gold,* perhaps one of the few times in history when pure gold was used to commit a fraud. Or was it a fraud? The matter was called to the attention of the highly respectable German company which embarrassedly asked that the bars be returned immediately. There an investigation was launched, and the matter was quietly hushed up. Was it a case of a melting error? Or one where a dishonest employee hoped to defraud a customer, perhaps with help of an accomplice in the firm's accounting department?

In any case, the matter emphasizes how carefully all shipments must be watched in the precious-metals field. This I was thinking when I toured the plant to see its electrolytic refining facility and its production line, where workers in blue-denim smocks drilled, milled, turned, stamped, and polished gold into watch and jewelry components.

Whenever I am in a central bank, a gold shop, or anywhere else with a stock of precious merchandise, I always have a morbid fear that something will disappear while I am on the premises. Then, the finger will point inexorably at me. I will become tongue-tied, unable to defend myself, and the web will tighten around me.

There's the time, for instance, when I visited De Beers' offices in Johannesburg. The De Beers Group, which is also led by Harry Oppenheimer of Anglo, is the royal house of diamonds, the company which controls the world diamond market. I was there to see diamonds, in the rough, by the pailful, polished, any way that officials cared to show them to me.

My guide happened to be E. T. S. (Ted) Brown, then an executive in diamonds, now a director of the Anglo Group, a big, hearty man of enormous vitality. And he was very willing to show me diamonds, in the rough, by the pailful, polished, in every way that they happened to be in the company's stock.

I thrust my hand into one bucket of diamonds, felt the stones run through my fingers, did it again so that an official could film me doing it. In 16-millimeter color movies, yet.

And so what happened? One of the diamonds disappeared.

I don't know how they discovered this, and so fast. I suspect that every time that a pail of diamonds is disturbed it is hurriedly placed on a scale which measures everything in milli-ounces. The disappearance of even one stone thus is immediately noted.

I wanted to shout: "I didn't do it." All I could do was glance furtively around, my throat so dry that I could feel dust on my tonsils.

"You don't mind," somebody said, gently, as if he might be ready to strap me in the electric chair. He bent down, felt my pants cuffs. Men still had cuffs on their pants, and that was the first time that I wished they hadn't.

"No. I don't mind," I said, in a thin, piping squeak. I was ready to extend hands for handcuffs, knowing full well that the missing diamond would be discovered somewhere on my person.

It wasn't. Somehow it had fallen onto the floor, rolled under a table, where it was found by one of the employees in this particular department. I departed, smiling with relief.

On the refining and primary fabrication side of the gold business the trend is for the large companies to become bigger and for the smaller ones to stagnate or to be absorbed by the larger firms. As gold's price has risen, the capital requirements of companies have soared. Small companies find it difficult to acquire capital to carry expensive inventories. Modern technology becomes more complex, making it harder for little outfits to introduce necessary mechanization. Research becomes prohibitively expensive, though vitally necessary.

The world's big three in this area are Engelhard, which not only has operations in the United States but also has plants abroad, too, Britain's Johnson, Matthey, and Germany's Degussa. Handy & Harman is another large refiner and fabricator in the United States. In Holland, Drijfhout & Zoon caters to the gold trade. France has its Comptoir Lyon-Alemand. Then, of course, there are the already-mentioned three refineries of the Big Three Swiss banks.

Engelhard is controlled by the Anglo American Group, which means that this giant South African company has a big piece of the United States' gold business. The close relationship between Engelhard and Anglo started long before Engelhard's death. In 1960, Anglo first acquired shares in Engelhard Hanovia, the Engelhard family company which controlled Engelhard Minerals & Chemicals. Then, in 1969, that interest was expanded to give Anglo control. Anglo remains much in the background, however. Silence is golden, especially when it involves a South African company selling gold in the United States.

Johnson, Matthey also has close ties with South Africa. Its two biggest shareholders are Johannesburg Consolidated Investment Company, Johannesburg, and Consolidated Goldfield Ltd., London based but South Africa orientated. Johnson, Matthey employs ten thousand people in plants around the world. Its subsidiary, Metalli Preziosi in Milan, is strong in Italy. It has a stake in an Indian refinery. It has close ties with many customers in the vital Middle East.

Degussa, or Deutsche Gold-und-Silber-Scheideanstalt vormals Roessler, Frankfurt, West Germany, has been in business for more than one hundred years. Now it is much better known by its shortened name than by the ponderous title which was its only name until 1928. An estimated seventy percent of the fine gold sold in Germany passes through its hands. In addition, it serves customers outside Germany's borders, including many of Italy's jewelry manufacturers. One of its several subsidiaries is located in Milan, while world-wide employment is estimated at about sixteen thousand people. Most of the activity of processors is focused upon jewelry.

CHAPTER VIII

# Golden Jewels

That royal crown used for the investiture of Prince Charles is transported in a case which looks just like a farm mailbox equipped with a handle on its top and then lifted off its post. Open the end as if you might be looking for mail, and you see the crown in all its magnificence, a glittery, gleaming piece of jewelry which reflects the finest craftsmanship of this century.

"It is a very good symbol for the whole world's jewelry," says Graham Hughes, that tall, trim Englishman who serves as an apostle for the jewelry trade everywhere in his post as director of London's Worshipful Company of Goldsmiths. Adds he: "It is probably the only royal crown made in the twentieth century."

That remark says much about the decline of kingly power in this century. But the crown itself says less about aristocratic politics than it does about the symbolism which often cloaks fine pieces of jewelry. A golden orb about the size of a golf ball sits atop the crown, signifying the world and worldly influences. The dragon engraved on its surface is the emblem of Wales, that section of Great Britain which has Charles as its prince. Superimposed diamond stars held on a tiny frame over the orb are arranged in the shape of Scorpio, reminding us that Prince Charles was born in November. Seven precious stones in the crown suggest the seven deadly sins and the seven gifts of God under the domination of a small cross which surmounts the entire crown. That cross is symbolic of Christian spiritual power, while smaller crosses at the sides denote protection. A fleur-de-lis indicates purity. And so it goes, with every line and feature of that crown following traditions and symbolism as the art of the jeweler (Louis Osman in this case) created far more than a golden circlet to rest upon a head.

This has been the task of the goldsmith for millenia. Sometimes a goldsmith acquired great fame as was the case with Benvenuto Cellini or with Fabergé, the French jeweler who worked at the court of the tsars in Russia at the turn of this century. More often than not, the goldsmith worked in anonymity, leaving only a trail of jewelry to mark his passage through life. He hammered and chiseled, bent and twisted bits of gold into exquisite shapes, employed precious stones and other materials to enhance the product, and tried to combine everything into a symbolic whole which would tell its own story to the beholder. Even the simple gold wedding ring tells its own tale of the binding of two people in marriage, while women may see their own symbolism in a jewel from a suitor.

> *Dumb jewels often in their silent kind*
> *More than quick words do move a woman's mind.*

In India, where goldsmithing and jewelry-making always has been a sacred profession, the symbolism of jewelry and its relationship to cosmic forces is impressed upon anyone who makes an acquaintance with the fabulous collections to be found in temples, museums, and lordly personal treasures. In Bombay, in the teeming gold market, I once listened to a venerable goldsmith as he discoursed about the radiating power of noble metals and precious stones.

Tiny clapboard and brick shops of goldsmiths lined alleys and cross-lanes for blocks. Sari-clad women brushed shoulders with black-bearded Afghans, with Gujarati merchants in white gowns, with Hindu shoppers in dhotis which flapped against skinny legs. One seldom sees a fat man in India, even among gold and jewelry shoppers who might be expected to eat much better than the average.

"The Vedas, our great epics, tell us about jewelry, and some five-thousand-year-old documents describe the relationship of metals and colors to man's well-being," my new-made friend said. He had a hawk nose, shrewd, dark eyes, and a tuft of beard under his chin which wagged up and down as he talked. A salesman's good cheer radiated from his bony frame. But he talked for sheer enjoyment, not for purposes of a potential sale, for I had told him I was a journalist and that had seemed to instantly mark me as one of the intellectual rather than the materialistic caste.

"Gold, you know, is the sacred metal, the purest of all and the closest to the gods. This is why it is so popular in our industry," he said.

"Even, today, when the price is so high?" I asked.

"Yes." His tuft of bearded wagged again. He shuffled to the rear of his shop where a safe sat in the gloom, returning with a gold bracelet.

"Look," he said. "This is a very old piece, probably from the time of Asoka." Tiny pea-sized "tears" of gold were linked by invisible binds into a flexible bracelet, with even tinier pearls interspersed in a pattern in gaps between those golden globules.

He fondled the bracelet in his slender fingers, eyes bright as he gazed at it. "This has a strange power," he said. "Any woman who sleeps with her husband when she has this on her wrist is sure to become pregnant."

I glanced keenly at him, wondering if he might be ridiculing some superstition. But I could see from the expression on his face that he believed firmly in the fecund power of that piece of jewelry.

"If that's the case, you should be able to make some money renting that out," I said.

He nodded. "I do."

Most women don't rent or buy jewelry for fertility purposes. But it is interesting to trace the superstitions and legends which have become associated with jewelry.

Naturally, jewelry does not have to be gold. Every metal in ordinary use has served as a material for jewelry at one time or another. Yet market surveys show that gold and jewelry are closely associated in the public mind. One survey made in the United States showed that seventy-five percent of the people queried thought of jewelry when the word "gold" was mentioned.

A market survey in several countries done for Consolidated Gold Fields, Ltd., in London showed that in all countries, women overwhelmingly preferred gold to other metals in jewelry. Asked to cite their preferred metal, women responded as follows:

|  | BRITAIN | FRANCE | ITALY | UNITED STATES |
|---|---|---|---|---|
| Gold | 77% | 68% | 59% | 60% |
| Silver | 11 | 7 | 7 | 15 |
| Platinum | 9 | 23 | 31 | 19 |
| No preference | 3 | 2 | 4 | 6 |

For this reason, it is ironic that nine-carat gold is even labeled as "gold" in the United States. Anything so titled contains only 37.5 percent gold, with a less noble metal comprising the remainder. Perhaps it might be better to label this as "a gold-bearing base metal." But that wouldn't sell. A salesman's job is to sell dreams, and few people dream of base metal. Nine-carat gold undoubtedly is popular with mass producers of jewelry, however, for it does offer a wide range of colors.

Historically, goldsmithing has been a cottage industry. Shops were small, undercapitalized, with little marketing know-how. Often proprietors seemed more interested in pleasing artistic souls rather than in meeting needs of commerce.

Today the machine has assumed many of the simpler tasks of the goldsmith and some of the very complex jobs, too. Mass production reigns. Often, the shop has become a factory with long lines of machines cutting and grinding, stamping and squeezing, milling and drilling. Jewelry may have lost in the process. No machine has yet been built which can produce the true work of art, and there are some commercial plants where the jewelry has but one fault: it's junk. There are others where the quality reaches a level of delightful mediocrity. And it must be admitted that machine-made jewelry has reduced prices to the level of people who otherwise might not have been able to afford it.

At the top end of the consumer scale, artist-craftsmen cater to the tastes of those who want something different to dazzle neighbors or to suit their own tastes. These goldsmiths create pieces to please themselves, then find customers who like originals.

Sometimes their jewelry pioneers new design roads. For Andrew Grima in London, Gilbert Albert in Geneva, Henry Shawah in Boston, Arthur King in New York City, or scores of other artist-craftsmen, there is no pandering to the mob, though crowds may be attracted to their works. Gerda Flöckinger, an energetic Austrian-born woman who now is a Londoner, is the first living jeweler to have been honored with an individual show at the prestigious Victoria and Albert Museum in London. She employs no semifinished components at all in her pieces. Everything is literally handmade, developed under her fingers from raw metal, stone, and gems into dazzling works of art.

"My pieces are an extension of my own personality," she says, emphatically.

Indeed they are, and so they are also when produced by any master goldsmith and jeweler.

Most designer-jewelers operate studios of their own; but they should not be confused with the many small goldsmithing shops serving the commercial market. These latter face ever stiffer competition from the big fabricators. Still, the tradition of the small shop is too firmly fixed to disappear overnight. In Italy, the world's jewelry leader, about ninety percent of the country's twenty-five hundred goldsmithing shops employ fewer than thirty people each.

Valenza, Italy, has thirteen hundred registered goldsmithing establishments, each averaging only eight employes. Vicenza, home of Palladio, the great Renaissance architect, has four hundred, many located within the old medieval walls of the town.

Once in Vicenza I spent a half hour driving up and down Contra San Francesco looking for Biffi, which had been described to me as one of the biggest goldsmith businesses in the town. The twenty-five-man plant sits flush on a street of houses and apartment buildings, looking like the town house of a wealthy merchant. Only a nameplate beside the steel door indicated that I had reached my goal.

Giuliano Tortoli, Biffi's president, greeted me enthusiastically, showed me the factory, which is separated from his office by a green patio. He is a former Italian Air Force pilot and he proudly explained the significance of some of the military career photographs on his walls. Then he talked about his employes.

"My workers are like my family," he said, with sincerity.

Some of the small firms are family businesses, with skills handed down from father to son like precious possessions, or perhaps like the secret ritual of a mystical society. Goldsmithing in ancient times used to be akin to a priestly rite, with the goldsmith regarded as possessing some special god-given talent for working this noble metal.

In the old days, the quality and caratage of the gold alloy depended upon the skill of the goldsmith. He brewed his batches of metal almost like the alchemist, working with his own recipes, adding a touch of this and a pinch of that. And he guarded his formulas with extreme secrecy. Introduction of controlled processing by melters in the nineteenth century paved the way for mass production, and struck a blow at the small-shop commercial jeweler.

Mass production is only possible when commodities going into plants are uniform. Today, melters have tight control over their alloys, and the machine now dominates the jewelry business.

Few companies have done better than Italy's Gori & Zucchi in wedding the machine to jewelry production. In South Africa, I found gold-mining executives speaking with awe at the way this plant in Italy could devour gold, churning the yellow metal into delicate pieces of attractive jewelry. In Moscow, the USSR, I heard Soviet foreign-trade executives speaking enviously of the machines developed by Gori & Zucchi for its own production, and the Russians hinted that they meant to create a jewelry industry of their own with the help of some of these Italian-made machines. (This proved to be a futile hope, for the Italian jewelry concern saw no reason for assisting the Russians to become competitors.)

Leopold Gori, diminutive partner in Gori & Zucchi, is an unusual combination of shrewd businessman, paternalistic employer, and ideologist. His silvery hair and pencil moustache blend with a pixyish smile. Despite his eighty years, he has energy to burn lavishly for promoting Italy's gold industry. His company is the General Motors of the world's gold jewelry business, big enough to consume five percent of the Free World's new gold production annually.

Carlo Zucchi, his partner of forty-five years, is less extroverted, thin and bony with gray hair combed straight back, eyes hidden behind dark glasses. He is a quiet man, not given to boasting. Yet he can boast that: "We began from nothing in a small workshop."

Today, their plant is the world's largest in the gold jewelry industry, employing fifteen hundred people and consuming up to sixty metric tons annually, about a third more gold than all the mines in the United States produce in a year. The plant manufactures over six thousand items ranging from necklaces to medallions and from wedding rings to plaited-gold women's handbags.

The modern factory sits on the edge of Arezzo, along a road where green fields start replacing the tile-roofed houses of the town. Beyond, the colors of the Arezzo plain merge into the dark green of the Tuscan hills.

The plant may be deceptive for anyone not familiar with the company's trademark. A huge sign erected near the gate of the fence surrounding the property advertises "Uno-A-Erre." It was only when I stopped at the gate, where a guard is housed in a glass gatehouse, that I learned that this indeed was the plant which I sought.

"Uno-a-Erre is our trademark," explained the guard at the gate, with a rather disapproving shake of his head. Everybody in Italy knew the sign. Therefore I should too. "It is the sign of quality," he added.

That trademark is the Italian pronunciation of the hallmark which is stamped upon the jewelry produced by Gori & Zucchi: 1AR (Arezzo 1).

The three hundred thousand-square-foot plant is of red brick, with a red-tiled roof and windows which are shaded by green venetian blinds. Greenery about the factory creates a parklike atmosphere. Two guards leaped to attention when we walked in, wanted to know our business. Grilled gates into the factory are like those of a bank, with a porter allowing entry only after checking a visitor's credentials.

The interior, including all melting areas, is as clean as a hospital, airy and bright, with a linoleum floor which has been swept so often that it has a polish. When gold-bearing dirt on the floor may run $180 a pound, cleanliness becomes more than a virtue; it is financially rewarding. Even the air in the plant is passed through filters to collect any minute traces of gold which might be floating around.

A line of furnaces smoked along one wall in the smelting department. Molten gold glowed brightly, an attendant closely watching temperature gauges. Gold may be heated too far above the melting point. Then, it collects oxygen and the resulting metal may be slightly porous when poured. This is just one more fact I learned as I followed the path of a bar of gold from the melting furnace to a jewelry case in the firm's exhibition hall.

"Most of our customers want eighteen-carat gold," explained Sergio Celli, a graduate of the University of Paris and an eight-year veteran of Gori & Zucchi, who conducted us through the plant. He was still in his twenties, enthusiastic about his job, thoroughly acquainted with every cranny of the factory. Then, he added: "And we don't allow any tolerance at all against the customer. If we stamp our gold at eighteen carats, it must be eighteen. To be sure, we sometimes overallow to make certain that we never come under the caratage which we mark."

France and Scandinavia also like eighteen-carat gold but prefer it to be red. The United States likes fourteen-carat yellow gold, while English jewelry purchasers show a distinct preference for nine- and ten-carat yellow. Italians like white gold, and so do some buyers in America, especially with gemstones. This I was told while strolling through the plant watching gold being rolled into sheets, stamped into blanks, squeezed into wires, and poured into tiny castings.

I also learned that the soaring price of gold in recent times has increased interest in silver jewelry in several areas. Whether or not this is a permanent trend or just a passing fad remains to be seen. A factory such as Gori & Zucchi's can work with silver as well as gold, for its craftsmen are proficient in either metal.

When walking on an overhead ramp we looked down at hundreds of workers at machines or workbenches. On one side of the ramp, production was automatic, with workers tending machines that spewed wedding rings, chains, and other items. On the opposite side, artisans finished pieces by hand. One girl held a tiny sliver of gold in tweezers, fitted it onto a brooch, and touched it lightly with a small, gas torch. Looking closely, I saw that she had fastened the golden head of a butterfly onto a body of lapis lazuli held together in a frame of gold.

Another worker, a man with the seamed features of one who has seen much of life, hammered a thin sheet of gold into a maple leaf for a brooch. At another bench, several girls seemed to be plaiting thin strands of straw into mats. Then I saw that these were not fibers but gold wires. What looked like mats were textiles of gold which would be fashioned into smart handbags.

In the medallion department, I peered over a designer's shoulder as he drew a plate-sized design for a medal on his drawing board. He was working over the portrait of an American astronaut. Nearby were finished medallions of the Pope, of John F. Kennedy, of the emperor Haile Selassie, of Richard M. Nixon. There also were commemorative pieces for the Olympic Games in Munich, for various moon landings, for civic anniversaries of various cities, and for independence days of numerous African countries.

The design is recreated in clay, molded to bring three-dimensional life to the figure on the face. The clay model is baked hard then placed in a copy machine. When a needle is activated to pass lightly back and forth over the pattern, that device feeds information about the model's face into the apparatus. Cutters go to work to repeat that clay model in steel, matching every indentation.

Those cutters may be set so that the metal replica will be any size desired, from the plate-sized original down to less than the size of an American quarter of a dollar. Once a metal model has been made in the appropriate size, it may be utilized as a die to stamp medallions from discs of sheet gold. A skilled craftsman may touch up edges, polish surfaces.

While Gori & Zucchi, like other large jewelry-makers, has its own designers, it also reaches out for ideas, purchasing designs from outside, Dr. Antonio Cangiano, secretary-general of the company explained. Cangiano is a young-looking Neopolitan who has been with Gori & Zucchi for eight years. He has close-cropped hair, a rounded nose and quick, dark eyes which gleamed everytime he talked about jewelry. The Italians seem to have this business in their blood, perhaps as a throwback to Etruscan ancestors.

"Louis Ferraud, the Parisienne couturier, is making a collection of designs for some of our rings, bracelets, and necklaces," Cangiano said, enthusiastically.

Such cross-fertilization of ideas is becoming common. I knew that

Tapio Wirkkala, the Finnish industrial designer, creates gold jewelry in his spare time. Picasso worked brilliantly in any art form, including jewelry-making. Arnoldo and Gio Pomodoro are Italian sculpturors who work in jewelry as well as in stone.

Geographically, Italy offers the most bargains in jewelry, for merchandisers accept lower markups than anywhere else. There, every $100 worth of jewelry sold by the manufacturer retails for an average of $200. This compares with $250 in West Germany, $300 in Switzerland, and $320 in France at retail. American markups, generally, are at the high end of that listing.

Sometimes people advocate jewelry purchases as a form of investment in troubled times. Usually this is bad advice, for jewelry markups are high, a hundred to two hundred percent, and even higher.

Take the simple wedding ring, which accounts for more gold consumption than any other piece of jewelry. These usually are produced from fourteen-carat-gold wire of about the diameter of a wooden match. The wire goes into automatic machines which literally disgorge finished rings into pails faster than the eye can follow. Italian factory records show that labor costs in the manufacturer's price represent only three to four percent of the total, including profit.

A ring which might cost you $50 to $60 retail probably didn't cost any more than $20 to make, even if the manufacturer paid $150 an ounce for his gold. Once you purchase it, the only resale value you have with the average ring is its gold value, which would only be fifty-eight percent of that ring by weight provided that it were fourteen carats. A little computation may show that the free-market price of gold may have to triple for you to even get your original investment back. Some investment, that one!

Italy's jewelry manufacturers sell their products by the pound, as if those glittering baubles might be butter, or cheese, or potatoes. In the sales office of Gori & Zucchi, I watched as one customer placed an order for several pounds of rings, a dozen pounds of chain, and a few pounds of brooches. This seemed to be carrying the commercialization of jewelry just a little too far, like selling paintings by the yard.

While Italy is the largest gold jewelry manufacturer, the United States is number two and easily the largest purchaser of such jewelry, and the largest consumer of gold. In 1972, for instance, U.S. mines produced about forty-five metric tons of new gold while consumption amounted to two hundred twenty-six tons, most of which, of course, came from imports.

Of that gold consumed, about sixty percent of it, or one hundred thirty-five tons, went into jewelry and the arts. Engelhard Industries and Handy & Harman are key suppliers to industry, though Homestake Mining Company, San Francisco, the biggest gold producer in the United States, also sells gold bullion directly to the industrial market. American Express, Inc., Mocatta Metals, Franklin Mint, the Republic National Bank of New York, and numerous other banks and firms are now supplying the retail market. In addition, there are about four thousand firms in the business of fabricating gold articles, the majority in jewelry.

New York City and Providence, Rhode Island, are the principal jewelry manufacturing centers in America. Zale Corporation, the chain outfit, is the biggest jewelry retailer in the world. It manufactures and assembles its own jewelry, with heavy emphasis on rings and watches.

About half the total fine gold used by the jewelry industry goes into class, engagement, and wedding rings. Egyptians started the practice of wearing rings more than four thousand years ago, but nobody has matched the Romans in this regard. Not only did they wear rings on all fingers, but on toes as well and even had summer and winter rings. Americans have not gone this far, nor do American women like the old Gaulish custom of wearing the wedding ring on the thumb.

Most class rings are of 9.5 carats though marked for 10 carats. Brooches, necklaces, cuff links, and other such jewelry usually is of 10 to 14 carats, with 18 in top quality lines. Recently, as gold's price has soared, a tendency has developed toward lowering the caratage of gold in the product.

In the United States, jewelry manufacturing costs are high compared with Italy. The skilled craftsman in America may earn $9 to $12 per hour versus less than $2 an hour in Italy. So America is unlikely to undersell Italy in the jewelry field.

Still, America can show the rest of the world how to merchandise jewelry, and New York City is its sales capital. The most prestigious jewelry firms in the world make certain they have outlets here. Harry Winston may be better known for his work with diamonds than with gold, but the two go together. Tiffany has made its name a household word throughout America. Hans Stern, that enterprising

Brazilian immigrant who now is a fourteen-nation international jeweler, has a New York shop.

Stern represents the type of self-made man who often is encountered in the jewelry industry. His family fled Germany in 1939 just ahead of a Nazi police patrol to settle in Brazil. In 1945, at the age of twenty-two, Stern established a small jewelry business, his only capital the $200 received from the sale of an old accordion. Today, he owns a nineteen-story building in Rio de Janeiro, a world-wide jewelry business, and a new accordion which he still plays when in a mood for relaxation. Like other industry leaders he finds it necessary to have a shop in New York.

"Everybody has to be in New York," insists an employee of Paris-based Van Cleef and Arpels. Other Paris firms seem to agree; Spritzer & Fuhrmann, the chain headed by energetic Charles Fuhrmann, has a New York outlet in addition to a chain of shops in the Caribbean.

But jewelry selling in America is far more than a New York industry, and there are all types of businesses from the craft shops of Boston's Henry Shawah, the first American ever to have a one-man show at Goldsmiths' Hall in London, to department stores like Gimbel's, and from chains like B. D. Howes, Los Angeles, to mail-order houses like Traub Company, a Michigan firm which sells over a million of its "Orange Blossom" engagement rings annually.

American jewelry usually is a half carat under whatever designation it carries, because merchandisers are allowed a half-carat leeway. Anything between 9.5 to 10.5 carats would be labeled 10-carats gold. By a not-so-odd coincidence you seldom find an article in which the half-carat leeway favors the customer. Gold labeled as 18 carats is closer to 17.5, while 14-carat gold is likely to be 13.5.

In the United States, there is no central assaying office or any government hallmarking system to support caratage claims. Standards are maintained through the industry's own self-policing Jewelers Vigilance Committee. The system may seem lax, but penalties may be heavy when false declarations violate U.S. consumer-protection laws.

Britain has by far the oldest and tightest consumer protection in gold. Hallmarking means the stamping of a symbol or mark upon a metal to denote its quality. Marks are only applied after assaying. In London the task is handled by the Worshipful Company of Goldsmiths, which has its granite-block edifice in Gutter Lane. The building is as solid as the white cliffs of Dover, with a marble staircase inside the main entrance like that of a ducal palace.

Heraldic flags of guilds jut from poles along interior walls. A great dome forms the ceiling over the staircase. Statues of cherubs stand on bannisters. On a landing there is a gilded gold statue of St. Dunstan, a figure which was the prow of the Worshipful Company's barge on the Thames in the seventeenth century. St. Dunstan was a medieval monk of a thousand years ago, who became Archbishop of Canterbury and who now is the patron saint of goldsmiths.

The Company obtained its present charter in 1327, and it has been in business ever since. Yet an assaying office had been hallmarking gold and silver items in London long before the present company was formed. The fraternity or guild of goldsmiths is known to have been in existence before 1180.

"Gold and silver plate, whether made in this country or imported from abroad, may not legally be sold until it has been taken to an assay office, assayed, and, if found up to standard, hallmarked," John Forbes, deputy warden of the company, explained. The company's hallmark is a leopard's head, the oldest of marks of origin, probably taken from the royal arms.

Britain has three other assay offices, in Edinburgh, in Sheffield, and in Birmingham. France and Holland have like compulsory hallmarking. Belgium has a weak voluntary system. In Italy, the manufacturer marks his products with his own fineness mark, and the customer depends upon the honesty of the producer. Germany has no control of any kind. Now, the European Common Market is trying to harmonize hallmarking in the nine-nation grouping, but it may take years to win agreement of all countries to any uniform system.

Ofttimes in gold, the buyer must beware. Some Hong Kong gold dealers, for instance, reduce the gold content of their alloys when selling to tourists, following the philosophy that the traveler won't know the difference anyway. Not long ago, one Johannesburg jeweler received an offer of some nine-carat-gold jewelry which a Taiwan seller promised would all be marked fourteen carats. The dealer's price would be for nine-carat quality, permitting the jeweler to sell at fourteen carats and pocket the profits. The jeweler rejected the offer.

British buyers may know exactly what they are purchasing but United Kingdom mass-produced jewelry is unimaginative in design, aimed at conservative customers who do not revise life patterns with ease. Johnson, Matthey is the leading company in the semifinishing of gold jewelry, probably accounting for around sixty percent of the business. Engelhard's British subsidiary has about twenty percent, according to one reliable estimate. Sheffield Smelting Company follows with around fifteen percent, with the remainder divided among smaller firms.

If Britain has rather conventional jewelry for the masses, most of it in the nine-carat range, it also has some of the most imaginative jewelry designers in the world, who are catering to those clients who want something other than a mass-produced item. Thanks to the Worshipful Company of Goldsmiths, to numerous art and design schools, and to an encouraging atmosphere, Britain has a whole coterie of artist-goldsmiths who are making their mark in the world of jewelry.

Hughes is an articulate promotor of goldsmithing who perhaps is more responsible than anyone else in Britain for the revival of this ancient craft in this country. In addition to his post with the Goldsmiths' Company, he also is joint chairman of the British Craft Centre, an agency which provides an opportunity for distinguished and rising goldsmiths and jewelers to exhibit their works.

Germany's jewelry manufacture is concentrated in and about Pforzheim, "the Golden City" on the northern edge of the Black Forest. Degussa, biggest company in the industry, has facilities here for the fabrication of jewelry components and semifinished products, while nine hundred small shops are located in the town or in the neighborhood.

This is a land of rolling hills and pine forests, where swift running streams course in the valleys. Tourism is the principal industry. But everyone in Pforzheim seems to have some connection with the gold industry.

A few years ago when George Lauer, one of Pforzheim's shops, celebrated its seventy-fifth anniversary, it conducted an international jewelry contest to commemorate the event. Three of the best-known jewelry retailers in the world served as judges: René Kern of Dusseldorf, Schilling of Stuttgart, and Charles Fuhrmann of Curaçao, the Dutch Caribbean possession; the South German Chamber Orchestra presented a concert on award night.

"Imagine! A little town like Pforzheim and three of the biggest jewelry firms in the world are represented here at our celebration," one of the town's burghers told me. He indicated clearly that he had been most awed by Fuhrmann, the cheerful and effervescent head of Spritzer & Fuhrman, who bubbles with energy as he merchandises jewelry through his seventeen shops in the Antilles Islands plus one in New York.

Everybody who comes to Pforzheim, however, usually makes a point of visiting the town's chief attraction, the jewelry museum housed in the Reuchlinhaus. This is a modern cultural center built in the Stadtgarten at the southern exit of the town. Here exhibits are changed twice a year, providing an opportunity for many to view a different jewelry show every time they visit the town.

The German gold industry produces eight-, fourteen-, and eighteen-carat jewelry for the home market, nine- and twelve-carat for export to Britain, and ten-carat jewelry for Latin America. German consumers, generally, go for the cheaper ranges of jewelry, and here design is geared toward the mass market. Quality jewelry is handled by designer-dealers such as René Kern or Paul Hartkopf in Dusseldorf, or Schilling in Stuttgart.

In the last few years, Spain, helped by a massive tourist boom, has almost caught up with Germany as a consumer of gold. It consumes around fifty tons of gold in jewelry annually, much of it going into hand-tooled pieces of conservative styling. The best work is in fourteen to eighteen carats.

Atop Spain's jewelry social-structure are dealers like Alexandre Grassy who immigrated to Madrid from France over forty years ago. Now his jewelry shop in the Spanish capital is like a museum, with eight hundred clocks from his collection forming backgrounds for the jewels on display. He is a gray-haired, distinguished gentleman, with black-rimmed spectacles which shade eyes that peer intently at a visitor. His work represents the traditional, the timeless, the deluxe pieces which are designed for the carriage rather than the bus-tour trade.

In Madrid and Barcelona, some goldsmiths aver that Spain ultimately will be challenging Italy as a manufacturer of gold jewelry. However, Italy now has the edge in its greater mechanization. Thus export prices of Spanish jewelry, generally, are a shade higher than are prices of Italian mass-produced items.

Paris is the center of France's jewelry industry, one which consumes about thirty-two metric tons of gold annually in carat jewelry plus about another fifteen tons in plated jewelry. Plated and cheaper grades of jewelry have been winning a larger share of the market as the free-market price of gold has climbed.

Legally, all of the solid-gold jewelry sold on the domestic market is eighteen carats, the only permissible standard if it is to be called gold. Oddly, though French citizens like to hoard gold in the shape of coins, medallions, and small bars, they do not purchase gold jewelry for its store of value. For this reason, it is easy for the purchaser to shift downward, from a solid-gold article to one that is gold-plated should the design of the latter have appeal.

The chief semifabricators are Comptoir Lyon-Alemand, Métaux Précieux, the Swiss Bank Corporation subsidiary, and Caplain St. Andre. Flamand in Angoulême is the largest manufacturing jeweler. While Paris is the industry's capital, it is a divided city. On the one hand there is the section of industry serving average buyers, probably depending upon Italian imports. On the other hand, there are international jewelry designers and retailers who represent the finest workmanship to be found, all presented in a *haute couture* atmosphere in accord with the ambience of France's perfumerie, fashions, and cuisine.

Atop this structure in the jewelry field are five Parisienne shops which have formed an elite association, *La Haute Joaillerie de France*. Firms are: Boucheron, Cartier, Chaumet, Mauboussin, and Van Cleef and Arpels.

Their business, like that of the great jewelry houses around the world, is international. All are located in the heart of Paris on and around Place Vendôme, that magnificent square which evokes the splendor of the seventeenth century. At any one time in any of these shops, a visitor is apt to encounter a South American millionaire, a Texas oil man, a Portuguese coffee planter not long away from his Angola plantation, a Park Avenue debutante, someone from the jet set, some Lord or Lady from Britain, and almost anyone else from the wealthy population of almost every country you might name that allows citizens to pile up money.

The French, who take jewelry seriously, divide jewelry into four categories, and each classification has its fans. The categories are:

1. *Bijouterie en métaux précieux.* This often is referred to simply as *bijouterie*. This consists of solid jewelry made principally from precious metals.
2. *Joaillerie.* This is jewelry which is primarily valued for its precious stones.
3. *Bijouterie de fantaisie.* Americans or English would call it costume jewelry.

4. *Bijouterie en or plaqué-laminé.* This is gold-plated or rolled-gold jewelry.

The largest single jewelry market in the world is the Beirut Gold Market, which is located in the center of this Lebanese seaside city. Phoenician traders established the city long before the time of Christ, and the modern gold dealers have all the bargaining instincts of their ancestors.

"We buy. We sell. We make a profit," says Kamal Nawbar, a partner in one of the ninety-eight street-level retail shops in this mart. At thirty, he already is a veteran gold dealer, a wavy-haired, friendly retailer who switches with ease back and forth in five languages. Now he explained that several hundred more shops, most of them manufacturers and wholesalers, are located in upper floors of the gold souk area with its narrow streets and cavelike passages.

"Our market is seventy-five percent tourist and twenty-five percent Lebanese," explains Nawbar. Most of the tourists are Arabs, wealthy oil sheikhs from Kuwait, from Abu Dhabi, from Qatar, and from other Persian Gulf states, merchants from Bahrain, Iraqi landowners, Mecca pilgrims. At any one time $40 million worth of jewelry and gold, nearly all of eighteen carats, may be on display in this rabbit's warren of retailing outlets.

In one shop, Georges Mouzannar, a third-generation jeweler, drops a woman's gold-mesh evening bag onto a counter and casually says it is a steal at $4,000. A Gucci ring is in a case of rings which includes the products of some of the shops upstairs. There's no gold under fourteen carats in the market, he says emphatically, as he sweeps his hand to encompass literally scores of gold chains which are hanging in his front window.

Nearby, Abdel Khassal, a Medina, Saudi Arabia, jeweler, purchases a stock of gold lockets for necklaces. Explains he: "We get much business during the Hadj from pilgrims who come to Mecca. They all want to take some gold souvenir back with them."

Some of the shops sell antique jewelry as well as modern products. In one such shop, I commented about the lack of lustre in the gemstones contained in one gold bracelet. I was told that, before the fourteenth century of the Christian era, jewelers did not know how to polish diamonds and other precious stones. Thus, before that time jewelers turned to precious stones only in unusual circumstances, probably for royalty or for temple priests.

"A piece of gold jewelry then had to be attractive in itself, not something designed to show off a precious stone," I was told. This same jeweler also told me about the inventory problems of today's shops, what with the gold price having quadrupled in four years.

"Look!" The shopkeeper reached into a case, took out a gold necklace which had been fashioned in the time of the Crusades, and several bracelets which had once decorated harem ladies of an eastern potentate. "These are worth $50,000 and I can put them all into one pocket of my jacket, and this is only a small part of my inventory."

I agreed that it must cost a considerable amount to carry such inventories in this day of high interest rates. It is gold's scarcity, of course, which gives it such worth, along with its beauty, and yet, as scarce as it is, gold is much more plentiful, today, than in olden days.

Understandably, there are no accurate records of the amount of gold mined since the dawn of time. Yet gold is a commodity which has been carefully watched since man first put a value on it. So it is possible to make crude estimates of how much gold has been produced from about 3000 B.C. to the present.

Studies made by Consolidated Gold Fields, Ltd., London, suggest total gold production through 1972 of about 80,000 metric tons. Recently, R. C. J. Goode, a director of Union Corporation, Johannesburg, and past president of the South African Chamber of Mines, presented another estimate, 105,649 tons. It probably is safe to conclude that total output is somewhere in the 80,000 to 100,000-ton range, with the estimate clouded not only by lack of early figures but by the fact that Russia has been supersecretive about its production since the late 1930's.

In any case, total production up to 1492 only amounted to 10,000 to 12,000 tons, which means that gold was very scarce indeed in olden days. The bulk of the gold now in existence has been mined in modern times, three-quarters of it in the twentieth century and around half of it since the end of World War II.

For most of history, silver rather than gold served as the ordinary money medium, with gold providing the monetary reserves to support the currency. It was only after the discovery of America by Columbus that gold was in sufficient supply to become a medium of exchange able to support modern economies.

It was gold that beckoned Columbus westward, glittering and shining on the horizon before the prow of his good ship *Santa Maria*.

Baron von Humboldt, writing in his *Fluctuations of Gold,* said: "America was discovered not as has been so long falsely pretended because Columbus predicted another continent, but because he sought by the west a nearer way to the gold mines of Japan and the spice countries in the southeast of Asia."

Columbus himself revealed his feeling about gold when he said: "Whoever possesses gold obtains what he will in this world, nay even by the payment of masses brings many souls into paradise."

The Spanish greed for gold sent many souls into the hereafter, too, for literally millions of Latin American Indians paid with their lives for Spanish avarice, either as slaves in mines or as victims in battle. Mexico, Peru, Colombia, and Brazil became producers of the yellow metal, adding to Europe's store of wealth. For a brief period, Russia reigned as the world's leading gold producer. Then, California introduced the half-century era of the individual miner, when a man could stake a claim on the banks of a stream and then strike it rich through hard work laced with considerable luck.

Still, it was the gold mines of South Africa, corporate empires created by financial magnates, which introduced gold's modern era. This was an era which was to see South Africa account for forty percent of the stock of gold accumulated over the whole world through all history.

# CHAPTER IX

# Today's El Dorado

In the spring of 1917, Ernest Oppenheimer was looking for money, and he arranged a meeting in a suite of London's Savoy Hotel. The hostelry is one of soft carpets, velvet drapes, and impeccable service, the sort of place where you don't seem to need money or you wouldn't be bedding there. Still, the easiest way to raise money is to create the impression that you don't really need it. Oppenheimer needed money.

He had visions of launching a new era for South Africa's gold-mining industry. He already had made a fortune in diamonds and in the Witwatersrand gold-mining industry. This wasn't enough for what he wanted to do, for he had become interested in the theories of W. L. Honnold, an American mining engineer on the payroll of Consolidated Mines Selection Company, the firm for which Oppenheimer now was resident director in South Africa.

Honnold believed that the gold discovered in South Africa up to that time was only a small part of the yellow metal in the quartz rock of the Witwatersrand Reef. He contended that the reef might form an underground bowl which stretched for miles across the veldt. By drilling along a line traced through outcroppings of gold-bearing rock, a company might strike a new bonanza.

Oppenheimer, a short, sinewy man of immense drive, not only was a shrewd business executive, he had the imagination to visualize how a company with financial resources could literally create a whole new industrial empire at the southern end of Africa.

He had broached the idea to the board of directors of Consolidated Mines, a gray-bearded group which was dominated by an acute respect for the status quo that was already profitable. The chairman had grumpily said that he "was not prepared to monkey about with the capital of the company."

Oppenheimer, having given his employers an opportunity to attempt to capitalize on Honnold's ideas, felt free to see what he could do by himself. He always had been adventurous financially, though his size and mild manner left an initial impression almost akin to meekness. He was the sort of man who talked loudly with a soft voice, using persuasion rather than belligerence to get things done, and winning cooperation because events usually proved him to be right.

He had been sent to South Africa when only twenty-two by a London diamond firm to head its Kimberley office. Enthusiastically, he worked on the job, often sitting down with his employees and helping them sort the diamonds being purchased for distribution in London. But the harder he worked, the less respect he seemed to draw from his fellow workers. They regarded him as an eager-beaver lad just out of knee pants, though handy to have around since he showed willingness to work like an ox.

"Every day I go there, and I work as hard as anybody in the firm, if not harder. I sit down and sort diamonds with them, yet they don't respect me," he griped to a friend, Leander Starr Jameson, a man who later was to become prime minister of the Cape Province.

"That's the trouble," said Jameson. "Of course they don't respect you for working hard. Don't sort diamonds: let them do the sorting."

It was good advice. The aspiring executive doesn't climb the ladder by becoming one of the boys on the production line. He lets the others do the physical labor while he directs. He visualizes new and better ways of handling an operation, then has them implemented.

Oppenheimer took the advice, and he started his upward climb. He got his first taste of champagne while celebrating his next promotion, liked it so well that he declared he would drink nothing else once he had reached success. Long after, his son, Harry confided: "It was one of his sadnesses that by the time he could afford it, he had already come to prefer whisky and soda."

Now, in London, the new corporation which he visualized was taking shape in his mind. It would be his company, one in which he would be in position to follow some of the ideas he had developed about mining. Honnold had arranged a meeting in the Savoy with another American mining engineer who could help with the financing.

That mining engineer was named Herbert C. Hoover. Oppenheimer told him about the possibility of South Africa's gold-bearing reef stretching for several hundred miles in a great arc. Hoover liked the concept of the mining company that Oppenheimer sketched to capitalize on this possibility. He agreed to seek financial help from the J. P. Morgan clan in New York City.

The financing was arranged. In September, 1917, the new company emerged as Anglo American Corporation of South Africa, with half of the initial £1 million of capital subscribed by J. P. Morgan & Company and the Newmont Mining Corporation. The new corporation was to become the vehicle through which Oppenheimer did prove his point, that the rich gold reef of South Africa could be followed like a line on a chart to produce the richest gold field ever known to man. Oppenheimer, Sir Ernest before he died in 1957, always stood head and shoulders above others around him in capacity to command, though physically he wasn't built very high off the ground.

South Africa's gold fields stretch in a 350-mile arc through the southern Transvaal and the Northern Orange Free State. Not only are the gold-bearing reefs the largest deposits of gold ever found, they are the most consistent known to man, a guaranteed, regular source of supply. This wasn't readily foreseeable in the infancy of the industry, when springbok and wildebeest roamed across the veldt and when engineers and geologists might have to dislodge a pride of lions to complete a survey.

After the initial discovery of gold on the Witwatersrand Reef in 1886, South African production increased to the point where in two years the Transvaal accounted for 4.3 percent of the world's gold. This was good, but not sensational. South Africa's gold was not alluvial and close to the surface to be scooped up without trouble.

The gold-bearing ore lies far beneath the rock of the Transvaal, necessitating deep mining. It occurs as a layer of gravel which looks something like gray asphalt with white stones in its body. The layer or reef is usually about eighteen to thirty-six inches, sandwiched between quartz rock overlaid with granite. Only a third of an ounce of gold and sometimes even less is found in each ton of ore. This means that huge amounts of rock must be mined, crushed, and milled in order to obtain the gold.

So laborious is that task that, within a few years of the Witwatersrand discovery, pessimists were predicting an early end to the gold-mining industry of the Rand. Separating the gold from the rock was just too difficult to be profitable as mines drove deeper and deeper into the ground. But shortly after discovery of gold on the Rand, three scientists in Glasgow, Scotland, developed the cyanide process of extracting gold from crushed rock.

The Scotsmen, John S. MacArthur and Robert and William Forrest, patented their process in 1887, and in 1889 it proved easily adaptable to the mining industry of South Africa. Gold has an affinity for cyanide. By mixing this chemical with the crushed ore of a gold mine, the yellow metal could be extracted from the rock. The addition of zinc dust drew the cyanide away from gold in the solution, leaving the gold as a black slurry which could be refined in furnaces.

Overnight, mines in South Africa embraced this new process. By 1892, fifteen percent of the world's gold was coming from this nation at the southern end of the African continent. By 1898, South Africa seized the world leadership, accounting for more than a quarter of the world's output of fourteen million troy ounces in that year. South Africa lost that leadership only for a brief time during and just after the Boer War, regained it, and has held it ever since.

Obviously, this is no mining operation for the amateur, for the entrepreneur equipped with only a pick, a shovel, a pan, and an ore rocker. Fortunes could be made in the 1849 California Gold Rush by the individual miner, the first time that gold and free enterprise went hand in hand at the production level. From the start, the mines of the Witwatersrand were corporate ventures, and it was the financier rather than the lone miner who made history on the Rand. Men like Cecil Rhodes, J. B. Robinson, Barney Barnato, Solly Joel, H. W. and Fred Stuben, Charles Rudd, Alfred Beit, and others launched the industry. Later they were joined or followed by the likes of Sir Ernest Oppenheimer and his son, Harry F., W. J. Busschau, Clive S. Menell, and others. It is significant that Anglo American, the biggest gold-mining company of them all, got its start in a hotel room at the Savoy Hotel in London over a financial discussion, rather than through some particular strike on the Transvaal.

Cecil Rhodes was too busy with his empire building and diamond interests to leave much of a mark on South Africa's gold industry. Others left their own personal stamp on everything they did. J. B. Robinson lived out his swashbuckling life, after acquiring the site of the original Witwatersrand gold discovery to become South Africa's richest man, and to win a knighthood from Britain. But when he died in 1929 at the age of eighty-nine, the Cape *Times*, Cape Town's influential daily, published a biting article attacking his meanness, and termed him immune "to any impulse of generosity, private, or public."

The cynic might say that if one is to be unmasked, what better time than after dying at the age of eighty-nine, after spending most of one's life as the richest man in the country. Robinson, however, was unpopular on the Rand, and everywhere else, long before his death. Hard, suspicious, a loner by nature, he believed in expanding his wealth by any means allowed to the free-booting financial magnates of the nineteenth century.

One South African who had more than a slight acquaintance with Robinson, says: "When Robinson passed by, men spat after him in the street, but never hard enough to touch his boots, and never when he could see them do it."

Barney Barnato, a much more likeable character, came to South Africa as an entertainer, and sometime-unemployed magician. He proved better at juggling corporate finances than at making things appear and disappear in his hands, and soon he had a mining empire under his control. But he never lost his love of the footlights, and even when he rated as one of Johannesburg's richest men, he sometimes would appear on the stage of a local music hall to show his histrionic talents. Usually he drew heavy applause, for at that time he owned more of Johannesburg than anyone else in town, and to the audience it seemed more prudent to clap than to boo.

Once when Barnato was playing Othello on the boards, one rugged miner couldn't conceal a guffaw during a particularly tense scene. Barnato halted his dramatic presentation, strode to the edge of the stage, pointed a finger at the culprit.

"You wait," he shouted. "I'll be seeing you after the performance."

The easily-amused miner didn't wait for the end of the performance. By the time the curtain came down he already was on his way to an unknown destination.

Barnato, a Cockney Jew with the build and temperament of a bantam rooster, left England almost penniless, yet became the first of numerous South African millionaires who made their fortunes from diamonds and gold. This land at the southern end of the Continent has been good to the Jew throughout most of its history. Hard-working Afrikaans citizens are bible-reading people with an affinity for the Old Testament who see themselves almost as a race apart, as Jews have been through most of their history. Thus, Afrikaaners are able to identify with Jews, and South Africa has been one of Israel's strongest supporters in modern times.

Barnato was a shrewd operator who was seldom rooked in any business deal, even though he was in an industry where the swindler and fraud artist has thrived ever since men have thought they could get rich with a gold mine. Even he, however, was bilked in one notable instance, which proves that when greed is the driving force, the supposedly-astute magnate may be no shrewder than the farm hick, but his fall may be more precipitous, since more money is likely to be involved.

When a gold strike was made at the Buffelsdorn Mine near Klerksdorp, the word soon got around financial circles in Johannesburg that this was a particularly rich discovery. Not mentioned was the fact that drillers had struck a granite ledge deep under the ground where the gold reef should have continued through the rock. The South African Witwatersrand Reef can be like that. Sometimes the reef may lie in an unbroken shield which miners can follow for miles. Then it may break off, reflecting the fact that some primeval shifting of the earth may have lifted a granite mass upward, shoving the reef far down, or to one side. If the reef is too scattered, the property may not be worth mining. If the reef is lost, expensive drilling may be necessary to locate it.

Barnato heard about the richness of the ore which had been assayed at Buffelsdorn. He presented a bid for an option on the holding, outfaced competition, and bought the mine. It was only after he had signed the contract that his engineers checked the property, and gave him the bad news.

Buffelsdorn had problems, serious problems. Eventually, Barnato lost nearly $5 million in the venture, enough to have put the ordinary man out of business.

Gold's long history is studded with tales of frauds, of the "salting" of mines with dust and nuggets to create an illusion of rich ground, of gold mines being other than what they originally seemed to be. Opportunity for wealth attracts shysters as well as capitalists, and sometimes a man may be both, which is one of the reasons why capitalism sometimes has a bad name.

America's gold-mining history has many stories of mine-salting with a shotgun. Gold dust would be fired into the rock of a claim or of a mine before a prospective buyer appeared to make an assay. Then the seller would innocently look the other way as the buyer caught sight of the flecks of gold.

Such practices occurred in the early days of South Africa's mining history, too. Then prospective buyers grew more sophisticated with their assays, and the shotgun passed into history as a gold-mine sales tool. But ingenious frauds still were perpetrated.

There is the case of one mining property offered for sale near Johannesburg by a man of rather dubious character. The prospective buyer hired a skilled assayer to analyze the property, and the latter was cheerfully greeted by the seller, a cigar-puffing gentleman who apparently couldn't stop smoking.

He followed the assayer around as the ore expert collected his samples, regaling him with stories about the property's worth. Occasionally, he would flick ash from his cigar into one of the sample bags the assayer was collecting, ostensibly to guard against starting a grass fire.

The assay revealed particles of gold which added to the value of the land, and the sale was concluded. But not a speck of gold was found on the property when a more careful search was conducted to determine where drilling might commence for operations. The seller had carefully rolled his cigars himself, first sprinkling the tobacco liberally with gold dust.

Such frauds are only penny-ante games beside some of the stock frauds which have occurred, often leaving rooked investors with only pieces of paper in exchange for their money. Sometimes, when speculative fever is high, a report may sweep through the community to the effect that a drill-core sample has revealed a rich strike at a particular mine. The stock of that company may zoom upward overnight. Only after owners have unloaded their shares does the suspicion arise that perhaps the core analysis may have contained some false figures.

The big mining houses of today can't afford to become involved in any such deals, for they are in business on a permanent basis, not for the quick killing before departing. In the early days of the industry, and in any speculative fever since, there sometimes have been cases of shares being touted loudly when little existed behind the glowing reports. In the first six months of 1933, after the world went off the gold standard, two score new gold mining companies were registered on the Johannesburg Stock Exchange. Most of those companies never paid a dividend, even though shares may have soared along with the whole market, as the average gold share nearly doubled in price.

In 1893, there were 183 gold-mining companies in the Transvaal, most of them headquartered in Johannesburg. Of this total, 104 of them had never produced an ounce of gold. They were described by zealous promoters as being in a "state of development," a condition from which few of them ever emerged.

South Africa's corporate group system (about which more later) has eliminated some of the chaos which formerly existed in the gold industry in this country. Nevertheless, anyone who invests in gold-mining shares must understand that this is a risky business, with numerous pitfalls. There are no easy routes to wealth despite all the glib talk by "boiler room" stock operators. In stock markets, a boiler-room operator is one who sells equities in a company when there isn't much more to it than an office and a telephone.

The California Stock Exchange, established in San Francisco in 1872 to finance development of the gold and silver mines of Nevada, acquired such notoriety that its members were popularly known as "The Forty Thieves." Nonexistent companies were floated, with brokers sometimes touting stocks which they knew to be worthless. Any real strike in the Nevada mines was loudly publicized, with implications that great fortunes were being made. Then, the worthless shares would be offered and they would be soon sold on the wave of euphoria stemming from the get-rich-quick atmosphere.

In London, the first great mining boom in stocks developed somewhat earlier, in 1825, when investors in the City, the London financial district, became obsessed with the idea of growing rich in gold, silver, copper, and other mining shares. But gold had the greatest allure, for this is the commodity which offers the best chance of big capital gains should a strike be made.

In that one year, forty-four mining companies were floated on the Exchange, most of them paper concerns launched by shrewd promotors. Any mine with a South American locale was especially popular, for London hummed with rumors of rich gold strikes on that continent. So when a company like the Anglo-Chilean Mining Association was launched with shares at £100 each, all were immediately grabbed by enthusiastic investors. Shares soared to £400 each before the bubble burst, and investors discovered nothing lay behind the fine-sounding title of the company. Almost the same thing happened with the Real Del Monte Mining Association, which introduced its shares at £100 each, then saw them soar to £1,350 before collapsing to a few pennies each.

In more modern times, Toronto has had more than its share of gold-mining companies which consisted of little more than offices for selling stock shares.

"Form a company with gold in its title, keep the price low, and you can always sell a few thousand shares even if there's nothing behind the title," one veteran Canadian broker said once when discussing the phenomena of "penny shares" on Canadian markets. A five-cent price on a share is not a bargain when the company involved consists of little more than a title.

Of course, few of the crooks would make any money were it not for the greed of the victims, who buy gold shares with dreams of easy money, of yachts on the Caribbean and of suites at the Waldorf. Gold always did have the ability to disturb men's minds, even when appearing only as promises on gaudily printed paper.

Moreover, there is something about gold which inspires spending. In Stillfontein, a gold-mining town west of Johannesburg in South Africa, they still talk about the goldminer who bought a new automobile a few years ago. Before the month was over he had traded that car and six succeeding new ones for still newer automobiles. Why? "Well," said he, "no car is perfect."

Sometimes in the gold business, a buyer may be bilked by circumstances. When gold was discovered in West Australia in 1893, fortunes were made by some men, lost by others. Five partners seemed to be in the former category when they found a rich vein near Londonderry. So confident were they in their strike that they named their mine "The Hole Full of Gold." Gleefully, they worked the property, banking eight thousand ounces of gold in a few weeks. That would be worth $1.4 million at a price of $180 an ounce, which provides a clue to the worth of this property—or so it seemed.

The partners certainly couldn't be blamed for thinking that they had one of the richest mines ever found in Australia. A representative of a group of British investors, one Lord Fingall, thought so, too. He offered the partners £100,000 for the property, an amount which probably would be equal to more than $2 million in purchasing power today. The deal was closed.

He took over the property, and had it sealed while a company was floated with a capital of £250,000 to exploit it. When the company proceeded to work the mine, it found there was no gold in it. The partners had encountered an extremely rich but isolated vein. They didn't know it, but they were virtually at the end of that pocket when Lord Fingall had appeared with his moneybags, offering to buy. Fortunately for the partners, but unfortunately for the investors, the five men decided it was better to enjoy their new-found wealth rather than work the mine to accumulate more.

Sometimes, too, in the gold industry there have been hoaxes unrelated to outright crookery. In the same West Australian gold rush, a priest at Kanowna was given a glimpse of a huge gold nugget which was shaped like a curved blade. His excitement grew when he lifted it, feeling its weight. Later that day, still agitated by the feel of that yellow metal, he blurted the story to some friends. Soon the word spread. A wild stampede developed for the particular valley where the nugget had been seen, with several thousand madly staking out claims. Nobody found any gold. And it is doubtful that the priest had much to say when he found he had been the victim of a hoax. The blade-shaped nugget was only the iron cutting-edge of a farm tool which had been gilded with gold paint.

Sometimes luck seems to play an important role in the success or failure of a gold-mining enterprise. However, when all the facts are analyzed, that "luck" may have been given a favorable push by some of the engineers and executives working for the successful concern.

R. B. Hagart, a big, broad-shouldered one-time banker who spent a lifetime in Anglo American's executive suite, once answered a question about why Anglo American should have been so successful as it forged the mightiest gold-mining empire ever created. Said he: "The superficial observer might attribute it to the luck of the Oppenheimers. Certainly, there has been a good deal of luck. I have often heard it said that Ernest Oppenheimer made his fortune—and, incidentally, benefited his fellow shareholders—by 'backing his hunches.' If that is taken to mean having a wild gamble, then I can only say that, in my knowledge and experience over thirty years of very close association with Sir Ernest, the element of gambling in his success was so small as to be insignificant. But if it is taken to mean pursuing with courage, determination, and perseverence policies and ideas that had been carefully and logically considered and finally decided upon, then indeed it is true that Sir Ernest built up the great organization of which he was the architect by backing his hunches."

The "luck" of Anglo became evident early in its history when the corporation turned its attention to the Daggafontein Mine, a decrepit property about twelve miles east of Johannesburg. The mine had been launched as a separate company early in this century, after engineering reports indicated it could be a paying proposition. But payable ore eluded miners. Millions of dollars went into tunnels, shafts, and facilities. Little returned to meet the mounting costs of the operation, and the mine was shut down after £1,250,000 had been lost in it. Daggafontein seemed to be one more of those thousands of failed mines which have cost investors a lot of money from Australia to the wilds of Canada and from Ghana to Bolivia.

Anglo appeared on the scene, and its executives, led by Ernest Oppenheimer, thought Daggafontein could be made to pay. So Anglo won control of the defunct property and once more engineers surveyed the area, drilled for samples, and plotted activities. A borehole produced payable ore, and the old mine began to hum and roar with the sound of rock drills biting into rock, headgears hoisting ore to the surface, and mills hammering that ore to fine dust.

In 1933, the mine paid its first dividends, four South African cents for the year. Whereas shares were selling in the four-to-six-shillings-a-share range in 1928, by 1950 units hit £5 each on the London market, or a hundred shillings a share. By 1952, the mine reached its dividend peak, paying out ninety South African cents.

For thirty-six years Daggafontein produced returns which gladdened shareholders, finally petering out as all mines eventually do. Clean-up operations ended in December, 1968, and the last revenue from the mine was obtained in 1969. As for Anglo, it has grown into a mighty complex of 150 companies and subsidiaries in a wide range of activities from mining to chemicals and from steelmaking to foodstuffs, with properties administered by the Group valued at about $4 billion. Yet, gold remains a basic product. In 1974, the Group was responsible for forty-one percent of South Africa's gold output, equivalent to thirty-two percent of world production (excluding Communist countries.)

Anglo American Corporation's headquarters is in Johannesburg, the thriving city of 1.5 million which is the world's gold-mining capital as well as South Africa's financial metropolis. Tall skyscrapers tower over yellow mining dumps which mark sites of some of the old mines that helped transform this city from a wild mining-camp into a sophisticated center. One towering shaft of concrete thrusts several hundred feet into the air like a fat pole, a revolving restaurant on its top. The new Carlton Center forms a "Rockefeller Plaza" of tall buildings around a concrete court where at lunchtime office secretaries sit in the sun beside a circle of flags which flutter above an artificial ice-skating rink.

Only a third of the city's population is white, the rest are black and brown, Zulus, Xhosas, Swazis, Basutos, Pondos, and other black tribesmen, along with brown men whose forefathers came from India two generations ago to work in the sugar plantations of Natal. On Commissioner Street, several Basuto mine-workers troop down the arcaded street, colorful blankets over shoulders, wide-brimmed straw hats sitting like lampshades atop heads. An Ndebele woman, weighted down with beadwork around her neck and on her arms, pauses for a traffic light, muttering to herself, while the baby on her back sleeps unconcernedly.

Here in South Africa, the black tribesmen are known by the generic term of "Bantu," while mulattos and detribalized Africans are called "coloreds." Sometimes race-conscious white South Africans refer to Africans as "kaffirs," a derogatory term akin to the "nigger" of America. Blacks have always played an important role in South Africa's gold mining industry, and today the mines employ 370,000 Bantu, along with 44,000 whites. This is why South African gold-mining stocks are sometimes referred to as "kaffirs" in brokerage parlance.

Anglo American operates under the group system, as do other corporate mining empires in South Africa. This is a uniquely South African system whereby a holding company takes a group of mines under its wing, managing operations and performing staff function so that an individual mine has all the advantages of bigness such as buyer discounts, research, A-1 managerial talent, assistance with manpower, and specialized engineering facilities.

Financing is perhaps the key advantage which a mine obtains from the group system. A group such as Anglo American has its own shares outstanding, and it has immense borrowing power with banks not only in South Africa, but in England, Germany, Switzerland, and elsewhere around the world. Mining companies are floated as individual concerns with public shareholders. But, the parent holding company takes a sizeable percentage of the shares and maintains financial control over its daughter mine.

Whereas a new mine might have difficulty in raising the necessary capital, a company which is backed by one of the big South African mining groups may obtain initial funds from its parent. Moreover, the very fact that such backing is forthcoming attracts investors to purchase shares of the new company on the market, while borrowing powers of the mine are considerably enhanced. This is important considering that South African gold mines are huge industrial enterprises necessitating substantial investments for start of operations. It cost $150 million, for instance, to launch the Western Deep Mine, an amount which an unknown mining company might not have been able to raise. Anglo American could do it. In fact, it raised much more in the late 1940's and 1950's, about $500 million to sink into the gold mines of the Orange Free State.

The major groups in alphabetical order are:

Anglo American Corporation of South Africa, Ltd.
Anglo-Transvaal Consolidated Investment Company, Ltd.
General Mining and Finance Corporation, Ltd.
Gold Fields of South Africa, Ltd.
Johannesburg Consolidated Investment Company, Ltd.
Barlow Rand, Ltd.
Union Corporation, Ltd.

These mining houses are responsible for about eighty-five percent of the value of minerals produced in South Africa. At the end of 1973 these groups had forty-one gold mines under their aegis plus several new mines which are under development.

Mining groups work closely together through the Chamber of Mines of South Africa, an organization which is more than a mere trade association. It attracts and hires labor for the mines. It operates the Rand Refinery, biggest gold refinery by far in the world. It administers welfare services, negotiates labor contracts, conducts research and maintains statistics.

"We are quite an organization in our own right," says John Lang, spokesman for the Chamber.

Among other things, the Chamber has one of the best libraries on gold to be found. Still, the librarian apologetically reported that files contain very little about Harry Frederick Oppenheimer, chairman and chief executive officer of Anglo American and of De Beers, its sister organization in the diamond business. I had met the South African mining magnate several times in the past, knew much about him, but was searching for more background.

"Why don't you try Anglo's library?" the girl asked, with that embarrassed note which librarians sometimes have when referring a researcher to another library for a specific item. The absence of a file may ruin a librarian's day, while the presence of a long-sought fact may arouse ecstasy.

Anglo's library wasn't much more productive. There, a pleasant woman who looked as if she might have been employed in that library for many years, said: "Our chairman discourages the collection of any clips about him."

This is quite a contrast to some industrialists in America who employ public-relations advisors who are given the task of publicizing not the company but the chief executive officer (on company time and pay, of course). Oppenheimer is not a seeker of publicity, though he probably is the most important industrialist on the African continent. His companies produce a third of the free world's new gold, which is far more than Croesus ever saw in his lifetime.

In southern Africa when people want to emphasize wealth they don't mention Rockefeller or Getty, they say that someone is as "rich as Oppenheimer," or perhaps that he is "another Oppenheimer." Harry Frederick Oppenheimer's twenty-first birthday present from his father was 10,000 shares of Anglo American stock.

Ask Oppenheimer how much he is worth, and there is only a shake of the head and a blank stare. He isn't enough concerned about his wealth to keep track of his net worth. Perhaps it is a rude question anyway, though it is one which people, especially Americans, like to ask of any man of wealth. This may be due to envy, or because wealth often is the criterion of a man's success on the treadmills of America. Perhaps you can't take it with you, but then the seeker after wealth is not planning to depart just yet if he can help it.

Anglo's headquarters sits in the financial district of Johannesburg, where the mining houses are clustered so closely together that a short walk might cover all of them. The gold-mining fraternity is a chummy crew which likes to meet at the Rand Club for lunch, perhaps to arrange financing for a new mine. Competition is keen when it comes to exploration, but cooperation is the word in just about everything else. So you find cases like the Buffelsfontein Mine which is managed by General Mining, yet General has only a 17.5 percent equity interest whereas Anglo has a quarter interest. Blyvooruitzicht Mine is in the Rand Group, but Gold Fields of South Africa had a bigger interest in 1972. The world's richest mine, West Driefontein, is in the Gold Fields of South Africa stable, but Anglo owns a healthy 14 percent of it. So it goes, with interlocking relationships often found between the great mining houses of South Africa.

Anglo's blocky, limestone building has the appearance of a Sumerian temple in ancient Mesopotamia, with entrance sculptures deifying mammon and like gods of wealth, the whole constructed to withstand any seige by the world's antigold forces. When Sir Ernest consulted his architect about erection of the new headquarters in the late 1930's he said: "I want something between a bank and a cathedral."

The architect succeeded so well that a visitor doesn't know whether to make the sign of the cross or to reach for his wallet.

Harry Oppenheimer occupies a comfortable first-floor office painted in glistening white, as antiseptic as a hospital corridor. A couch and easy chairs decorated with a floral design, and several tasteful horse prints, provide a homey touch which is accentuated by the graciousness of Oppenheimer's welcome. The prints are more than an affectation. He is a horse breeder and owner of a racing stable, though not a betting man, and in different circumstances he might have been a gentleman farmer rather than a mining magnate. His taste in art, however, goes well beyond horsey prints. The reception room of Brenthurst, his mansion (also painted a glistening white) in a Johannesburg suburb has four Renoirs, a Degas, and a Bonnard on its walls.

Oppenheimer is small of build, with receding hairline and a wisp of a graying moustache. Educated at Oxford University, he served as an intelligence officer in the Western Desert in World War II, returned to South Africa to enter parliament with the opposition United Party. He switched from that to the Progressive Party because he opposed the United Party's acceptance of the apartheid line of the ruling Nationalist Party. Oppenheimer has always had enlightened views on race relations in South Africa, believing that there should be one rate for the job regardless of color. This stand makes him unpopular in government circles, for apartheid is the official policy.

There is nothing about the office or about Oppenheimer to tie him to gold. One might have expected to find gold ashtrays on the desk and side tables, or perhaps a gold bar being used as a paperweight as I noted one time when interviewing the chairman of a major Swiss bank. There is nothing so ostentatious about Oppenheimer. In fact, he has a self-deprecating, almost shy manner, as if afraid that a visitor may be overawed in his presence. As an executive, he has a reputation within the company for delegating tasks to subordinates, expecting them to make decisions on their own.

"Businessmen," says he, "like all men of action, must be prepared to act on incomplete evidence and on what appears to them to be the balance of probabilities."

And sometimes he likes to quote a favorite remark of his father: "If the wise man thinks too long, the fool does some thinking, too."

During any visit with Oppenheimer, it doesn't take long for his liberal (for South Africa) views to appear. The gold-mining industry depends upon its three hundred seventy thousand black workers, and Anglo American has been leading a campaign to raise wages and upgrade the status of black employees.

"We must provide better training and better jobs for our black employees," said he. "Our ultimate goal must be to establish a uniform wage scale for black and white."

"Won't your white mine workers object?" I asked. In South Africa, it isn't the government as much as it is white trade unions which bar Africans from rising to certain jobs. Lower-paid white workers fear the competition of blacks, and they are the most militant in trying to "keep the Bantu in his place."

"White unions are coming around," said Oppenheimer. Then, he explained how a recent wage increase to white workers had been used as a vehicle to persuade the white Mine Workers Union to remove some of the barriers to black advancement. Moreover, wage increases in 1973 averaging around fifty percent have helped upgrade pay scales of blacks.

"Wages still are too low," I said.

He nodded. "I agree, and the best way to increase wages is to train the black workers in order to increase their productivity."

South Africa's mines are built upon cheap labor without a doubt, just as gold through the ages has depended all too often upon strong backs driven to work through force or necessity. Admittedly, the fixed $35-an-ounce price of gold which pertained for thirty-seven years didn't give mines much leeway for raising wages. So the labor pattern which has developed in mines is one of unskilled, poorly educated tribesmen coming from their kraals to the mines to work for periods of a year or two. Sometimes men will sign over and over again. The bulk of them come for short periods, to obtain *lobola* or the price of a bride, to pick up money for an extra cow, to obtain cash for building a house.

They live in single-men's barracks, eat and drink well (4,800 calories a day), have medical care, and work their shifts, under direction of white bosses, like black automatons unable to think for themselves.

Because the system is so paternalistic, with everything from *mahewu* (native beer) to Wild West movies supplied free to workers, it is difficult to compute exact pay scales in American or West European terms. Estimates are, however, that the average black working in the mines was receiving under $100 a month in 1974, when costs of food, lodging, social services and such were included. Take-home pay, of course, was much less.

Often, outsiders refer to such statistics then indicate that they would like to see the present society in South Africa shattered to bits. But in South Africa, many black leaders warn that advancement for

the African must come through a stable and economically progress-
ing society, not through violence which may destroy everything the
black has created along with white civilization.

Gold and apartheid are linked, but Oppenheimer is not alone in
pressing for evolutionary changes to upgrade the black. Even some
Afrikaners, those citizens of Dutch extraction, now advocate such
change. Such a one is Adriaan Louw, chairman of Gold Fields of
South Africa, a tall, moustached executive who is one of the few men
with an Afrikaner background to reach the top in a gold-mining
industry founded and dominated by South Africans of British origin.
Moreover, when appointed chairman in 1965 he was probably the
youngest man to reach that position with a major South African
mining group in the previous thirty-five years.

"The increase in the gold price was one of the best things which
could have happened for blacks in this country," said Louw when I
encountered him behind a desk in his sumptuous office. He is an
outdoors man by choice who now finds himself tied to a desk while
his heart still lies with the mines from whence he climbed upward
to his present position.

Carefully, he explained that mines now have the means to do
better for their black workers than they have in the past. "I believe
in equal opportunity for everyone," he declared, emphatically.

To him the apartheid idea of forcing Africans back to their home-
lands is a "pipedream," for the structure of black and white societies
are so interlocked that there can be no turning of the clock backward, as apartheid suggests.

But, C. B. Anderson, chairman of Union Corporation, which has
seven gold mines under its wing, emphasizes a factor which seems
to be unknown to many people not living in South Africa. Says he:
"Three quarters of the African miners come from outside the Republic, from Mozambique, from Swaziland, from Lethoso, and places like
that. Wages paid in the mines are better than these blacks could earn
at home, so they come here."

It was at Anderson's suggestion that I toured some of Union Corporation's mines in the Evander area. South African gold fields sometimes are viewed as part of one immense field, and they are, if the
Witwatersrand Basin is seen as one, huge saucer, as geologists view
it. But, because gaps exist in the continuity of that reef, South Africa's
gold-mining areas may be divided into seven fields, with Evander the
furthest east, and the Orange Free State field at the opposite end of
that 350-mile-long arc.

Evander is rather unusual because Union Corporation has this particular field all to itself, with control of the Kinross, Leslie, Bracken, and Winkelhaak Mines.

Hugh Corder, slender, bespectacled intelligence officer with Union Corporation, served as the guide-chauffeur on the seventy-five-mile ride to the Leslie Mine, east of Johannesburg. We drove through the city's heavy early-morning traffic, past small, tin-roofed houses with porches, which probably were built years ago for workers in the mines. Mine dumps rose like yellow mountains beside time-worn buildings of defunct mines. A low pall of smoke hung over the ground, the smoke of industry, tinged with sulfur and biting to the lungs.

Then, we were in open country, on grassy veldt which was brown in the August winter sun, with scattered stands of eucalyptus shielding lonely farmhouses. South Africa is a land of open spaces, much like the American West in many respects, where the blacks are the Indians, living in thatch-roofed rondavels often set in clusters, or kraals around which cattle brouse. Villages have a wide main street down which the highway knifes past arcaded stores. On the edge of one village, a negro couple drove a wagon and mule team, he huddled in an old army coat, his female companion wrapped in a colorful blanket, with only her bereted head exposed.

Once, Corder slowed to point to a deserted group of buildings beside the road. "This is one of our old mines, the Van Dyke," said he. "It's been closed awhile now."

I knew the Van Dyke. In August, 1941, when hopes were high, workers at the mine established a new shaft-sinking record of 461 feet in one month. Basically, a gold mine consists of a shaft driven vertically into the ground until the reef is reached. This shaft provides means for raising and lowering workers, tools, equipment, ore, and anything else. Tunnels, called crosscuts, are driven from the shaft to the stope, or working face, of the mine where the ore of the gold-bearing reef will be mined.

It costs a lot of money to open a mine. Nearly $200 million in capital already have gone into Western Deep Mine, $150 million of it just to get production started. Investments don't pay any return until production starts. Thus, the faster that miners can drive the shaft down to start the mine, the sooner will gold begin to come from the property, and the sooner will dividends be paid to shareholders. So shaft-sinking has become something like a competitive contest at new mines. The record is now held by Buffelsfontein, which sunk 1,251 feet of shaft in March, 1962.

This I was thinking when I stared at the collection of forlorn buildings of Van Dyke, clustered around a mine headgear which towered into the blue sky. (A headgear is the derricklike framework of steel which is used to raise and lower lifts into the shaft.) Lofty ridges of waste rock rose behind, grass growing on slopes.

Soon we came upon the industrial ruins of Brackpan, another defunct mine. "We are passing through an area of dying or dead mines," said Corder.

"Every mine is a dying mine from the first day it starts producing," I said.

He nodded. There is just so much gold-bearing ore in a mine. Eventually all mines peter out, though modern technology does keep providing new assists to the mining industry. Fifty years ago, for instance, a deep mine was one of four thousand feet. Today, Western Deep is geared for mining at over twelve thousand feet. A little more than fifty years ago, miners used hand drills to bore holes into rock. Today, it is done mechanically with air jackhammers.

The oldest mine in South Africa is the Rand Group's East Rand Proprietary (ERPM) Mine, which declared its first gold in September, 1894. It still is producing, accounting for 557,128 ounces of gold in 1972, worth $55.7 million at $100 an ounce.

The Leslie Mine is one of those so-so properties, never a great mine in the manner of a Vaal Reefs or a West Driefontein; it milled its first ore in 1962 and now has only about a half dozen years of life left, though rising gold prices may extend that. But there was an air of neat order about the red-brick buildings with roofs of painted galvanized steel. Africans in slickers, helmets on heads, waited near the headgear for the "Mary Anne" to take them down. Garbed in boots, oilskins, and helmet with flashlight on its crown, I joined them, walking into the battered steel cage which waited for us.

It started slowly, with a squeak and a groan, only a dim light glowing overhead as darkness surrounded us. We dropped faster and faster. Lights flashed by, the lights of side tunnels which we were passing like an express train roaring through way stations. Ears popped. Moisture dropped onto my helmet, flowed down the front of the slicker. There was a rush and a hollow rumble as if the sound of our descent were plunging to the bottom of the shaft, then reechoing to us.

At the 3,000-foot level, the cage stopped at a brightly lit tunnel with a railroad track running along its floor. A water pipe snaked along the ceiling on one side. A mine train rolled down the track toward us, followed a switch, and disappeared somewhere into another crosscut. The air was hot and heavy with moisture, and after only a few yards of walking along the track, perspiration coursed off my body.

The crosscut led to the stope or mine face. Here the work area was just high enough to allow crews to crawl forward with their jackhammers, explosives, and shovels. Standing in the crosscut, I peered down the stope. It was no place for anyone with claustrophobia, and I wasn't sure visitors would be allowed to clamber down that forty-inch-high passage.

Eric Collier, the sandy-haired former British naval submariner who was underground manager, took everything nonchalantly, determined that I would obtain a full understanding of his mine.

"Mining really is a simple process," he explained, then added, "Duck your head."

Crouching on all fours he led the way into the stope. I followed with a squirming hand-crawl to a point where a white miner was directing a crew of two Bantus. There didn't seem to be room enough for the three of them, let alone for the four more in our party.

At this depth there was a pressure of 4,000 pounds per square inch inside the rock, with the pressure increasing with the depth. In deep mines, the pressure sometimes is so great that rock will explode like a bursting grenade, spraying deadly chips in all directions. A few years ago, one such explosion killed a half-dozen miners in South Africa.

Helmet lights gleamed, providing the only illumination. Noise of the air drills thundered and roared with a staccato cadence in the low passage. One of the blacks balanced a drill with a booted foot as he lay on his back, the handles in his fists. A crouched assistant helped apply pressure on the tool. Wood-and-rock pillars supported the tremendous weight of the rock overhead.

Collier signaled to the white crew-boss. The deafening noise halted so suddenly that Collier seemed to be shouting when he explained how the men were drilling holes to charge them with explosives. After a pattern of such holes are drilled along the face, the blaster packs them with the explosives, departs to a safe place and fires the charges. That blows rock loose that winch scrapers gather. Mechanical loaders lift that gold-bearing rock onto cars for transport to hoists. Above ground, the rock is pounded to a dusty fine power in revolving mills. The ore then is mixed with cyanide, which separates gold from the rock. Zinc dust is added to attract the cyanide from the gold. The resulting slurry is melted and refined in electric furnaces, then poured into 1,000-ounce bars for transport to the Rand Refinery in Germiston, a Johannesburg suburb.

Some blasé souls contend that when you have seen one mine you have seen them all. I haven't found it so. Essentially, every gold mine might seem the same, yet there are differences. Gold mines in South Africa are like ships which ply the world's trade routes. They are self-sufficient units, employing men who have been thrown together to complete a job. Mines have their own recreational grounds (segregated, of course), their own shops and service facilities, their own cinemas, their own clubhouse. (At Stillfontein the Strathvaal Club boasts of a 126-foot bar, long enough to accomodate a lot of miners when the drinks flow.)

The mine manager is like the captain of a ship, the boss, who is in charge. If he is a good manager, he looks after the welfare of his men, both white and black, as well as the ore-hoisting and milling rates of the property.

And each mine has its own history, its story to tell. A few years ago in the Crown Mine, before it finally closed, I could feel that history as I stepped off the cage into one of its deep-level crosscuts to be greeted by a helmeted mining official who said:

"Welcome to the richest mine in all history."

In its long lifetime, about 1,370 metric tons were taken from this one mine, which may have been close to the total volume of gold cornered by Alexander the Great after making himself master of most of the ancient world.

Engineers have plotted a life of over sixty years for the giant Western Deep mine, which means that it ultimately may surpass Crown Mines as the richest in history. Walking down its tunnels, one wonders what the gold-mining industry will be like in 2035 A.D. or thereabouts when this massive mine will be on its last legs. Will gold still be sought as desperately by men as it has been thus far in history? Probably? That lust for gold has not faded after more than five thousand years, so there is little reason for believing that chrysophobes can dim gold's lustre in the next sixty years.

After I visited that mine, it added a bloody chapter to its young history, when a dozen rioting black miners were killed by police. A wage dispute had gotten out of hand. Demonstrators milled before a line of policemen, and one of those tragic events occurred in which panic affects fingers poised on triggers of guns.

The tragedy was compounded because in the average mine there is a camaraderie and good relationship between white employees and black miners which is surprising considering the segregation practiced above ground. When in the Leslie Mine, we paused once at an underground first-aid station where a white miner and a black miner were sitting side by side, waiting for the administrations of a white medical man. Explained Collier: "When a man is hurt his color doesn't count down here. The important thing is to do what we can for him." Then, he quickly added: "And the best thing we can do is to try to make sure he isn't hurt in the first place."

I was trudging down a long crosscut several thousand feet below the ground with a young engineer in the Western Holdings Mine in the Orange Free State one time. He was explaining to me how mines continually stress safety to employees, seeking to minimize accidents.

"Mining is a hazardous occupation, but so many accidents are due to pure carelessness," he explained. Then he cheerfully shouted something to an African miner who appeared momentarily in a pool of light which marked a side tunnel.

"Have you seen the lion's paw?" was the gist of his remark in the Fanakalo dialect of the mines, he later explained to me.

The answer came back in hollow, sepulchral tones from the African: "Mena ikona buka lo nyeou ka lo gonyaan." ("I have not seen the lion's paw.")

"Lion's paw" means danger in the African vernacular. Translated into English, the question would have been: "Are you safe?"

One time at the East Geduld Mine, before that venerable property ceased production in 1970, I watched a demonstration at the mine school for Africans. This is a facility which is duplicated on all the gold mines of South Africa. On a lawn was a life-sized figure of a man made of sheet metal except for an extended hand, which was of clay.

"This is the way we emphasize the danger of explosives to our blacks," explained an instructor, pointing to the clay hand. "We put a fuse into that hand, then explode it when everyone is standing back to watch. Of course, the clay hand is blown to bits."

A few minutes later, I suppressed a startled jump at the explosion, then listened to the "ohs" and "ahs" of a dozen blacks from tribal kraals as they gazed at the shattered pieces of the clay hand.

I learned more about Fanakalo at the Vaal Reefs Mine, another of South Africa's great gold mines. Blacks from fifty different Bantu tribes, speaking forty-four different languages, work in the gold mines. To cut through that Babel of tongues, the mining industry has developed its own language, a sort of pidgin dialect which Bantu and European miners speak as easily as their native languages. Fanakalo has about two thousand words in its vocabulary, but a man may do well with five hundred.

"Tina qala sebenza maze," says a white shift-boss to a dozen blacks waiting for him by the mine cage. ("We are going to start working now.") They nod.

At the 6,500-foot level below ground, one licensed white blaster tells an assistant: "Zunki skatpas op lo dopi." ("Be careful with detonators.")

I. W. Swain, the training officer at the mine, said: "If you speak Fanakalo you can drive as far as Malawi in central Africa and you will find someone all along the way who speaks the language."

Deep in Vaal Reefs Mine I forgot about Fanakalo as I followed one shift-boss to the stope face in the 87-degree Fahrenheit temperature of the 6,500-foot level. Air conditioning is necessary to keep temperatures that low, and there the forty-inch-high stope slants at about a thirty-degree angle, adding to the difficulty of crawling along in that tight space.

"You know, I read something not long ago in one of your American magazines," said the white shift-boss as we inched along. "The writer was saying that we make our Africans work in tunnels which are only forty inches high."

"So what are we doing down here?" I asked, knowing full well that every gold mine keeps its stope as low as possible.

"Yeah," he said. "I'm down here every day and so are other of our white miners, too. It isn't just the blacks who work down here."

"I know what you're driving at," I said. "You have to avoid taking out any useless rock or you won't be in business long. So the stope has to be low."

"Yeah," he said, "and that's the way they mine gold anywhere else when the reef is a thin seam sandwiched between worthless rock. But some of your people can always find something to criticize insofar as South Africa is concerned."

I didn't say anything. When you are a stranger, 6,500 feet down in a passage forty inches high, you hardly want to start any argument with your guide. Anyway I got his point, for a little earlier I had heard about the nineteenth-century Notre Dame des Victoires Mine where the prissy manager organized the operation so that stopes were high enough to enable him to make his inspections without removing his top hat. The company went broke not long after starting operations.

Today, tunnels in mines usually are about ten feet high, plenty high enough for anyone to walk on stilts if he so wished. But at the stope face the height is forty inches, and it is kept to forty inches as the stope moves deeper and deeper into the reef, unless the reef, itself, widens.

Vaal Reefs rates as the world's biggest gold mine according to the number of miners working in it and the amount of rock which is moved to the surface and milled. It employs thirty-three thousand black and twenty-eight hundred white workers and in 1972 the mine hoisted 6,145,000 tons of ore to the surface. That produced 2,122,285 ounces (66 tons) of gold, or $212.2 million worth, at $100 an ounce. A mine merger is making Vaal Reefs even bigger.

The richest gold mine from the standpoint of gold content is West Driefontein of the Gold Fields of South Africa Group. In 1972, this lone mine produced 2,418,398 fine ounces of gold, an amount equivalent to 75.2 metric tons. That is considerably more than the total annual production of all the gold mines in the United States.

The sheer size of South Africa's gold-mining industry is staggering. At the Harmony Mine, for instance, there is the largest elevator in the world, one which is authorized to carry 150 persons at a time. At Government Areas Mine is the highest rock dump, a pile 357 feet high, nearly as high as the Great Pyramid of Cheops in Egypt.

The richest gold mine in all history was the Crown Mine, a Rand Mines, Ltd., property. In its seventy-seven years of life, it produced more than forty-four million fine ounces of gold, which would be worth nearly $8 billion at a price of $180 an ounce.

# CHAPTER X

# Lust for Gold

Graham Greene in his *Travels with My Aunt* tells the story of a gold bar which was stolen from a shipment at London's Heathrow Airport. Thieves didn't see any quick way of escaping with that ingot while the search for it was hot. So they rolled the bar in black tar and used it for a doorstop until time had dimmed the passion of the search. Then, they cooly lugged the "doorstop" through the gates of the airport.

"That happens to be a true story," said one employee of London's Heathrow Airport in the departure lounge when the usual crowd was milling about. "There's more gold stolen at London airport than at any other place in the world."

This last was said with evident pride, as if Heathrow's superlatives might redound to the credit of anyone who happened to be working there. Perhaps it is human nature to seek pride in exterior things when one has no personal accomplishments from which to draw dignity. London has frequently been the locale for heists of gold bullion, for it has been a focal point on the world's gold trail for years. Still, his remark was an exaggeration.

The biggest gold robbery of all time wasn't in England. It was the Spanish Civil War seizure by the Russians in November, 1936, of Spain's gold reserves of sixteen million fine ounces. This was worth $560 million then but would be worth around $2.8 billion today, a coup which no group of gangsters has ever matched anywhere else, before or since. In 1957, Alexander Orlov, head of the Russian NKVD (secret police) operation in Spain during the Civil War, defected to the West. He appeared before a Senate committee in Washington in that year and told enough to prove the close political tie-up which existed between Republicans and Communists.

When Republicans seized assets in the Spanish Central Bank, Stalin immediately demanded those assets as security for payments for arms and aircraft for the Republican side. The Communist-infiltrated Republican command obliged, then looked the other way when Orlov had the gold loaded on a freighter at a Spanish port and transported to Odessa, where it disappeared. Nobody in the West has seen it since. That robbery soured Spanish-Russian relations for years. But the Kremlin, for all its alleged disinterest in gold, learned long ago that gold might be more durable than diplomatic friendships.

Spain was the victim of another robbery in 1810, when Napoleon's army was occupying the country. France dispatched a commission to the Escorial Palace outside Madrid to collect all the gold and silver treasures to be found. There is no way of estimating the value of the art objects which were seized and melted down to meet Napoleon's need for funds. But it is known that the French destroyed the largest collection of gold and silver art objects then existing in Europe, with ten camp wagons needed to transport the loot to Paris.

Today, the world's richest gold trail, between South Africa and Europe, is so well protected that criminals have had little success trying to heist any of that rich cargo. In early, 1965, however, it looked as if that fine record was finally ended. When the Union Castle liner *Capetown Castle* docked at Southampton, England, on February 5, after a voyage from South Africa, twenty gold bars of 400 ounces each were missing. At that time the gold was worth $280,000, a figure which would be about $1.4 million at the present free-market price of the metal.

The gold had been transported in armored trucks from the Rand Refinery near Johannesburg to the Durban docks, where it was placed aboard the Union Castle liner. Destination: the Bank of England. In the loading operation, 729 wooden boxes, each containing two 400-ounce bars, were carefully lowered through a hatch into a strongroom on the ship. This room was sealed.

Another 144 boxes, also with two bars each, couldn't be fitted into the strongroom. So a special cargo locker on the port side became a second, unofficial strongroom. After bars were loaded into this locker, the hold was locked and welded shut. Then five iron bars were welded across the entrance to make it impossible, apparently, for anyone to tamper with the cargo.

Yet, twenty bars were missing.

The ship's master, Captain H. L. Holland, notified the Castle company, and police were called immediately. Said the Captain: "I don't think anyone from the crew is responsible."

Southampton detectives invaded the ship, checked the passenger list, contacted some of them at homes and hotels, started grilling the crew. The mechanics of the robbery became evident immediately. Thieves had entered a cargo locker adjacent to the temporary strongroom. A wire grille in a ventilation shaft had been clipped open with heavy shears. Robbers had wriggled through an eighteen-inch passage along this shaft to the strongroom. Another grille had been removed at that end to force entry into the vault. Then the ten boxes containing the twenty gold bars had been passed along the tunnel, to disappear.

By the time the robbery was discovered, the ship already was tied up at the Southampton dock, and half of its crew of 485 had been paid off. Two dozen detectives and a dozen customs officers started a stem-to-stern search of the liner, figuring that perhaps the gold had not yet been removed from the ship. Nothing was found.

Police carefully reconstructed the scene, tried to narrow the focus of their search. Whoever had entered the cargo locker adjacent to the strongroom had needed a key, for the door was kept locked. This seemed to point to some member of the crew, eliminating passengers, though one or more passengers might have been in league with one or more crew members. Investigation, however, showed that any of dozens of crew members might have had access to keys to lockers.

Tools used for the job probably had come from the boatswain's locker or from the engine room. Here, again, however, any number of the crew had access to them. All members of the crew were questioned, either on shipboard or ashore. Nobody had anything to contribute to the search.

Twenty gold bars at 400 ounces each represents 8,000 troy ounces or 500 avoirdupois pounds. That is a lot of weight for a robber band to be carrying around. Thus, it seemed that the first step taken by robbers would be to hide their loot, waiting for an opportunity to remove bars one by one to some safe location ashore. Then would come the job of breaking up the bars and selling them through fences who might be only too glad to accept gold bars at a fifty percent discount.

But the *Capetown Castle* had been searched from bow to poop deck and nothing had been found. The ship's log, however, showed that, after leaving Durban, the liner had stopped at East London, Port Elizabeth, and Cape Town in South Africa and Las Palmas in the Canary Islands. Could the gold have been removed in one of these ports? At that time there had been no alarm about missing gold. Since no theft ever had been made, heretofore, from the gold traffic, customs officials might have been lax.

And a second possibility occurred to police, too. Other vessels had lain beside the *Capetown Castle* at those particular ports. The gold could have been transferred from one ship to another, from robbers to accomplices on another ship. There was a fleet of Castle boats plying between Britain and South Africa, and crew members often switched from one ship to another of the line. Men on the *Capetown Castle* thus would have friends on the *Athlone Castle*, the *Windsor Castle*, and other ships.

Cables were dispatched to police in the port cities, seeking cooperation and warning them that perhaps the lost gold might reappear in their localities. Police were also asked to check shipping logs to determine which vessels may have moored beside the *Capetown Castle* on its voyage north.

The investigation warmed when it was learned that a cargo ship, the *Apapa*, had moored beside the *Capetown Castle* at Las Palmas. And two men, Edward Okonkwo, aged twenty-seven, and John Paul Ajunonwo, aged sixty-four, were caught red-handed in Liverpool, trying to sell a one-kilo bar of gold. Ajunonwo had been a crewman aboard the *Apapa*.

"I got the bar off a fellow on the ship," Ajunonwo told detectives.

The case seemed to be cracking. Then, as in the plot of a detective story, this lead collapsed. Chemical analysis showed that the Liverpool gold was different from the South African gold. Wearily Southampton police admitted there was no connection between the arrests and the *Capetown Castle* robbery.

Police searched the liner again, questioned some members of the crew a second time. Nothing was turned up. The gold had disappeared as effectively as if a helicopter had met the ship somewhere enroute to haul away the gold.

On February 11, when a sister ship, the *Windsor Castle*, docked at Cape Town, police sealed off the area, subjected ship and crew to an intensive search. It developed that the *Windsor Castle* and the *Capetown Castle* had lain in adjoining berths at Las Palmas, the *Windsor* on its way south, the *Capetown* on its way to Southampton. Passengers were asked if they had spoken to anyone from the *Capetown Castle* or had seen a gray Rolls-Royce on the quay at Las Palmas.

The search proved futile.

Meanwhile, longshoremen in Southampton were busy unloading cargo from the *Capetown Castle*. On February 12, in a hold which had contained hides, police found ten bullion boxes, the same kind as those in which the gold had been loaded.

The boxes were empty.

Southampton detectives continued their investigations, tried to follow movements of crewmen who had left the *Capetown Castle* after the gold-haul voyage from Durban. A passport photographer provided a little information. On the February 5 morning that the ship had docked at Southampton, the photographer remembered that one of the crewmen, Neil Francis Hawthorne, aged twenty-six, had passport pictures taken and had inquired if the pictures would be all right for Australia.

There is nothing wrong about wanting to go to Australia, of course. Moreover, it developed that Hawthorne was an Australian. But when questioned again by detectives, he refused to make any statement without consulting his attorney.

Other sailors confided that Hawthorne's good friend on shipboard had been one Raymond Messer Williams, a twenty-seven-year-old Gloucester resident. Williams, too, was called in for further questioning, and he seemed ultranervous, admitted that he had been suffering from migraine headaches ever since the *Capetown Castle* had docked in port.

When being questioned, he blurted to Police Sergeant J. McCullough that: "This has worried me a lot. When I read in the papers how much the gold was worth it shook me. I will be very pleased when you get the stuff back."

"Where is it?" asked Detective Chief Inspector Bertram Adams.

Hawthorne and Williams exchanged glances. Then Hawthorne seemed eager to be first to speak. Said he: "Six bars. Top Number six small sand locker, starboard side, permanently open. Bars in there with thin layer of oil, grease, and cement over them."

Williams interjected, as if afraid silence might be held against him. "Fourteen bars in air-cooling, well deck. Lift trap door. Descend iron ladder. Turn right. After that you will have to crawl to the end of passage. Bars are covered with concrete."

That night both Adams and McCullough took a plane for South Africa to meet the *Capetown Castle* in Durban. On March 9 they boarded the ship, found six gold bars hidden in a sand box as indicated.

The search intensified. Late that night, police found the other fourteen bars in a narrow passage near the engine room. The bars had been sprinkled with concrete, sand, and water, creating a hard lump which looked like refuse left by ship repairers who had been working near the engine room. When the *Capetown Castle* steamed north again, the twenty bars again were in a strongroom aboard, destined for an insurance company which had already paid the claim on the stolen bars.

On July 23, 1965, Hawthorne and Williams were found guilty of theft at the Hampshire Assizes in Winchester, England, and each was sentenced to ten years imprisonment. In retrospect, their bid to steal that gold appears to have been an amateurish stab at a crime which was doomed to failure from the start. But being stupid over gold is a common failing among criminals. Often the criminal not only counts his chickens before they are hatched; he also counts the eggs before they are laid. When he does encounter the egg of gold, he finds it to be much heavier than he expected, and this compounds the disposal problems.

If you visit the bullion vaults of the Bank of England in London, you will find that gold bars are not stacked high in glittering gold piles. No. Bars are in low mounds spread all over the concrete floor. Notices warn that loading must not exceed 784 pounds per square foot, even though this happens to be a reinforced concrete floor.

Gold is slippery to handle, too. A novice might drop a heavy bar on his foot if he didn't handle the ingot with extreme care. This wouldn't hurt the ingot. It could crush a foot.

Then, there is the problem of sale. First the gold must be melted into smaller bars. This not only destroys telltale marking numbers, but when poured into smaller sizes, ingots are easier to sell or to smuggle to some foreign land.

So the successful gold thief needs strong muscles, a solid truck, an adequate storage place, a miniature foundry, and some sales contacts. It helps if the owners of the gold are careless in their habits and thoroughly convinced that crime doesn't pay. In London in the 1967–69 period, some gold holders were so negligent that it seemed as if robber gangs would corner the bullion market. In one week, $500,000 worth of bullion was robbed in three different jobs. But the biggest haul of any by far was that of May 1, 1967, when over a ton and a half of gold bullion was robbed from a truck of the London Gold Market, the record gold-bullion robbery for jolly England.

May 1 is a holiday in most of Europe, the Labor Day on which Socialists celebrate their proletarian rituals. It is a simple workday in Britain, however, and just before 10:00 A.M. the 3¼-ton navy blue Commer truck of the Royal Mint Refinery of N. M. Rothschild & Sons left the garage for its regular Monday run. Walter Clements, the forty-seven-year-old driver, noticed that traffic was heavy but this wasn't surprising in London's financial district, where seventeenth- and eighteenth-century lanes still serve as streets. The truck wasn't armored, but this didn't worry Clements or the two guards, Jack Chandler, forty, and Richard Brew, fifty-one. N. M. Rothschild figured that an armored truck could attract the attention of would-be robbers. A plain truck might be mistaken for a vegetable delivery or perhaps a furniture van. The bank failed to recognize that today's smart crooks may trail a vehicle for weeks to identify its cargo and the delivery habits of its crews.

The Bank of England opens for business at 10:00 A.M., and Clements turned into the Bank's private drive at 10:10 A.M., and wheeled into an interior loading dock after identifying himself at a check point. Inside the bank, the three-man crew watched as 188 gold bars, each weighing 400 ounces, were loaded, along with a small bag of grain silver. At today's prices that cargo would be worth more than $13 million.

The first call on the truck's route was at Johnson, Matthey (Bankers) Ltd., the gold-bullion dealer and fabricating company which has a facility in Hatton Gardens in the financial district perhaps a half mile from the Bank of England. The delivery sheet called for forty-eight of the bars to be dropped off here, a shipment which was made on schedule without incident. It was 11:30 A.M. when the truck left the Johnson, Matthey freight dock for 14 Bowling Green Lane, only a few blocks away. Orders were to drop off the bag of grain silver at this address, the least valuable of the shipments on the truck this particular day.

Traffic clogged Bowling Green, a short street in an area of tenementlike apartment buildings and smoke-begrimed factories. Clements searched vainly for a parking position before No. 14, couldn't find any. So he parked a few hundred feet up the street. Chandler jumped to the ground from the rear of the truck, took the bag of silver, and walked back with it to the building occupied by Clare Press, while Clements lounged in the driver's seat and Brew sat upon some of the gold bars.

This delivery, too, was made without incident, Chandler noting the time as 11:42 A.M. as he took the receipt for the silver. He started back up the street, empty-handed, paying no attention to the taxi and several automobiles which were parked by the curb, nor to the several men loafing beside the vehicles. London is not the sort of place where one normally thinks of crime on the streets, especially when it is almost high noon.

Says Chandler: "I was walking along the street toward our van, when all of a sudden, bam, somebody conked me on the head from behind."

Dazed, he felt himself being seized before he could fall. A blindfold was slipped over his eyes. His arms were rudely jerked behind his back, and his hands were pinioned with adhesive tape. Two men half carried, half pushed him toward the van.

Brew, sitting on the gold bars in the truck, heard a knock at the back door. Thinking it was Chandler returning, he lifted the roller door at the rear, then gasped as a shot of Mace or some like chemical squirted into his eyes from a vague figure on the pavement. This was Brew's last clear recollection of the hijacking.

At almost the same moment, the identical thing happened to a relaxed Clements in the cab. Chandler was pushed into the truck. Several men tumbled behind, quickly bound Brew and Clements. Both were in agony from the chemical.

In seconds, a gang member held the wheel of the gold truck, others occupied the gold compartment. The truck rolled away. And nobody on the street even noticed anything amiss.

The first alarm didn't sound until fifty minutes later. Three miles north of the hijacking scene, Mrs. Alice Summers, a London housewife, joined three other neighborhood women for their regular Monday-afternoon bingo session at a hall in the Islington section of the city.

They heard the muffled sound of voices and a thumping coming from a truck parked along the curb. Says Mrs. Summers: "I thought they were taking us on because we were laughing as we went along. I thought it was somebody havin' a lark, until I heard a voice saying, 'Please, please phone the police. We've been locked in.'"

Even then the women thought it was all a joke until one of them peered through a crack at the door of the vehicle and saw the three men lying on the floor. There was a shriek from one of the women, and they all scattered to the nearest houses to get help, and to call for the police. Soon police arrived, to find themselves confronted with the biggest bullion robbery in Britain's history.

Fortunately, forty-eight of the gold bars had been delivered before the hijacking. This still left 140 unaccounted for, 56,000 ounces of

999.9 fine gold which then was worth $1,960,000 but which would be worth over $10 million at a price of $180 an ounce, today.

In a marvelously understated comment, one police official said: "This was obviously an extremely well-planned job by professionals." It was evident from the first, of course, that 56,000 troy ounces (3,500 avoirdupois pounds) of gold wasn't easy to handle. Still, this gang had been able to seize the bullion truck at 11:45, drive it three miles north through heavy traffic, yet find time to stop somewhere to transfer 3,500 pounds of gold and to get away with the whole works.

Ironically, a fluke telephone call almost led to police entrapment of the gang while the gold transfer was underway. At about noon-time, Mrs. R. Purcell, a housewife living on Elthorne Road, peeped through her curtains toward an empty house and garage next door. This is a row-house area where everybody on a street usually knows what everybody else is doing, and this particular house had been empty for two weeks. She noticed several men entering the garage of the house.

She didn't have a telephone. So she hurried across the street to an auto-repair shop, told Frank Tarrant, the manager, that something odd was happening in the house next door. Strangers were about, and they seemed up to no good. Tarrant didn't know if he were dealing with a nervous woman or with trouble. To make sure, he casually strolled across the street, glanced up the driveway. Says he: "From the gate, I could see a light van parked crossways in the garage, and a man in a cap walking round the front."

He didn't wait to see more, but hurried to his telephone, called the nearby Holloway Station. "Suspected loiterers on premises" calls are routine at any police station and most of them are easily-explained misunderstandings. A squad car was dispatched to investigate. It arrived after the "loiterers" had departed. It was only after news of the robbery was broadcast that police related the trespasser call to the robbery. A recheck of the garage showed that this, indeed, was the place where the robber band had transferred the gold from the bullion truck to a vehicle of their own.

All customs points were alerted to watch for attempts to smuggle the gold to the continent. That evening the small 500-ton Dutch freighter *Thea* was halted in the lower Thames by a police launch. A thorough search failed to reveal anything, and the ship proceeded on its way to Rotterdam. A few days later police in Lima, Peru, arrested three Argentines who had a 200-pound gold bar in their possession.

Was this part of the loot? It wasn't. But the London robbery had alerted police around the world to be on the lookout for illegally moving gold. Some authorities believed that the gold would be placed on smuggling routes through contacts with criminal syndicates. In fact, within days, police informants provided information that some of the gold was being smuggled to Switzerland and sold to a Swiss bank.

Police suspected that funds on sales might be flowing back to London for splitting with various members of the gang. Requests for cooperation went to Switzerland, while authorities in London solicited help from London banks concerning any oddities which might appear in accounts of clients. Sources tipped off police about some newly opened accounts at the Bank of Bilbao, Barclays Bank, and Westminster Bank in London, into which funds were flowing from the Geneva branch of the Union Bank of Switzerland, one of Switzerland's Big Three and a highly reputable bank.

Swiss banks deal in gold every day, buying and selling as casually as if they might be dealing with potatoes or bananas. So a few smuggled bars might disappear into a bank's vaults without any member of the bank being any wiser or having any intent of rewarding the criminals behind the operation. Just as you or anyone else would not commit a crime if you innocently accepted a forged bank note, a Swiss bank may accept illicit gold without realizing it.

But it so happened that the Union Bank of Switzerland's Geneva branch had received sixteen gold bars in May from one source, an André de Bec, all offered to the bank for sale. And the bank had accepted them.

Sixteen gold bars of 400 ounces each totals 6,400 ounces. That would be worth around $640,000 today, but in 1967, at a price of $35 an ounce, it represented $224,000. Still, that is a considerable volume of gold to be selling, especially at a time when troubles in the Middle East were increasing buyers' interest in gold as a hedge against currency problems. Smart investors were buying gold at that time, not trying to dump it.

So Union Bank checked those gold bars, found that all sixteen had been dispatched by the Geneva branch to the bank's gold refinery, Argor S.A., at Chiasso, in southern Switzerland on the Italian border. A call to Argor revealed that ten of the sixteen bars already had been melted down. The other six still were in Argor's vaults. The bars were examined and found to be identical with those lost in the great bullion heist.

London police were told that payments for the gold sales had been telexed to accounts of Ronald Stafford at the Bank of Bilbao, Leslie Neame Alldridge at Barclays Bank, and Norman August Margrie at the Westminster Bank in London. Subsequent investigations in London showed that Stafford had been credited with £18,044 on May 9 and that £14,400 had been collected the same day by Brenda Desmond, with a check signed by Stafford. On May 11, £20,910 was sent by the Union Bank to Alldridge's account at Barclays Bank. On May 18, £21,500 arrived from Switzerland for Margrie's account at the Westminster Bank, and that amount was paid out the same day to a gentleman who claimed to be Margrie.

Police established a watch upon accounts which still retained funds. On May 25, Miss Desmond, a twenty-three-year-old switchboard operator, appeared at the Bank of Bilbao armed with a check from Stafford to collect more funds from the account. She was arrested. Shortly thereafter police apprehended Alldridge, a thirty-seven-year-old television repairman, and Margrie, a thirty-year-old architect's assistant.

Police announced that all were being held in connection with the great bullion robbery. Six of the 140 missing gold bars were returned to London. Bank accounts involved were sequestered. Yet there was a feeling that much of the case still lay unsolved. Stafford, the most important character in this particular group, was still free. Those arrested didn't look like criminals, and they seemed more than eager to cooperate with police, except perhaps for Miss Desmond where Stafford was concerned. She was in love with him.

Stafford was a forty-one-year-old surveyor who liked fast cars, bright lights, and travel. Later he was to be described as "a sort of James Bondish character." The police description of him was terse:

> He has a fresh complexion, receding light brown hair and blue eyes. He is about 5 feet 9 inches tall and is known to have a British passport. He may try to disguise himself by dyeing his hair and wearing sun glasses.

As the investigation proceeded police concluded that Stafford was "undoubtedly the principal factor" in the great bullion robbery. Stafford's father, a man in his early eighties, was a voluble fellow who talked a little too much for his son's good. Sure, his son had been in Switzerland, the elder Stafford said, and he knew it because he had been along with his boy and Miss Desmond. The time? Well, it was about May 5, and the elder Stafford remembered it because May 5 was his birthday. He didn't know anything about any gold bars.

But when police checked the Mercedes, they found particles of gold in the trunk.

Alldridge admitted he had done a favor for Stafford. Stafford had given him the name of a man who had a couple of heavy suitcases at Dunkirk on the English Channel. Alldridge had picked up the suitcases and had then driven to Geneva with them. For this, Stafford had paid him $480. He made the first such trip on May 8, and had followed this with a second trip with another two suitcases a few days later.

It was on May 8 that a Mr. de Bec appeared at Union Bank of Switzerland's Geneva branch with four gold bars to sell.

In early June, two letters sent by Stafford to Miss Desmond in Holloway Prison were intercepted by police. In them, Stafford apologized to her for getting her into trouble, and promised to do everything he could to see that she was cleared, along with the other two men involved. And he asked her to press hard for bail.

Net effect was that nobody was given bail in this case. The prosecuting attorney pointed out that only a small part of the stolen bullion had been recovered. He told the court: "With that sort of money about I feel there would be a reason that these defendants would not appear for trial."

But where was the gold? Had the rest of it been smuggled successfully to the continent where it could have found numerous markets? Was most of it buried in England somewhere waiting for the search to grow cold?

In late July, police informers told authorities that a man on London's northwest side was trying to sell gold bars. Detective Sergeant P. Boorman of London's Flying Squad, accompanied by one of his men as a witness, arranged a rendezvous at a London apartment, posing as a potential buyer of gold. Everything went smoothly. There detectives met Anthony Cavanagh, who averred that he had gold to sell, all the gold that anyone might want to buy.

"I can only supply one bar at a time," Cavanagh said, according to the detective's version of the conversation. "The people that I get it from are very cautious."

"My father is a jeweler in Victoria," explained Detective Boorman. "Of course, he is in a position to dispose of anything like this. He can

supply the ready cash, provided the goods are genuine. I have come
to do the business for him because he does not like showing his face."

"Don't worry," Cavanagh said, cheerfully. "It's genuine, the real
thing, twenty-two or twenty-four-carat solid gold, and you can check
it before you buy."

Another rendezvous was set up at a pub in a London suburb.
Boorman brought along a friend whom he introduced to Cavanagh
as his father. After a round of beers, Cavanagh invited the detectives
to his house in Anglesmead Crescent to have a look at the gold bar.
There he unwrapped a heavy package covered first by a piece of
carpet and then by brown paper.

"It's gold, all right," said Cavanagh, opening the package.

Boorman looked at it, had no doubt that this was a gold bar, glittering in the light of the living room. "How much are you asking for it?"
he asked.

"Three and a half grand," said Cavanagh, speaking in British
pounds sterling. At that time this was the equivalent of $9,800, with
the official price for such a bar at $14,000, which explains why gold
thieves find buyers for their products. Sometimes robbers may extend an even greater discount to move their products. A jeweler who
buys such a bar may eliminate all the evidence as soon as he melts
down the ingot.

"Did the bar come from the big gold job?" Detective Boorman
asked, casually.

"Yes." Cavanagh nodded. "That was a nice job they pulled. I wish
I had done it."

As he rewrapped the bar, he added: "If you have this one I can get
you as many as you like, but only one at a time. They have them
buried somewhere. I wish I knew where."

Boorman departed, ostensibly to raise the money, promising to call
back in a few days. In a few days, he did return, with a police party
to raid the house. Cavanagh was arrested along with Michael Benja-
min Harris, a forty-seven-year-old trucker who happened to own the
house.

Cavanagh, however, wouldn't tell the police any more about the
source of his gold supply. So police regained only one more of the
missing bars, with 123 still unaccounted for.

The arrest did alert police and customs officials elsewhere that a
considerable number of those gold bars might still be in Britain,
seeking buyers. Collapse of this particular sales outlet might make

the gang decide to smuggle more of the gold to the continent, the police reasoned. Watches at boat docks and railroad stations were intensified. And the vigilence paid off.

At smoke-begrimed, gloomy Victoria Station, passengers on July 31 were embarking aboard the night train for Paris when a customs guard noted that one of two gentlemen walking down the platform had a peculiar gait, almost as if he might have been drunk. But he seemed sober enough when halted. A check showed the two men had tickets in order, everything seemed all right. But the customs officer had a hunch. He signaled for reinforcements and suggested that the men submit to a search at a nearby customs office in the station.

The search revealed why one of the men had been walking with a staggering gait. Thirty-nine-year-old Ivor Bloom, a furniture maker, had forty-five small gold bars, worth about $25,000, concealed in a smuggling jacket under his suit. The weight of the gold had thrown him off stride everytime he took a step. He was arrested along with his companion, Michael Edward Kenrick, who identified himself as a businessman.

It was evident that the bullion robbers were finding much more difficulty in selling their haul at a fair price than they had estimated. A smuggling operation to Switzerland had collapsed after sixteen bars had been dispatched to that country. A sales outlet to unscrupulous jewelers in London had been closed by police. Now, this attempt to melt bars into smaller sizes to get them out of the country had failed, too.

It is not known whether these abortive attempts to sell the gold affected Stafford in any way. But on August 11 Detective Chief Inspector Robert Harris of the London Flying Squad received a telephone call from a lawyer. Stafford was in the lawyer's office and wanted to surrender to police. He denied any connection with the bullion robbery when charged by police with participation in the crime.

Then, on August 14, at Newhaven, an English Channel port, another piece in the puzzle slipped into place. Customs officials were making a routine check along a queue of automobiles waiting in the early morning for the cross-Channel ferry *Valencay*. A brand-new Triumph Herald waited in line, nothing untoward to call attention to itself. But customs officials looked again at it.

There may have been a gold detector beeping somewhere. Perhaps a tip had warned officials to watch for this particular automobile. Subsequently, it developed that a race driver, Squire Francis Waterman, had purchased two high-temperature furnaces for the melting of metals shortly after the bullion robbery. While there is no crime in that, police and customs officials were ready to take a hard look at all recent furnace purchasers no matter how respectable they might appear. The driver was Waterman, accompanied by his girl friend, Avril Beatrice Preston.

So customs officials searched the Triumph Herald, courteously questioned the driver and the woman with him. Authorities found nothing. Yet, things didn't jibe. Customs officials develop a sixth sense for detecting the smuggled package, the bag of narcotics, or the illicit merchandise. And, admittedly, they may have been tipped off by an informer.

Officials directed Waterman to pull out of the line. Now, authorities launched another search, not the routine trunk inspection, but a careful bolt-by-bolt investigation of the automobile, its engine, its body, and its chassis.

Twenty-six small gold bars were found in the chassis of the automobile, bars contoured to fit snugly into the frame. Documentation in the case reports that: "The concealment was so effective that it was not until the car was examined by forensic-science officers that the point of entry was found. The plate over the entry was cut from a metal sheet and this had been positioned in such a way that it was nearly invisible. It had been sprayed with paint the same color as the car and the edges had been filled and covered with dirt and oil."

"Split" Waterman, a speedway driver known all over Europe, and his girl friend were charged with conspiring to evade the prohibition on the export of gold and with receiving it knowing that some of the bars were part of the great bullion robbery.

Shortly after their arrest, police raided a Bedfordshire farm where Waterman and his girl friend had been living. They found several smuggling jackets, a "veritable arsenal of weapons," dies for making gold coins, and an electric furnace able to reach a temperature of 1,150 degrees centigrade. (Gold melts at a temperature of 1,063 degrees centigrade.) A smuggling jacket, which usually is made of heavy duck or some like fabric, looks something like a hunting vest, with many small pockets into which gold bars may fit snugly. With such a vest, a strong man may carry as much as fifty pounds of gold, or around $140,000 worth at early-1974 prices.

Police noted that the smuggling jackets found on this farm were exactly like the jacket that Ivor Bloom was wearing the night he thought he was taking the night train to Paris from Victoria Station. Police did not find a single gold bar on the farm, though they used metal detectors and scoured the entire property. The 26 bars in the Triumph Herald had been poured from 2 of the large 400-ounce bars stolen in the great bullion robbery. These 2 big bars plus 2 melted to make Bloom's small bars meant that 21 of the 140 stolen ingots were accounted for, all that police ever were able to recover of the loot.

At his trial, Stafford told a fantastic tale of encountering two Frenchmen named Max and Charles who had hired him to smuggle gold from France to Switzerland on behalf of some wealthy Nigerians. He had taken the job as a lark, arranging for the sale of the gold through André de Bec, a gold dealer in Geneva whom he knew. The court didn't believe him. He was found guilty of conspiracy to receive the proceeds of theft, and sentenced to eight years imprisonment. Miss Desmond, Alldridge, and Margrie were acquitted.

Anthony Cavanagh pleaded guilty to possessing gold unlawfully and was given a three-year sentence. Waterman and Miss Preston pleaded guilty to charges, and Waterman received a four-year sentence, while Miss Preston received two years, suspended.

As for that missing gold. It would be worth about $8.6 million at current prices, and it still is missing, at least to the law.

The craving for gold fosters a whole industry of smugglers who are ready to transport gold to any point on earth for a price, even though local laws may prohibit such transfers. Admittedly, the soaring price of free gold in 1972–1974 paralyzed smuggling routes of the world, temporarily, forcing creation of new patterns. The hijacker also proved to be the worst enemy of the smuggler, nearly eliminating the commercial airliner as the vehicle for illicit transport of gold. The resulting shakeout in the smuggling world still is underway.

The Big Three Swiss banks are key suppliers to this trade, not because they want any connections with smugglers, but because they do not ask any questions of gold buyers. Since Union Bank of Switzerland, Swiss Bank Corporation, and Swiss Credit Bank maintain the world's largest gold-merchandising pool, the gold smuggler is likely to deal with them if he operates on a grand scale. The banks, of course, have nothing directly to do with the trade, except for the fact that they have the telex communications networks, the refineries to pour any convenient bar sizes including those which fit neatly into smuggling jackets, the credit facilities, and the distribution outlets at key places.

They aren't alone. The main London gold suppliers don't ask any questions about the business of a gold buyer in Beirut, a key smuggling point, or in Dubai, Hong Kong, or anywhere else. They pour bars in the ten-tolas size which Mideast smugglers like, too. The tola is a standard unit of weight in India and the Middle East, equivalent to 11.6 grams. Thus a ten-tolas bar, which is about the size of two dozen calling cards pressed tightly together or perhaps of a small book of matches, weighs 3.73 ounces (0.116 kg).

On a plane from London to Dubai one time, I found myself in the first-class compartment directly behind an executive of Samuel Montagu & Company, Ltd., a reputable bullion company which is one of the five members of the London gold market. He was on his way to Dubai to contact some of the firm's customers there, people who undoubtedly were in the gold-smuggling business. Given a choice, many smugglers prefer the Johnson, Matthey product to those of other merchandisers of gold. Moccata & Goldsmid and Sharps Pixley, two more members of the London market, also do business in the Mideast. Rothschild, the fifth concern in that market, is considered Jewish, and it has not made a dent in the business, at least not in the Arab segment of it, and Arabs have a big chunk of the total volume.

Ironically, though the Rothschild London branch now plays little part in the smuggling trade of the Mideast, it once was involved in one of the biggest smuggling coups of all time. In 1811, Nathan Rothschild and others of his family engineered a scheme which only the Rothschilds could have managed at the time.

The Duke of Wellington was in Portugal with his army, battling the forces of Napoleon in the Iberian Peninsula. The Iron Duke needed money to purchase supplies for his troops, and gold was the only recognizable money on the war-torn peninsula. The British government sought assistance from the Rothchilds, a plea which was particularly well placed. Through their ingenious network of financial agents on the continent, the Rothschild's smuggled $10 million worth of gold across France—the enemy country—and into Spain. French authorities actually helped, believing that the gold was being smuggled into France to escape the British government.

Proceeds were delivered to Spanish bankers who then were willing to accept the drafts written by the Duke of Wellington's supply officers. British troops ate well on the smuggled funds, fought well, and routed the French.

Of all the forms of lawbreaking known to man, smuggling perhaps is the one which provides the most rationalizations when participants philosophize about their activities. Just as the rum runner of the Prohibition Era in the United States saw himself as a vital cog in a service industry, the modern gold smuggler views himself as a benefactor who is helping prudent men to conserve their capital in a world which is filled with money-sucking governments which want to dissipate the savings of citizens.

Moral judgments involving smuggling depend upon the point of view of the judges. The businessman in Iraq, in Egypt, in Uganda or elsewhere may have no moral qualms about purchasing smuggled gold with his hard-earned local currency if governments are consistently debasing currencies. The Indian peasant, who has almost a religious veneration for gold, has no scruples about purchasing gold jewelry made from smuggled gold when his government prohibits importation of gold.

"We are not hurting anyone," a Lebanese banker told me one time as we sat on the terrace of the Saint Georges Hotel in Beirut. Waves broke easily on the rocks at the base of the terrace. Bikini-clad women sunned beside the hotel's swimming pool, which was enclosed on a point thrusting into the small bay. A line of snow-tipped mountains formed a backdrop for the ochre and pastel hues of Beirut's buildings, which were piled on ridges rising from the sea. Beirut is a sensuous and scenic city where everybody is in business for himself, trying to enjoy the fruits of someone else's labor. On the terrace, several tables away, four young men whom I knew were couriers were in close conversation, probably relating recent experiences on runs to Southeast Asia, at $500 per trip, with fortunes in gold hidden in heavy canvas jackets beneath suits.

"I keep hearing stories of feuds between smugglers, of killings," I said. I knew the banker was a key figure in one of the smuggling syndicates flourishing from this east Mediterranean base. But he didn't look like the television-screen idea of the gold smuggler.

He looked like . . . well, like a banker, with a neatly pressed charcoal suit, a bland, cheery manner, rimless glasses, and a receding hairline which made it difficult to estimate his age. I had found him to be a fan of impressionist art, and he had nonchalantly mentioned that he owned a Sisley and a Pissarro, talking so casually that he might have added: "Doesn't everybody?"

"This is really a very prosaic business, the distribution of gold. We have regular customers with whom we have been dealing for years. They know us. We know them. The trust we have between us is what makes everything possible, and no one wants to see that shattered. So don't believe all the gory tales you hear about gold."

"Why is Beirut such a center for the trade?"

He ordered another cup of Turkish coffee, his fourth, and said: "Beirut is the money capital of this part of the world. It has free currency convertibility. There are no restrictions upon the import, export, or ownership of gold. Banking facilities are readily available. We have over seventy banks, you know, and most of them have international connections."

"And Lebanese businessmen have that free-enterprise spirit which recognizes a profit when they see it," I said.

He nodded.

Earlier, I had seen a study of Beirut's gold market made by Charter Consolidated, Ltd., London, the affiliate of Anglo American Corporation of South Africa. It had mentioned that in 1969 the three principal firms operating in this gold trade were the Bullion Exchange Trading Company (of Lausanne), Société Bancaire du Liban, and Banque de Crédit National S.A.L., Beirut, Lebanon.

Business rises and falls according to the seriousness of currency crises, the weaknesses of governments, and the monetary panic of citizens. Before the collapse of the Allende government in Chile, some businessmen there were desperately seeking to transform some of their holdings into gold. Argentina has citizens who feel that gold bars are better to have hidden in haciendas than are pesos. Some Brazilians combat inflation by keeping a certain percentage of assets in gold.

Once in Dubai, that desert town of sheikhs and shops on the Persian Gulf, I was offered a share of a gold-smuggling venture. Shares sold at $800 each as if they might have been stocks in General Motors Corporation, though there were no certificates to verify the deal, only a handshake and a cup of Turkish coffee to seal the bargain. I had the Turkish coffee without closing the deal, for I have never hankered to be a gold smuggler. In Dubai that particular year there didn't seem to be much else going for the town. The gold-jewelry markets of Bombay, Delhi, Calcutta, and other cities of India were crying for the yellow metal at prices double the world price. Smugglers were only too willing to oblige, and Dubai was absorbing about a sixth of the whole world's supply of gold, nearly all of it for smuggling via dhows into India. The Dubai government has no laws against the export of gold, and nobody in Sheikh Rashid bin said al Maktoum's government saw any reason for interfering with the swift, diesel-powered dhows of the smuggling syndicates.

Establishment of the free market in gold dimmed Dubai's lustre as a smuggling port for gold, especially when the price soared above $100 an ounce. This came at a time when India suffered a drought and peasants were pawning gold jewelry with village lenders, rather than investing their meager funds in new purchases. So the Indian market faded, though it did not disappear altogether.

Meanwhile, restrictions on the import of gold into Japan were removed, and gold could flow freely into Tokyo and other cities without need for the smuggler to assist in the transport. And, above all, America retired from Vietnam.

All of these factors changed the gold-smuggling pattern drastically throughout Asia. War and social unrest always are conditions which benefit the smuggler, for then nations are likely to introduce restrictions aimed at conserving foreign exchange. The smuggler seeks to evade these restrictions by making it possible for citizens to exchange their money for gold, no matter what governments say about it. The war in Vietnam, for instance, had stimulated gold smuggling on a grandiose scale throughout Southeast Asia as profits of war filtered into hands of merchants, prostitutes, contractors, and nightclub czars in the form of United States dollars which then were traded for gold.

In 1967, seventy-two tons of gold were imported into Vientiane, the humid, sleepy capital of Laos, though local consumption in the gold market is about one ton annually. Some of the gold entered through the Banque de l'Indochine; most went to four Chinese gold dealers, directly from Big Three Swiss banks, in the form of one-kilo bars of 999.9 purity. Laos has frontiers with six other countries in Southeast Asia, North Vietnam, South Vietnam, Cambodia, Thailand, Burma, and China. South Vietnam had been the major market for the smuggled gold, with Thailand the second most important market.

Some of that Laotian gold went to support the narcotics racket, too, a trade which has not been upset by ending of the Vietnamese

War, or at least of America's involvement in it. The remote area where Burma, Laos, Thailand, and China meet is one of the wildest places on earth, an area where there is no central government to control the tribesmen who live in isolated green hills and mountains. The only industry is the cultivation of *Papaver somniferum* from which comes about ninety percent of the world's production of raw opium. And it is gold which helps to move this output through Vientiane to the outside world.

The American withdrawal has cut off the heavy flow of dollars into South Vietnam. But rich South Vietnamese merchants still are seeking to transform some of their wealth into gold bars, and some smuggling continues.

Hong Kong and Singapore are also key entrepôt centers in the world gold trade, though smuggling activities from these ports are considerably reduced from the golden smuggling era of the late 1960's. There are nine authorized gold dealers in Singapore: the Banque de l'Indochine; Hong Kong and Shanghai Banking Corporation; Chartered Bank; Overseas-Chinese Banking Corporation; Overseas Union Bank; United Overseas Bank; Intraco Limited; Kim Bian Seng Co., Limited; and Yee Shing Co., Limited.

Hong Kong's dominant gold importer is Jardine Matheson, an affiliate of London's Johnson, Matthey. Others in the business are Mount Trading Company, Ltd., Commercial Investment Company, Ltd., and Premex, Ltd. Three main jewelry manufacturers are Chao Tai Fook, Chao Sang Sang, and King Fook Jewelers. The latter firm also owns the Miramar Hotel, one of Hong Kong's most ornate, which has the unusual distinction of possessing a nightclub with walls which are plated with 300 ounces of gold ($54,000 worth at today's prices).

Macao, which long was an important gold entrepôt center in the Far East still functions as a distributor. But there is an air of déjà vu about it, as if the gold business is as run down as some of the baroque buildings in the city.

Gold smuggling has taken a hard rap from radio-isotopic detection devices. But the hijacker has given the smuggler the roughest blow of all. Today an air traveler never knows whether or not his baggage and his person will be carefully inspected by airport ground personnel. This makes it very hazardous to be caught wearing a smuggling jacket where local laws may prohibit exportation or importation of gold without licenses. To smuggle gold by air, today, requires the purchased connivance of members of a plane's crew, probably with payoffs arranged for customs people at the point of arrival.

The free price of gold has gotten so high that there isn't much of a margin anywhere for the smuggler to undertake such additional expenses. So the volume of smuggling has fallen off drastically, and those adventurous young couriers who were hauling gold across continents a few years ago now are trying to slip pot and other drugs across borders in suitcases or in bodies of old clunker automobiles.

Meanwhile, the bullion robber faces tougher problems. Not only must he worry about getting rid of his ill-gotten gold at a profit, he is finding it more difficult to hijack gold cargoes in the first place. Brinks-MAT, a joint bullion and money moving company formed in Europe by Chicago's Brinks and by MAT Transport, a Swiss company, recently put on a show for newsmen in London, explaining how the company is making bullion criminals think twice before attempting a hijack.

John Patoux, managing director for Brinks-MAT, claims that his company now handles more than half of all the bullion moving in and out of London, using fully armored vehicles. One of their trucks looks like a railroad freight car pulled by a truck-tractor which is so high off the ground it takes a ladder to reach the driver. The $60,000 vehicle is equipped with all types of devices aimed at frustrating holdup men, including those armed with bazookas, grenades, and gases.

Peter Cox, operations director for the security hauling company, says: "In the past, a security company would alter times of travel and colors of vehicles and stand a fair chance of fooling the cloth-cap-and-jimmy-type criminals who were armed with more daring than dynamite. But you will not fool today's highly sophisticated and organized criminal with these methods. We must make the possibility of a successful robbery as remote as we can by using every modern device available within the bounds of the law."

The new vehicle is capable of making a 650-mile-journey without refueling, at speeds of up to sixty miles per hour. A unit can carry up to twenty tons of gold at a time, which is over $115 million worth at $180 an ounce. That would be quite a haul if hijackers ever succeeded in escaping with a loaded truck, though a tour through the unit indicates that it might take considerable military power for such a job.

The windshield glass, specially made by Pilkington, the British glass maker, can withstand a high-velocity bullet. Radio communications are provided between cab and office. The interior has built-in bunks, kitchen, and toilet, and the three man crew can live aboard for four days. The body of the truck looks as it it might be able to withstand dynamite, land mines, grenades, and bazooka shells.

Risks of hauling bullion around streets and highways of Europe are indicated by the fact that the insurance charge for coverage of $1.5 million worth of gold on a shipment from London to Zurich via surface transport is $40,000.

# CHAPTER XI

# Treasure-troves

The published proceedings of Britain's Royal Geographic Society for 1861 contain a paper prepared by Richard Spruce. It details the story of the Inca Treasure of the Llanganati, a legendary gold hoard which may be waiting for someone to rediscover it. Like many of the tales of treasure-trove, it is one that quickens the pulses of adventurers, for gold often has been a reward for the risk-taker in life's stakes. And gold that is frozen into an antique pattern as coin or artifact is worth much more than its bullion value.

The story detailed by Spruce is a simple one. When Pizarro demanded his gold ransom for Atahualpa, the Inca ruler, his subjects in what is now Ecuador collected a substantial golden treasure from the northern part of the Inca's realm. Before the hoard could be delivered to the Spaniards, news reached Quito that the King had been murdered.

Inca nobles loaded the assembled gold treasure onto backs of human porters and led the caravan, not toward the Spaniards but deep into the eastern Andes. Porters snaked over mountain trails to the headwaters of the Rio Verde in the Llanganati Mountains. Indians dammed a small tributary, creating an artificial lake in a deep canyon. Into its depths, the sorrowful subjects of the Inca tossed golden cups, plate, figurines, and other artifacts which probably were worth many millions of dollars. Then, the whole troop departed to meet whatever fate the Spaniards had in store for them.

The secret of this hoard came into the possession of a Spaniard named Valverde after he married an Indian princess. He bequeathed the secret to his king upon his death, and the description of its location became known as the Derrotero of Valverde. An intrigued King of Spain dispatched agents to the Spanish colonial town of Latacunga, seeking the treasure. Nothing was found, for the exact location of the lake could not be determined. That fabulous treasure still lies in its watery vault, according to legend, waiting for some intrepid searcher to stumble upon it.

That Derrotero of Valverde is one of many maps and keys to treasure which lie in the archives of Spain, in records of the Dutch

East Indies Company, in British Admiralty reports, in maritime annals of wrecks, or in the hoary legends which pass from one man to another over a period of centuries. The Mystery of the Money Pit. The Lima Treasure. The Tongan wreck of the *Port au Prince*. The wreck of Sir Francis Drake's flagship, the *Revenge*. The *Die Liefde*. The H.M.S. *Association*. The *Nuestra Senora de Atocha*. These are only a few of the many treasure-troves which are sought by men with single-minded intensity.

On August 17, 1971, the London *Mail* published a treasure hunters' guide listing all wrecks along Britain's coasts which involved lost wealth. There's the *Die Liefde*, a Dutch East Indiaman wrecked in 1711 off the Shetlands, a vessel which already has given up at least five thousand silver guilders to divers. Not far away is the wreck of the *El Gran Grifon*, flagship of the Spanish Armada, which lost a vital battle to Drake's British fleet in 1588. Records show it was carrying at least $600,000 worth of coins and gold when it went down in a storm while fleeing British warships. The *Donna Marie*, another Spanish galleon, allegedly was carrying about $70 million worth of gold when it sank off the Thames estuary. The *Florencia*, the *Pereira*, the *Romney*. These are only a few of the vessels listed on that particular treasure guide.

So many wrecks have been salvaged off the coast of the United States that Florida, Texas, and some other states now have laws regulating the search for sunken treasure. States want a share of the proceeds if anything is found. So hunters must obtain licenses, paying for the privilege of being assigned specific areas for their searches as if they were prospectors staking claims for gold-bearing ground.

Today, the treasure-hunter lives in a highly competitive world, one where science has created new tools to assist him. But those same tools are available to anyone who has the price, and that adds to the competition. Simple metal detectors, for instance, have made it possible for the individual to scour land sites with a thoroughness which appalls legitimate archaeologists. The thoroughness of the amateur is seldom directed at preserving ancient relics but only at locating buried gold and jewelry. Thus, the metal detector has become the bane of archaeologists.

One letter to the London *Times* which appeared on August 9, 1973, underscores this situation. Written by Professor Leslie Alcock, archaeologist at the University of Glasgow, and Professor R. J. C. Atkinson, archaeologist at University College, Cardiff, it said:

Though archaeologists today employ a whole range of instruments for detecting soil anomalies, they use metal detectors only rarely, for recovering the components of hoards of coins and bronzes disturbed and scattered by deep plowing and earthmoving, and on a few excavations to obtain advance warnings of the presence of metal artifacts in graves.

Archaeologists deplore not the use of metal detectors as such, but the subsequent illicit digging. This destroys the archaeological context which gives a find its evidential value, and bears the same relationship to proper excavation as does crude butchery to surgical dissection.

Unfortunately, where gold is the lure, historical and archaeological considerations rank far down the scale among the urges which drive treasure-hunters to seek El Dorado. Certainly no amount of lecturing and sometimes not even the threat of legal sanctions deters the confirmed treasure-hunter.

The only thing which stops even more treasure-hunters from appearing is the cost. Maritime salvage, for instance, is being transformed into a business rather than an individual adventure because of the capital needed to finance an expedition. Skin-diving equipment, electronic gear, miniature submarines, and other such developments have opened huge areas of the ocean floor at great depths to salvagers. It takes money to even consider a search with such gear, though the skin-diver may have a try with only an aqualung and a rubber suit.

That equipment has helped spawn a new science in the last two decades, that of marine archaeology, and the treasure-hunter may find himself colliding with its disciples. The Spanish galleon may have historic as well as pecuniary interest, while any gold artifacts about may be valued more for their artistic and archaeological worth rather than for their gold content. Most marine archaeologists bitterly resent the amateur treasure-hunter.

But as long as one treasure-hunter in a hundred discovers a lost rich hoard, the other ninety-nine will be willing to take their chances. And there are enough finds to provide inspiration for new seekers of wealth.

On December 11, 1971, an auction of treasure found on the wreck of the *Le Chemeau* off Cape Breton, Canada, brought $199,680 at Parke-Bernet in New York. Yet that auction involved only 688 of the 4,000 silver and 500 gold coins which had been salvaged over three

years by David MacEachern, Alex Storm, and Harvey MacLeod, the
Canadian treasure-hunters who had located this wreck. The *Le Chemeau* had sunk in a gale on August 25, 1725, while transporting 82,000
gold and silver coins to a cash-short French Canada. About all these
treasure-hunters would say of their methods was that they used a
"search-and-find box" to locate the hoard.

At the November 27–29 "Golden Galleon Treasure Sale" at the
Waldorf-Astoria Hotel in New York, one single coin, a gold doubloon
struck at Mexico City in 1702, sold for $21,500. The coin was one of
several million dollars worth of treasure salvaged by the late Kip
Wagner's Real Eight Company off the coast of Florida. This company
certainly can claim to be one of the most successful of the many
treasure-hunting corporations which appeared on the scene in recent years drawn by the promise of ancient archives and stimulated
by modern salvaging devices which require capital to assemble.

The key target for this company was an eleven-ship convoy which
went to the bottom south of the present Cape Kennedy off the
Florida coast. It was a rich convoy, too, which sailed from Havana for
Spain on July 24, 1715; five vessels carried silver bullion and other
cargo, while six ships carried gold, emeralds, and pearls. One French
ship joined the convoy for the expected voyage across the Atlantic,
fearing the threat of pirates if it sailed alone.

When less than a week at sea, the convoy encountered a severe
storm which drove the ships relentlessly toward the Florida coast. On
the early morning of July 31, winds accelerated, cracked masts,
smashed riggings, and opened seams in the hulls of the hapless Spanish ships. Eleven vessels foundered, drowning one thousand sailors
and officers and taking about $14 million worth of treasure to the
bottom. Only the French ship survived to carry the story of the
treasure convoy's demise.

Kip Wagner and associates traced the facts through available records, searched the waters off Florida for the wrecks, and located
them in the late 1950's. A decade of work yielded a reported $4
million worth of old coins and of gold and silver valuables plus
enough artifacts to stock the Museum of Sunken Treasure which has
been opened at Cape Kennedy.

Florida now has strict rules regulating treasure-hunting in the state
or its adjacent waters. It takes the view that all treasure lying within
its territory belongs to the state. Treasure-hunting licenses are sold
for $600 each, with hunters required to put up a $5,000 bond to

assure that the state will get its share of anything found. A license covers only a specific area of eighteen square miles for a year. The state claims at least twenty-five percent of any treasure discovered, while the hunter must bear all the loss if nothing is found.

"Of all the speculative ventures, treasure-hunting is the riskiest," admits Carl Clausen, marine archaeologist with the Florida Board of Archives and History.

Because of state regulations, federal income taxes, and the possible claims of descendants of wrecked mariners, treasure-hunters sometimes prefer to work in secret. News of finds may attract competitors, too, and a wreck on the bottom of the sea is difficult to guard.

In 1972 a rash of gold coins, including Dutch gold ducats dated 1724 and earlier, appeared in numismatic markets. At first there was considerable speculation concerning their source, since all evidence indicated the coins were genuine. Was this a long-held collection being sold by heirs? But why the heavy concentration of Dutch coins of the early eighteenth century? Then the secret emerged. Sponge divers operating off the coast of Norway had located the wreck of the Dutch East Indies Company vessel *Amerendam,* which went to the bottom two hundred and fifty years earlier. They had salvaged more than $1 million worth of coins and had quietly sold them to international coin dealers.

There is no way to tabulate the number of wrecks which may have been discovered and quietly looted by salvagers who sold proceeds to coin collectors, antique dealers, and museum curators with a minimum of publicity and with no taxes paid to anybody. But in the summer of 1969, one case became a *cause célèbre* in Texas, resulting in the passing of a new salvage law by the stage legislature.

The story broke when Jerry Sadler, state land commissioner, announced that "pirates and plunderers" had looted "tons of valuable historical treasures" from the floor of the Gulf of Mexico off the coast of Texas. This was the first time that many people ever heard there was treasure off that coast, though confirmed treasure-hunters had known the facts for years. Long ago another golden convoy had departed from Vera Cruz, Mexico, with a rich cargo of bullion and coins being dispatched by Luis de Velasco, the Mexican viceroy, to Charles V, the King of Spain.

The ships headed northward to catch the prevailing westerlies across the Atlantic. But in that April, 1554, there were no westerlies blowing across the Gulf of Mexico. The fleet encountered a bitter northeaster which blew ships with gale force ever westward, smashing them on the shores of what is now Texas. Seven hundred men perished when ships went down, but three hundred managed to reach shore. Only one man of those three hundred survived the overland trek back to Vera Cruz.

Three of the shipwrecks had been located earlier off Padre Island in thirty feet of water. But over the centuries the sea had deposited ten to twenty feet of sand over the wrecks, as is often the case with sunken ships. Army mine detectors had verified the finds and Platoro, Ltd., a salvaging company, had been formed by Gary, Indiana, treasure-hunters. Officials of the company claim that $30,000 subsequently was spent on the salvaging operation which retrieved 46,000 pounds of cannon, ballast, and various iron artifacts plus several hundred ancient coins.

Immediately a legal hassle developed concerning the find. Sadler, as land commissioner, contended everything found belonged to the state of Texas. The city of Corpus Christi argued that it had a right to the discovery. A private group sued to have artifacts preserved in a local museum. Platoro, Ltd. contended that this was a case of finders-keepers.

Cleburne Maier, regional commissioner for the United States Customs, claimed jurisdiction, reminding everyone that the Tariff Act of 1930 requires that all salvage from shipwrecks be cleared by U.S. Customs. There aren't any duties on items which rate as antiques. But failure to declare findings may result in confiscation.

Only one of the three known wrecks had been salvaged. It seemed pertinent to recheck the other two. Then it was that Sadler discovered that where one of the supposedly unsalvaged ships had been lying, nothing remained but a hole in the ocean floor. When sand covers a wreck, salvagers may use suction to pump up sand and salvage together. On shipboard the sand is sifted for anything of value, then dumped over the side. This seemed to have been the formula followed by the wreck poachers. Thus, they looted the site and departed before anyone was the wiser.

An indignant Texas State Legislature hurriedly passed a bill creating the Texas Antiquities Committee with the right to assert state ownership of all artifacts found on state lands or in adjacent waters. It was definitely a case of trying to close the ocean bottom after the wreck has been stolen.

Squabbles over wrecks are common among treasure-hunters, for it often is impossible for the original finder to prevent kibitzers from arriving on the scene with aqualung and rubber suits, eager for a try at locating treasure, too. The wreck situation usually adds to the problem.

While a steel ship may hold together for decades after sinking, wooden ships soon break up under the pressure of underwater currents and batterings against rocks. Metal and waterlogged planks sink to the bottom while jetsam floats away. Thus an old wreck may not present the appearance of a ship at all, but may be visible only as a few cannon, some scattered pieces of metal, piles of ship's ballast, and waterlogged planks spread across an area larger than a football field. Coins may be scattered like a handful of pennies thrown onto a sandy beach then left for the winds to bury. Finding them again years or centuries later may be a colossal task. And if a treasure-hunter does find a few gold coins or something else of value, he is almost sure to have company on the bottom once the word gets out, unless the wreck site is so far away from civilization as to be reachable only with an expedition.

In 1967, an undersea gold rush was underway in the Isles of Scilly off the southwest coast of England after the wreck of the H.M.S. *Association* and sister ships were found. Admiral Sir Cloudesley Shovel's Mediterranean fleet was wrecked on this rugged coast where two hundred shipwrecks are known to lie. The naval vessels went down with two thousand men in a hundred feet of water after striking reefs in a fog in 1707 while returning to England after a successful foray against Spaniards. The convoy was so far off course as to raise doubts about the Admiral's seamanship. He didn't survive to present his case before a naval court of inquiry.

"The H.M.S. *Association* was an admiral's flagship," explained Lieutenant Commander Alan Baldwin, the Royal Navy officer who led a team of nineteen divers from the minesweeper *Puttenham* in the summer of 1966. "She was returning from the wars after the sacking of Barcelona."

Estimates of the salvage value range up to $14 million, though as is often the case with wrecks, nobody really knows. When treasure-hunters aren't sure of a valuation, they are apt to add a zero or move a decimal point over to the right.

The Royal Navy was interested in the *Association* in a historical way, though it probably would have regarded any gold bars around as legitimate salvage, too. After all, the Royal Navy once was involved in what may have been the biggest gold salvage job of all, the recovery of most of the treasure which went down with the *Laurentic* when this fifteen thousand-ton armed cruiser hit a mine off Lough Swilly on the British coast in World War I. The vessel had been dispatched from Liverpool to New York with £5 million worth of gold, an amount which would be worth around $200 million today.

The Admiralty started the salvage job in 1919. After seven years of work with the primitive diving equipment then available, the Navy had hauled up 3,057 gold bars of the 3,211 which had been on board.

In the case of the *Association*, however, the Navy lost interest and retired to make way for a small army of treasure-hunters. The *Daily Telegraph*, a national newspaper, counted thirty-eight divers who were in the Scillys in the hunt for the wrecks of the *Association* and its sister ships, the *Romney* and the *Eagle*.

One of the first on the scene was Roland Morris, then fifty-eight, a one-time professional diver who had retired to operate the Admiral Benbow Restaurant in Penzance. The lure of treasure attracted him back to the sea, as head of a team of divers, with the H.M.S. *Association* and the H.M.S. *Eagle* as its goals.

In Britain, all unclaimed wrecks belong to the Receiver of Wrecks, an agency which grants search rights to applicants with the provision that findings must be given to the Crown. The treasure-hunter usually is rewarded with a third of the value of all salvage. Heirs of seamen lost in wrecks may claim part of a discovery but must prove that anything found was the personal property of the ancestor, a rather difficult task.

In this case, an unnamed seventy-year-old woman from Hampshire claimed to be a descendent of Admiral Sir Cloudesley Shovel, and she felt she was entitled to her share of the *Association*. It was a futile claim, though the *Association* did yield a substantial haul for Morris and his crew.

But diving rights were clouded. The H.M.S. *Association* wasn't an unclaimed wreck. It had an alleged owner, the Royal Navy, and the Department of Defence figured it had the right to grant diving rights. Morris thought he had those rights; but there are numerous wrecks in the vicinity of the *Association*. When Morris sought to bar trespassers, he was asked to prove that he was, indeed, working on the *Association*. Maybe it was another ship. Maybe he was the trespasser.

For five years, the struggle to salvage the *Association* kept divers busy in the Scillys. Often they squabbled over who was trespassing, and courts sometimes were asked to intercede. In May, 1970, Morris seemed to have scored a major legal victory when a court granted him a temporary injunction and sole diving rights to the *Association* and sister ships. In June, other divers successfully appealed that decision and the injunction was lifted. Morris threatened to withhold his discoveries from the Receiver of Wrecks unless the government backed his position. The British Board of Trade responded by warning Morris that he would be "in breach of law" if he took this course.

Morris, a garrulous, convival type, provided good copy for British newspapers during his long and unsuccessful campaign to maintain exclusive rights over the salvaging of the *Association*. He and his group did better than any of the others in that salvage battle, though, admittedly, some finds by poachers may not have been declared to the Receiver of Wrecks. At one auction at Sotheby's in London in 1970 some of the maritime artifacts and coins salvaged by the Morris group were sold for $25,000, bringing the total value of discoveries to about $55,000. A third of this was the Morris share, which seems very small compensation for five seasons of dangerous work in a hundred feet of water off the Scillys. Swirling currents and hidden, jagged-edged ledges are constant hazards, while sudden storms may separate divers from surface tenders.

But Morris reveals the drive of the treasure-hunter when he says: "There's nothing quite like the first glimpse of guns and anchors under the water. You swim toward the wreck and you see the cannon and you know you're getting close. You've found the ship. Next stop, the treasure."

Next stop the treasure! But getting it out may not be so easy. That is what three New Zealanders learned after discovering the wreck of a treasure ship which went down in 1806 near the island of Haano in the Pacific island-kingdom of Tonga. In 1968, C. Prast, than a twenty-eight-year-old business executive with a taste for adventure, and two friends, R. H. Rossiter and B. J. Curtis, started a charter fishing company in Tonga. This seemed to be a pleasant way of earning a living while enjoying life.

Before long they heard the story of the *Port au Prince*, an English privateer which was burned off Tonga after her crew was massacred. On this voyage, the crew allegedly had sacked two towns in Peru and had captured several Spanish ships which had been unlucky enough to cross the *Port au Prince*'s bow. That loot had never been found, according to the story, and the reported value of the cargo seemed to grow with each passing year.

"That ship was carrying between ten and thirty tons of bullion," claimed one Englishman who resides in Tonga.

Excited by the tale, the three New Zealanders started searching for the wreck in November, 1968, using a glass-bottomed boat to first study the terrain, then making skin dives to examine anything which appeared promising. Since they already were a familiar sight along the coast of the island of Haano, they attracted little attention.

"We found the wreck in February," says Prast, "about forty or fifty yards offshore, just inside a very exposed reef on the windward side of the island of Haano. The first thing we came across were two really big anchors. Then there were two ten-foot cannons. They had been split in two by fire, so we knew we had come across the *Port au Prince.*"

And the three men claim to have found the treasure, too.

"The treasure was in one large strongbox, the size of a room, fourteen feet by eight feet by six feet. It had obviously been built into the ship as a strong room. We cut it open."

Inside, so they claim, were silver and gold coins, gold plate, candlesticks, and other items one might find in the loot of two sacked towns of the early nineteenth century. But the party's small boat wasn't large enough to transfer the treasure across the Pacific. And the three men had reasons for believing that Tonga might not allow such a treasure to depart, a conclusion which events justified. Under Tongan law, all treasure belongs to the government.

Pending the outcome of negotiations, the partners brought the treasure to the surface and then moved it "elsewhere." The Tongan government did, indeed, claim the treasure and King Taufa Ahau Tupou dispatched his own team of divers to search for it. They found the wreck, but nothing of value.

The New Zealanders prudently departed from Tonga and left negotiations to a lawyer. Their position was: either we get a cut of the treasure or everything remains where it is and nobody gets anything. The King of Tonga stubbornly held to the position that all treasure in his kingdom belonged to the government and he could take his time about eventually finding it. So the impasse rests.

But I was intrigued by the various claims concerning the value of that treasure. One report said $12 million was involved. Prast in one discussion with a newspaperman in Wellington, New Zealand, reportedly declared that the trio had found at least ten tons of bullion and "possibly as much as thirty tons."

Even without any historical value, a ton of gold bullion alone is worth about $5.8 million. This would place the claims in the $58 million to $175 million range, which, if the higher figure were right, would make the *Port au Prince* one of the richest treasure troves ever found. So, when I found myself in London, I decided to check old archives and records covering the last voyage of the *Port au Prince*.

The story of that last voyage of the *Port au Prince* is told in the two volumes of *Mariner's Tonga Island*, written in 1817 by John Martin. It is written in the archaic language of a hundred and sixty years ago in the narrative style of a diary, and it is the remembered diary of Martin, the cabin boy of the *Port au Prince* and the only person to survive the voyage.

The *Port au Prince* left Britain in February, 1805, sailing from Gravesend in search of prizes for an England which then was at war with France, and with the Spain which was controlled by Napoleon. But the ship, a five hundred-tonner, had some financial insurance in that it also was equipped as a whaler. If it couldn't earn anything at piracy, or privateering if you will, it always could hunt whales in the Pacific.

The ship rounded the Horn without incident, worked its way up the coast of Chile. At Conception, it dropped anchor, while the crew nervously studied the town through glasses, wondering if necks should be risked attempting to loot the place. Piracy had seemed to be a glorious adventure back in England, especially since it had the approval stamp of his Majesty's government. But a raid doesn't seem so enticing when one contemplates that there might be some shooting involved, with some of the shooting at you.

The crew noted that townsmen were putting into the harbor in long boats. Apparently Conceptionites had mistaken the ship for a trading vessel which had goods to offer. The townsmen were shopping, which meant they would have money. And so they did when they came aboard, expecting to be shown merchandise by the well-armed crew of the English ship. Instead, they faced the musket barrels of a crew with nervous fingers on triggers. Citizens of Conception surrendered their valuables without protest, leaving about $5,000 in gold and silver coins when they fled toward shore.

Further up the coast at Caldera Bay, the crew did raid ashore, taking a bar of silver plus some gold and silver jewelry from a defenseless populace. Then, probably fearing retaliation, the ship sailed across the Pacific to the Sandwich Islands (Hawaii) where in August, 1805, the town of Hilo was pillaged. The loot included silver candlesticks and chalices from mission churches plus some plate from a brig which happened to be in the islands at that time.

Then it was back to South America, for a raid upon the town of Chinca in Peru. There was almost no opposition as the crew stripped the local churches, the governor's mansion, and everything else of value in the town. How much did all this involve? Nobody knows, for the cabin boy wasn't privy to the secrets of the captain. Yet the account reads more as if tens of thousands of dollars might have been taken rather than millions. This is supported by the fact that after leaving Peru the ship turned to whaling, an activity one might not expect if millions of dollars worth of booty reposed in the hold.

In any case, on November 29, 1806, the *Port au Prince* found itself anchored in seven fathoms of water off the northwest point of Lefooga in one of the Tonga Islands. The ship required fresh water and the wooly-haired natives seemed friendly enough. Four of the crew went ashore. Several score natives were invited aboard ship.

At a signal, Tongans began swinging their long knives and axes at every Englishman in sight. Surprised crewmen fell before they could seize muskets. Except for Martin, the crew was massacred to a man.

Tongans valued the iron in the vessel more than any loot in a strongroom below decks. They pried nails from the hull, hacked fittings from the planks. Then, to free some of the iron, they set fire to the vessel, not knowing what happens to gunpowder when fired. With a roar, guns exploded. The blazing ship drifted onto a reef as frightened natives paddled desperately for shore. More explosions followed, and the *Port au Prince* settled into the green-blue waters, a charred hulk with a treasure of undetermined value within its strongroom.

A small fortune has been spent over the years trying to locate the British sloop *De Braak* which sank off the coast of Delaware in 1798 while allegedly carrying a substantial amount of gold recovered from Spanish pirates. Nothing has been found.

The world's longest and probably most costly treasure-hunt started in 1795 on tiny Oak Island off the coast of Nova Scotia. It has been continuing intermittently ever since with thousands of man-days and uncounted sums of money poured into what ironically has become known as The Money Pit.

The story opened when three boys noted a time-rotted block and tackle on a tree limb over a depression which might have been a hole sealed with earth. Immediately, they thought of buried treasure and started to dig. Their excitement grew when at ten feet they found an oak platform in a thirteen-foot-diameter hole which seemed to go on much deeper. At thirty feet they found another oak platform which had been carefully laid as if to seal the hole. By that time the digging task had become too much for three boys, and a syndicate took over.

More layers of sealing were discovered as the hole went down. At ninety feet, diggers allegedly found a flat stone on which was written: FORTY FEET BELOW TWO MILLION POUNDS ARE BURIED.

That stone however, has disappeared, if it ever existed. Digging halted when water flooded the hole. That only intensified interest of treasure-hunters when investigation revealed that the original diggers of that hole had constructed an elaborate 145-foot-long catchment system along the shore not far from the hole to harness a tidal inflow. This directed water toward the hole, apparently as a protective measure.

Such precautions seemed to indicate that the original hole-sinkers had been seeking to protect a fabulous treasure. But every attempt at finding the cache failed miserably. A drill once seemed to indicate the presence of oaken chests at the hundred foot level, chests which contained an unidentified metal. But the soft, watersoaked earth shifted and those chests couldn't be located again. Group after group futilely tried to solve the puzzle of The Money Hole, pouring enough time and money into the task to represent a sizeable treasure in itself. Yet, that hole remains an enigma, promising much and giving nothing, which often is the way with buried treasure.

There are easier ways for people to make money from gold if capital is available at start. Gold and gold shares hold a tantalizing promise, too, in periods when men worry about the stability of currencies.

CHAPTER XII

# Goldbugs in Action

In October, 1973, 420 investors from around the world gathered at the deluxe Chateau Champlain Hotel in Montreal for an international monetary seminar aimed at clarifying how participants might invest their money to maximize appreciation and to minimize losses. There was an air of seriousness about the gathering as Harry D. Schultz, the promotor of the affair, called the first session to order in the Grand Ballroom of the hotel. Money is a subject which merits earnest attention, especially when the wealth is one's own.

Each participant had paid $600 to attend, and an informal tabulation of the wealth possessed by that group added up to $500 million. At least half of those present were millionaires, some many times over. Nobody was on relief. All of them were worried enough about protecting their wealth to have traveled here from as far away as South Africa to hear some words of investment wisdom. Most of them were chrysophilites, "goldbugs," the chrysophobes sometimes called them; they preferred to term themselves "sound-money advocates." But if that assembly had put it to a vote, the world would have returned to the gold standard then and there.

With gold at $400 an ounce.

Americans predominated in the audience, slow-talking Texans, retirees from Florida who may have headed giant corporations a few years ago, Californians who valued their life styles in the sun, and others from elsewhere who worried about inflation, currency controls, investment problems, declining stock markets, and all those other anxieties which plague people who have money. Once a man has accumulated a fortune he is likely to concentrate upon keeping it, and the concentration grows along with the size of the pile. Perhaps it may be better to have the problems of keeping it rather than of getting it, but you would never be able to tell that from a conference of millionaires.

Harry D. Schultz, the American who organized the conference, is an advocate of sound currencies who often sounds un-American as he berates the way United States government authorities have debased the dollar in recent times. The first time you meet him he is likely to emphasize that he spells Schultz with a "c," which is his way of saying that he doesn't want to be confused with that fellow George Shultz who was the United States treasury secretary in Washington.

For years Schultz, the one with the "c," dispensed financial advice to all comers from his office in London at $750 an hour. When inflation pinched, he raised his rates to $900 then to $1,000 an hour, which is the sort of advice most of us would like to give. But his principal and ample source of income is his biweekly investment letter, the four-page *International Harry Schultz Letter,* with its $1,000-a-year subscription.

In appearance, Schultz is a fooler. You might expect a sound-money man to look like a pompous banker, with a paunch to fit his net worth. Schultz looks like a trendy hippie who can afford Pierre Cardin suits, as well as a different girl friend every time you see him. Moreover, he is surprisingly mild in manner for one who writes so boldly in his letters, and he is more a listener than a table-pounder at a luncheon session.

For years, he has been a bear on the United States stock market, vying with the erudite Eliot "Calamity" Janeway for the title of biggest bear in the investment-letter field. This may be the only area where they agree. Janeway is not a goldbug. Schultz takes pride in being cited by numerous financial editors as the doyen of all the progold militants, though some other financial experts like James Dines *(The Dines Letter)* and Franz Pick *(Pick's World Currency Report)* might challenge him to the dean's title among goldbugs.

"I was the first of the widely read American security analysts to turn bullish on gold in 1960," says Dines, with no attempt at modesty.

Pick is not so much a goldbug as he is a man who dislikes paper money, especially if the only thing behind it is the ink on the underside of the bill. If you followed Pick's advice you would use your paper money only for day-to-day spending, while investing most of your funds in solid things such as diamonds, gold, or land. He is a Bohemian American of unquenchable enthusiasm who sounds much gloomier in his writings than he looks in person. To read him is to conclude that the world is coming to an end, drowning in worthless paper currencies. Still, he sometimes suggests ways of grabbing for life preservers such as gold.

Schultz likes gold in solid forms, in coins, or in stocks. If you want to feel the pulse of goldbugs around the world, you come to a Schultz investment seminar. Interest in gold at the 1973 conference was so heavy that a flying trip to the Agnico Gold Mine had been arranged for relaxation. The tone of the affair was set at the registration desk where free matchbooks were available with the inscription in black letters on a gold background: "Gold, the investment for the future."

The theme of the gathering was Investment Survival in the Age of the Fluctuating Dollar. That's a title which has peculiar appeal to the gold-lover, for supporters of gold usually are pessimists who see the worst in everything except for their own investment ideas.

"In times of famine, invasion, national emergency, depressions and devaluations, nothing has provided better financial shelter and assurance than gold," Ira U. Cobleigh, conservative author and editor, told one session.

*Barron*'s, the New York–based financial weekly, summarized the preachments of this investment meeting this way:

> No significant increase in free world production of the yellow metal is likely before 1980. The continuing ban on legal ownership of gold bullion by U.S. citizens is a purely arbitrary abridgement of their rights. A depression is surely coming, but the exact timing is difficult to pinpoint. However, one needn't believe in an imminent credit collapse to consider gold shares a sound long term investment. Though formal foreign exchange restrictions will be imposed on U.S. citizens, they will be as ineffective as wage and price controls. Don't put all your financial eggs in one basket or keep all your assets in any one country. Invest only in liquid things that can be sold overnight.

Past history shows that in time of crises, investors turn to gold or to gold-mining shares. The history of Homestake Mining Company, America's biggest gold mine, is a good example. During the Great Depression of 1932 and 1933 the price of its shares ranged from $40 to $50. On January 31, 1934, the United States price of gold was raised from $20.67 to $35 an ounce. The price of Homestake stock shot upward, was split ten for one, and still shares were selling at over $50 each in a short time. Investors had made over one thousand percent on their money.

In recent currency crises, investors have found again that money could be made in gold and in gold-mining shares. Until January 1, 1975, it was illegal for Americans to hold gold bullion or coins minted after 1933 except with special dispensation. This regulation hasn't stopped some Americans from dealing in gold in foreign lands, Switzerland, for instance, where banking secrecy is practiced. *Pick's World Currency Report* of October 11, 1967, said:

> The once powerful gold dollar has gone through various stages of depreciation, becoming the paper dollar, the dollarette and by early 1967, the Mini-dollar, worth about 40 percent of its prewar buying value. At a 4 percent annual loss of purchasing power, about 110 billion Mini-dollars worth of the total public and private debt were simply wiped out during last year. It will be left to historians and professors of jurisprudence to consider the ethics of such procedures. . . . As savers became more desperate, the once respected American law forbidding ownership of monetary gold domestically or abroad lost its effectiveness. Gold was and is being hoarded on a world-wide scale by governments and individuals of all nationalities, including many United States citizens.

The dollar's problems mounted in stages, of course, through creation of a two-tier gold market in 1968, the ending of the dollar's tie to gold in August, 1971, the Smithsonian money agreement of December, 1971, devaluing the dollar, and the second dollar devaluation in February, 1973. These steps, and the lust for gold among investors and hoarders, pushed the free-market gold price up from $35 an ounce to a peak of $127 an ounce in 1972. When this gold conference opened, the price had fallen back somewhat. Still, that three-and-a-half-times jump in the price had spelled fortune for the world's goldbugs, lending credence to the doctrines they had been preaching for years.

Now, at this meeting, they insisted that the price rise was only a start, a contention soon verified when gold soared to more than $180 an ounce in early 1974. There is nothing more satisfying to the goldbug than to be proved right when his own money is involved, for this provides him with an opportunity to purchase still more gold. And prophets of the progold fraternity were advocating just this. Gold will be priced at $400 an ounce within a few years, James Dines boldly predicts.

Any such rise would earn more fortunes for those investors who might put money into gold and gold shares. One should be warned, however, that history doesn't always repeat itself, at least in the short term. And in the long term, as John Maynard Keynes used to say, we are all dead.

No investment area arouses such controversy as does gold among its adherents and its detractors. You can invest your money in oil, or cotton, or real estate, or in thousands of other ways and, if you practice a reasonable application of the Golden Rule, your morality and your ethics may not be questioned. If you invested in gold bullion, you not only break the law in many countries, there are those who may accuse you of immoral conduct, of debasing the monetary system, and of being a heartless reprobate who probably accumulated wealth through robbing widows and orphans.

Prior to the big upsurge in the price of gold in the 1968–74 period, chrysophobes took every opportunity to ridicule goldbugs for their alleged stupidity.

The inference then was that investors in gold or in gold-mining shares were throwing their money away, getting no interest in the case of bullion, and dealing with highly speculative companies in the case of gold stocks.

Nobody calls the gold investor stupid anymore, for many of them tripled and quadrupled their money on one gold-price upsurge, then repeated the action on another. Anyone who invested funds in American South African Investment Company, Limited (now ASA Investment), shares in 1961 saw a ten-times gain in his capital if he held those shares into late 1973 and a twenty-times gain if he still had them in 1974. ASA, which is traded on the New York Stock Exchange, invests its funds in South African gold-mining shares, providing an easy way for Americans to invest in gold.

To understand why gold arouses so much controversy as an investment medium, one must realize that gold frequently sits at the opposite end of a monetary teeter-totter from the paper currency of a nation. As the currency declines in value, the value of gold in relationship to that currency rises. The inflationists in government who are responsible for the balance often will blame gold rather than themselves for the reaction. People who don't know any better may begin to think that gold has something sinful within its metallic heart. America's law against holding gold was based upon the idea that citizens should not be given a free choice between holding gold or keeping dollars. The U.S. government feared that if people had that freedom, politicians then would face a rush of money from dollars into gold when profligate political leaders spent far more money than the nation was earning.

It can be seen that the goldbugs are believers in sound money, the sound money of gold or a currency strongly backed by gold. Antigold fanatics usually are believers in big government, in government spending allegedly to right any wrongs and in the creation of "managed" currencies which, hopefully, would outmode Gresham's law. (This latter says that bad money drives out the good, with good money being hoarded while the bad money continues to circulate.) The antigold fanatics want to make it impossible for the average citizen to turn to gold as printing presses emit a steady stream of paper dollars.

The gold investor, too, usually is an economic pessimist. If one expects a depression or a recession and a bear market in stocks, then gold and gold shares become more attractive. If one is an optimist who believes in growth and the possibility of a boom ahead, then other forms of investment are more alluring.

Seen in this perspective, it is obvious that the goldbug and the antigold nut are at the opposite ends of the political spectrum, the sound money man versus the managed currency manipulator, the pessimist versus the optimist, the defender of property rights versus the proponent of human rights at the expense of someone else's property. Being opposites in so many respects, the chrysophilite and the chrysophobe have almost no common ground for discussion. Each irritates the other. Each finds his own pet theories at odds with those of the other. Net effect is not merely disagreement but downright dislike.

So it is that investors in gold find politics, economics, and ethics interwoven into any analysis of investment possibilities. In recent years, however, it is the goldbug who has been laughing all the way to the bank, whereas the detractors of gold have been crying on the road to the poorhouse, the road everyone is on if he fails to pay attention to inflation.

There are four basic ways to invest in gold: through purchase of gold bars or gold futures, through accumulation of gold coins, through jewelry, or through creation of a portfolio of gold shares. Some investors follow all four avenues, though this is unusual. Much of the gold purchased in bar form goes into hoarding, and the hoarder is not usually sophisticated enough to know much about investing in equities. And the astute equities investor may be uninterested in putting his money into noninterest-bearing gold bars.

Still, the hoarding demand sustains the world's gold market, with hoarding sometimes being done in the form of jewelry in India and other places in Southeast Asia. Jewelry investment might not be profitable in western countries where other forms of investment are available, but in some Asian countries there isn't any other safe outlet for spare cash.

Why do men hoard gold? To many people around the world this is a stupid question. For most of man's history this has been a violent world of revolutions, of wars, of looting, and of robbery. During political upheavals, paper money often becomes worthless. The only acceptable medium of exchange is likely to be gold, as coins or bars.

Gold has been like insurance to many people during times of social unrest in the past. The German who managed to hide some of his hoarded gold through World War II had a stake with which to start a new life in 1945, when the country was a bomb-ruined economic desert. The Frenchman who survived the German occupation of World War II also could start afresh if he had hoarded gold rather than the paper currency which had become worthless.

Charles R. Stahl, president of Economic News Agency, Inc., and publisher of *Green's Commodity Market Comments,* in Princeton, New Jersey, tells a hoarding story involving not gold, but platinum. Still, the tale does illustrate the rationale of the gold-hoarder.

"During World War II, in order to protect some of our assets after the Soviet troops had occupied my native town of Lwow, Poland, my family had oven grills made out of platinum, hoping that if the Russians searched our home, they would not seize the oven grills. Since platinum oven grills were not handy to carry around, when my wife and I escaped from occupied Poland to Hungary in 1941, we had platinum nets made to fit under the lining of our coats."

In Hungary, the family wealth was hoarded in platinum, gold, and diamonds in casings of windows, to be reclaimed after the war. That hoarded wealth permitted purchase of an apartment block after the conflict.

The tale has an ironic twist, which doubly emphasizes the dangers of depending upon paper currencies rather than upon gold and other precious metals. That apartment building was sold for Hungarian pengös, the currency unit of the country, at a twenty-times profit measured in those units. But in the time between signing the sales agreement and receiving the cash, wild inflation had reduced the value of the pengö by a thousand times. The money was only enough for purchase of a dog.

The typical gold-hoarder is not buying gold in anticipation of a capital appreciation in the metal. He is a frightened individual who believes wealth, even in small amounts, has its advantages, and he doesn't trust the political wills of governments to fight the inflation which destroys the meager possessions of the poor along with the caches of the passive rich. So he is merely seeking to keep his wealth from being swept away.

Today, an estimated twenty thousand to twenty-five thousand tons of gold are in the hands of gold-hoarders around the world. Probably a quarter to a fifth of that total is in France, which is far and away the biggest gold-hoarding nation in Europe. Nearly the same amount is in the hands of hoarders on the Indian subcontinent.

As long as currencies keep losing buying power because of inflation, gold-hoarders will have solid reasons for preferring holdings in the yellow metal rather than in paper currencies. In India, social traditions play an important role in the hoarding of gold, too. According to Hindu tradition, women had no proprietary rights over properties of husbands. To give a woman some protection in event of her husband's death, it became customary for the bride to receive a dowry, or *stridhana*, at time of her marriage. This, usually presented in the form of twenty-two-carat jewelry, remains her property through life, her insurance against hard times, her guarantee that, in case of need, she will have something to leave with the village pawnbroker in return for a loan.

One study of the gold trade by Charter Consolidated, Ltd., a London-based mining house, indicates the place that gold holds in Indian households. It says:

> Attitudes to gold vary greatly. As a symbol, gold can represent wealth, excellence, goodness, holiness, permanence, etc., stemming largely from historical, religious and cultural traditions. In the underdeveloped countries, particularly in Asia, reverence for gold is more or less universal. In India, for instance, where gold is symbolic of Lakshmi, the Hindu goddess of wealth, it is hoarded in almost every household, and a gold dowry *(strindhana)* worth an average $400 to $670, is given at all Hindu weddings. Gold in India is the principal feminine status symbol and is even eaten as medicine as well as being hoarded for the usual investment and ornamental purposes.

In no other country in the world is the attachment of ordinary people to gold as strong as in India. There are few families, no matter how poor, without at least one article made of gold which is held for a rainy day as insurance against rising prices, famines, and other vicissitudes of fortune.

But even forgetting about the laws against holding gold, the average American investor wasn't likely to be much interested in hoarding gold. Despite all the troubles experienced by America in recent years, it still is an oasis of peace compared to many sections of the world, and banks afford safer places for wealth than does a hole in the backyard or the window frames of living quarters. Moreover, investments such as gold shares provide a return, whereas gold bars do not.

Admittedly, if you truly believe that America is on the point of collapse financially, and that the dollar will become as unstable as some Latin American currencies, then you might favor holding gold no matter what the government has against it. Still if anarchy lies ahead for America, merely holding gold isn't going to solve problems for the hoarders, unless they are ready to defend their hoards with tanks and bazookas. This is something that some of the progold investment letters never mention as they slyly hint that every man of wealth should hold some gold.

Of course, there are Americans who do hold gold in Switzerland or elsewhere through secret bank-accounts. Usually such holders are speculators, rather than hoarders. The hoarder purchases his gold with intention of keeping it as a form of insurance; the speculator buys with hope of selling later at a profit. The jump in the gold price from $35 in 1968 to over $198 in 1974 provided numerous opportunities for killings by gold speculators. Gold speculation, however, is not a game for the amateur, since the price may fluctuate sharply.

Looking ahead, the odds are that the price of gold is more apt to rise than to fall over the years for the basic reason that inflation is likely to be with us into the foreseeable future. But there will be periodic setbacks, and that predicted price of $400 an ounce may not come anywhere near as fast as speculators want. This means that, in order to make money speculating in gold, the plunger may have to know quite a bit about the market. The Russians are selling gold. That's a price-depressing factor. So be wary. South Africa is selling all of its gold on the free market yet the price holds steady. That's a tipoff to underlying strength in the market. The dollar weakens. So gold should be bullish. Conversely, the dollar strengthens. That normally is not too good for gold, though this is not always so if you are speculating in currencies as well as in gold.

The smart gold speculator, for instance, may buy into gold with dollars. He may take profits in German marks, waiting for another gold-investment opportunity. If, during that wait, the German mark appreciates, the dollar price of gold might remain constant yet he may be able to buy more ounces of gold with his money when he returns to the market.

The skilled speculator may switch from marks to gold to Swiss francs to gold to dollars to gold to Dutch guilders to gold and so on. It sounds complicated, and it is for the amateur who may be unfamiliar with the foreign-exchange market. Average investors, and many smart ones, find gold shares more profitable and easier to follow. The sharp rise in the price of gold in the last few years has drastically altered the situation in the coin market, too. Prices of gold coins have soared to record levels, as buyers began to realize the currency-hedge value of numismatic coins.

Gold coins have a dual investment nature, possessing both numismatic and intrinsic value. Even if a piece has little numismatic worth, its price will rise along with the market price of gold. If the demand for a particular coin increases, the premium above the intrinsic gold-content value is likely to rise, too.

There are dangers in this field, however. Today, so many fakes are in existence that a buyer should deal only with a well-known coin house if he is being asked to pay any substantial premium for a particular coin. One should remember, also, that the spread between what the coin collector pays and what he might get if he sold the same coin back to the same dealer ranges between twenty-five to fifty percent. Thus, if you purchased a certain coin today, its value on the market might need to rise by fifty percent for you to break even, if you resold it.

This should not be an obstacle if a person intends to invest in coins on any scale. There are volume discounts, which reduce that spread. And prices have been rising so sharply in recent times that anyone who has entered the gold-coin market two or three years ago may have quadrupled his investment even if he didn't know much about coins and the market. The collector who made a study of the market may have done much better.

Perhaps it isn't fair to cite individual coin sales, lest the casual reader assume that such sales are the norm. Yet, these do provide cues concerning what has been occurring in the gold-coin area.

In June, 1973, a 1927 double eagle $20 gold piece with a D mint-mark sold for $60,000. This same coin had fetched $32,000 when sold in 1969. A few months later, an 1838 United States $10 gold piece sold for $100,000. The last time this particular coin had appeared in a salesroom was in 1952 when, as part of the collection of Egypt's ex-King Farouk, it had been sold for $700.

Such bonanzas are not common, admittedly. Most speculators and investors in coins confine purchases to British sovereigns, Mexican pesos, and American eagles; these coins have a big mint volume and a low numismatics value. Between 1817 and 1968, for instance, Britain minted 1,046,794,339 gold sovereigns. In addition, an unknown number of fakes have been minted in Lebanon, Italy and, elsewhere. Thus, the total number available for potential buyers is substantial indeed.

Nevertheless, it is common to find premiums of 25 to 100 percent above the intrinsic value of the coin. Basically, demand in America for gold coins comes from three groups; the numismatic collector who buys individual coins which fit into his collection, the investor who purchases in volume, counting on a rising gold price to upvalue his acquisitions, and the jeweler.

As coins have become more popular, jewelers have found a rising demand for them in pendants, earrings, cuff links, tie pins, necklaces, bracelets, and such. Buyers should realize, however, that once a coin is pierced by a jeweler, its value as a numismatic coin disappears, leaving only its intrinsic value plus whatever art value the jeweler is able to introduce.

Some sources keep insisting that gold jewelry is a good investment in these times. This is seldom the case unless one happens to be living in some underdeveloped country where the currency is plunging downward at about a twenty-five percent annual rate. Then, of course, anything solid, not just jewelry, is better than holding the particular currency. In the Middle East, Moslems making the traditional *Haj* to Mecca often will load themselves with gold jewelry before returning home to Pakistan, to Indonesia, or elsewhere. This is their way of shifting funds from paper currencies into gold, which may be sold at a much higher price when home.

Generally, the retailer markup on jewelry is around 100 percent and even higher in some cases. Sales taxes add to the spread, which means that anyone who invests in jewelry may discover that it takes years before pieces can be sold at the break-even point, let alone with a profit.

One recent conversation with Moshe Schnitzer, the affable, dynamic president of the Israel Diamond Exchange, illustrates the point. I met Schnitzer in a pleasant reception room of his office in Tel Aviv where leather furniture and tasteful art works on walls creates the atmosphere of a cultured home. A closed-circuit television screen in one corner provided a view of the electronically-controlled steel door which guards the entrance to the office.

"The diamond business is off," Schnitzer said. "The world-wide recession is adversely affecting sales."

He is as smoothly polished as some of the gemstones he sells. But, unlike many people in business, he speaks frankly when business is bad, as well as when it is good. So you usually know exactly where you stand with him.

Now, he said, "Earlier this year, we were selling the larger gemstones at premiums forty percent or more over list prices. Today, the premiums are gone and we are selling at two percent discounts."

Often diamonds and gold are combined into jewelry. It was evident right there that anyone who purchased jewelry at retail in early 1973 took a financial licking before the year was over, provided that investment was the goal.

One product often sold by jewelers, however, has become fairly popular as an investment medium. This is the medallion. (A medal is an insignia of honor to be worn, whereas a medallion, usually larger than a medal in size, is a memorial to a person, an event, a city, or a society.) Medallions may be of gold, silver, copper, bronze, or other material. Gold is the most popular, especially today. The medallion to commemorate something was an idea of Pisanello, a fourteenth-century Italian artist. Famous goldsmiths like Benuvenuto Cellini welcomed this avenue for their talents.

Today, many people who are worried about the declining values of currencies are turning to gold medallions as a hoarding device. Medallions are made with gold ranging from nine to twenty-two carats in quality, and sometimes the caratage is not clearly evident to the buyers. In fact, some medallions are merely gold-plated, which may mean that the intrinsic value may be only a few cents.

Most investors favor gold shares when it comes to investments in the gold area. Gold shares have been particularly rewarding for investors in the last few years, too, while most other equities were plummeting.

Gold shares, generally, move with the gold price. When the price rises, market valuations of shares rise, too. Ditto in reverse, though changes in either direction may not occur on the same day as the rise or fall.

The London *Financial Times* index of gold shares, a reliable index, stood at 40 through most of 1970, at 96 in 1972, at 207.1 at the end of 1973, and at 424.3 on April 5, 1974. By merely "buying the market," the gold-share investor had a ten-and-a-half-times gain in his investments in four years, while collecting dividends which exceeded the value of the original investment. Smart investors selected individual shares rather than the market and did even better.

Some of the great market jumps of recent times have been made by certain gold shares. In April, 1974, a share of Vaal Reefs Mine was worth $81, versus $19.50 in January, 1972. In the same period, a share of Loraine Mine soared by eleven times, from $1.45 a share to $16. East Rand Proprietary Mine showed a per-share rise to $50.40 from $4.42, while Durban Deep spurted to $52.80 from $5.82. ASA, Ltd., a favorite among Americans, was selling for $29 in 1970 and for $99.50 in April, 1974.

As share prices soared, dividends mounted, too. Thus East Rand Proprietary had a dividend pay-out record of 9.9 percent at the start of 1974 even when the figure was computed against its much higher share price. Western Holdings paid 11.6 percent in 1973, while the West Driefontein pay-out amounted to 6.1 percent of its much higher price.

Some dividend pay-outs have been sensational, 16.8 percent for Grootvlei and 19.1 percent for Marievale. One must remember, however, that every mine begins to die as soon as production starts and a short-life mine may not have too many more years for those good dividends. Still, as gold's price rises, mines earn more for their output, and dividends may climb. Obviously, though, if the share price soars, the percentage of the dividend pay-out to the share price may decline until the next dividend increase occurs.

One table in the *Financial Times* of December 22, 1973, illustrates how dividends have been climbing for key South African mines. Figures which follow are dividends paid on specific dates in South African cents:

| | DEC. 1973 | JUNE 1973 | DEC. 1972 | JUNE 1972 | DEC. 1971 |
|---|---|---|---|---|---|
| Blyvooruitzicht | 35 | 20 | 15 | 14 | 12 |
| Buffelsfontein | 55 | 55 | 20 | 10 | 9 |
| Doornfontein | 35 | 30 | 19 | 15 | 11 |
| Durban Deep | 50 | 25 | 20 | 10 | 5 |
| East Daggafontein | 20 | 20 | 30 | 15 | 11 |
| East Driefontein | 10 | – | – | – | – |
| East Geduld | – | – | – | 5 | 8 |
| East Rand Proprietary | 65 | 12 | 12 | 3 | 1 |
| Elsburg | 3 | – | – | – | – |
| Grootvlei | 13 | 18 | 5 | 5 | 7½ |
| Hartebeestfontein | 50 | 65 | 35 | 25 | 5 |
| Kloof | 29 | 30 | 15 | 10 | 3 |
| Libanon | 35 | 30 | 27 | 27 | 23 |
| Marievale | 45 | 27 | 22 | 18 | 12½ |
| South African Land | 30 | 20 | – | – | 40 |
| Stilfontein | 25 | 22½ | 12½ | 5 | 2½ |
| Vaal Reefs | 65 | 50 | 30 | 25 | 25 |
| Venterspost | 20 | 23 | 14 | 15 | 12 |
| Vlakfontein | 12 | 10 | 12 | 10 | 14 |
| Western Areas | 26 | 9 | 10 | 6 | 4 |
| Western Deep | 80 | 42½ | 50 | 30 | 40 |
| West Driefontein | 140 | 120 | 90 | 80 | 60 |
| West Rand Consolidated | 6½ | 5 | 5 | 3 | 3 |
| Zandpan | 8 | 10.8 | 5½ | – | – |

The investor in gold has several countries for selection when it comes to investing, but, the confirmed goldbug realizes that South Africa offers the widest share choice. South Africa dominates the gold equity market because it produces three-fourths of the free-world's new gold. Canada is a poor second in the free world, with the United States third.

Perhaps the easiest way for an American to invest in gold is to purchase shares of the biggest U.S. gold-mining company, Homestake Mining. The already mentioned ASA or International Investments, a mutual fund investing in gold shares, also offer ways of getting into the yellow metal, while American Depository Receipts of three dozen South African mining and finance houses are available through brokerage houses.

These receipts, called ADR's, are certificates signifying ownership in specific foreign companies which have investment appeal. They were originated in 1928 by Morgan Guaranty. At that time it took so long to transfer stock certificates from foreign lands to New York that many potential American buyers were shunning foreign stocks. In effect, an ADR represents ownership of a share or shares of a foreign corporation, with those shares deposited in a foreign bank.

Applicable dividends are paid to the ADR holder, while ADRs may be bought and sold in the market like ordinary shares.

For those who worry about the political situation in South Africa, Canadian gold mines offer possibility, too. Dome Mines, and its sub-sidiary, Campbell Red Lake, the new Agnico-Eagle, Giant Yellow-knife Mines, the Dickenson Group, Camflo Mines, and numerous small operations offer investment possibilities.

An investor pays for that hope of political stability through high price-earnings ratios for Canadian shares. There are speculative risks in South African shares the same as there are risks anywhere when profit potential exists. There also are rich rewards for those who make the correct judgments, as records of the last few years plainly show.

Investing in gold shares may be a tricky business, however. There are no automatic guarantees of capital appreciation, even though the price of gold is likely to be higher two years from now and higher than that five years from now. In one study, *Gold and International Equity Investment*, made by S. Herbert Frankel, professor in the economics of underdeveloped countries, Oxford University, there is the following passage:

> Gold mining is an industry where the ratio of failures to successes is high, and the risks and uncertainties faced by the investor are, there-fore, higher than in most industries.

His study showed that of 116 gold mines which launched operations in South Africa in the period 1887–1965, thirty-six percent had a zero yield for their stockholders. Thus, historically, one in three mines never made enough to pay a dividend. Recent history supports this thesis. In the 1950's, the great Orange Free State Gold Field came into being in South Africa, with rich mines like President Brand, President Steyn, and Western Holdings.

The Jeanette Mine was floated there, too, with more unfortunate results. Two shafts were sunk to 5,500 feet, and development started. Thick shale hindered operations, and the mine was put on the shelf, a lemon for its investors. The Loraine Mine in the same area never proved to be more than a marginal proposition, though in 1974 its share prices soared upon hope.

Even the Vaal Reefs Mine, biggest in the world, had problems, and these illustrate the financial hazards of gold mining. The mine is located near Klerksdorp, a town west of Johannesburg which was the scene of a gold rush in the 1880's.

By 1888, thirty-four mining companies were operating here, along with seventeen pubs to serve hard-drinking miners. The mines included the Shamrock, the Star of Erin, the Nonpareil, and the Sunbeam. A stock exchange was established in 1887. When it moved into a new building in 1888, officials proudly announced that now the exchange had its own bar. Klerksdorp then literally was a town with streets paved with gold. When no gravel was available for laying out the town's grid of streets, city fathers used gold bearing ore from the mines. There seemed to be so much of that ore available that nobody cared.

But the ore wasn't as plentiful as imagined. One by one the mines closed as ore bodies petered out. If Klerksdorp didn't become exactly a ghost town, it was sufficiently asomatous that it seemed finished as a mining center.

Then, in the 1930's, Anglo American Corporation of South Africa started re-explorations in the area. Mining techniques had improved over the years. The increase in the gold price in the 1930's created a new economic picture. The Klerksdorp area seemed to be worth another look. But that search proved futile.

The gold wasn't there in amounts which justified spending huge sums for development. With drilling rigs about to be removed from the area, several of Anglo's engineers were disconsolately drinking in the bar of the old Palace Hotel. Conversation turned to the abandoned Orkney Gold Mine, south of Klerksdorp. The discussion led to a decision to sink one more hole on that property as a final fling before ending operations.

Those drillers hit what became known as the Ventersdorp Contact Reef. Anglo created Western Reefs Mining Company to develop it, and production started in 1941. In 1942, an Anglo exploration team found another much richer reef, the Vaal reef, over four thousand feet below the surface and under Ventersdorp Contact. A separate company, Vaal Reefs Exploration and Mining Company, Limited, was formed to exploit this new find, with production starting in 1956.

In 1971, Vaal Reefs and Western Reefs merged into one giant company under the Vaal name. Today, this mine has stockholders in fifty different countries, twenty-eight thousand miners working underground, and a milling capacity of over six million tons annually. No other gold mine comes close to that.

West Driefontein, however, can claim to be a richer mine. It mills only about half the volume of ore as does Vaal Reefs. But its ore was averaging 28.5 grams to the ton in 1973 versus 12.4 grams to the ton at Vaal Reefs. So West Driefontein's revenues from gold in 1973 amounted to $184 million compared to $112 million at Vaal Reefs.

Yet West Driefontein, rich as it is, also illustrates the hazards of gold-mine financing. Twice it has been the site of tragic accidents which might have destroyed a weaker mine, wiping out stockholders' equities without any warning.

In 1962, the ground under the main crushing plant of the mine opened up like a giant mouth, swallowing the facility in a cloud of dust and tons of debris. No one had known that a dolomitic sinkhole had been under the plant, bearing the weight of the operation. A subterranean shift deep within the soil sucked the works downward in one ghastly plunge. Twenty-nine African workers died in the disaster.

Adriaan Louw, now chairman of Gold Fields of South Africa, had been general manager of the mine but had been transferred to the Gold Fields Group central office just prior to the tragedy. He took charge, organized a salvage operation, launched the study to find a safe site for a new plant, and established an emergency system by which other of the Group's milling facilities at neighboring mines could handle West Driefontein ore. The working profit of the mine, about $40 million annually then, was maintained despite the disaster. Cost of the new mill, however, was $12.6 million, a figure which, of course, had to come from dividends which otherwise might have gone to the mine's shareholders.

Louw is an ex-bomber pilot from World War II who has been a whiz kid in South African mining circles. In 1972, the Sunday *Times,* a Johannesburg-published newspaper which is one of the most prestigious in the country, named him as one of the country's five top businessmen of the year. He probably was more deserving of an award somewhat earlier when he sparked a salvage operation at West Driefontein after a second major disaster at the mine.

West Driefontein is located in an area which possesses considerable underground water resources as well as rich gold ore. Between 1954 and 1959, Louw was directly involved in installing the pumps that were used to prevent flooding as the mine was being extended. Says he: "The inflow was only just behind our pumping capacity. It was at that time that we invented a series of underground water doors."

By 1962, these doors no longer seemed necessary. On a hunch, Louw had them left in place. And these doors helped save the mine when, on October 26, 1968, an underground river poured into tunnels and crosscuts of the property.

Such disasters have ended the lives of many mines, set others years behind. In this particular case, it wasn't only West Driefontein which was involved, but its sister, East Driefontein, a new mine then in the development stage. Thousands of miners were below ground when the water poured into the tunnels at a rate which reached a hundred million gallons a day. They hurried toward lifts, slammed underground doors behind them. Those doors allowed all of the miners to escape, and not a single life was lost. But the mine, then yielding a net profit equivalent to about $60 million a year, faced collapse.

Quickly, salvage crews were organized. Men battled the water deep beneath the ground. Both East and West Driefontein launched a massive pumping operation. Louw held daily press conferences detailing what was happening.

This was no simple mine tragedy, though, fortunately, no lives were at stake. This was a battle for the richest gold mine in the world. Not only would its loss be a national disaster for South Africa, it also involved a billion-dollar mine which had stockholders in two-score countries. Many of those shareholders were Americans, drawn by monetary anxieties into South African gold mines.

Business and financial newspapers around the globe carried stories of the underground battle. Shares plummeted to under $5 each and many investors saw themselves facing steep losses. For nearly three weeks the dramatic battle seesawed. Then, on November 19, 1968, Louw appeared at a press conference in Johannesburg to announce cheerfully that: "West Drie is saved."

Those courageous enough to invest in that mine at that time subsequently experienced a twenty-times gain if they held shares in 1974.

It should be evident that gold-mining shares merit study before plunging heavily into the field, especially after the sharp climb of

1973 and early 1974. One bit of advice along those lines was contained in *The Economist* in its May 19, 1973, issue. It said:

> In picking and choosing [gold shares], the smart money goes for the high-cost mines because they enjoy the added boost of gearing when the gold price rises. Durban Deep, for instance, had expenses of about $52 an ounce of gold mined last year. Its average selling price of around $55 gave it a profit of $3. But an average selling price of $87 this year and costs of, say, $60 would boost that profit per ounce to $27, a ninefold increase. On the other side of the coin, West Driefontein (a relatively low-cost mine) made a profit of about $35 an ounce last year. On a gold price of $87 that profit would rise to $65, an increase of only 85 per cent.

One should remember, however, that any speculative profit carries its speculative dangers, too. Gearing operates in reverse. It does not take much of a price decline to send the equity price of a highly geared mine plummeting downward, especially if the share has enjoyed a rise earlier. When you start from a low base, any gain may seem greater than when rising from a high base. Nevertheless, the IBM's and the Polaroids have done well for investors in industrial stocks over the years. Unless you are a gambler at heart, you may find more peace of mind with a longer-life mine which has lower costs.

Mine life is an important factor for investors to consider. It may seem cheap to purchase shares of a mine at $1 a share when the dividend pay-out amounts to 20 cents annually. This may be expensive if the mine has an expected life of four more years.

Nevertheless, if you are gambling on a rise in the gold price, sometimes the short-life mine may be a better buy than the long-life operation. The rising price may double or triple the anticipated life of the mine which had seemed to be nearing its close.

Taxes play a part in the valuation of a mine, too. South Africa has a complicated formula aimed at encouraging mines to drop to lower grades of ore when the gold price rises. This extends the life of mines, a plus for shareholders. It may mean that the profit rise in any particular year could be less than the percentage rise in the gold price.

Uranium holdings are another matter for consideration when contemplating a South African gold investment. Several mines produce uranium along with their gold, a big added plus in the energy-short era which is developing. Among them are Vaal Reefs, Blyvooruit-

zicht, Buffelsfontein, Harmony, Hartebeestfontein, West Driefontein, and Western Deep Levels. President Brand and Welkom also
have limited quantities of the atomic power mineral.

The factors affecting a mine, such as grade, life, costs, and milling
rates vary with even slight changes in the price of gold. So it is
evident that an analyst requires a computer to put all of the factors
into the correct perspective. As a rule of thumb, the high-cost, short-
life mine is the best choice for the bull who is positive the price of
gold will rise. A low-cost, long-life mine will have more stable prices
over the long term and is a better bet for the more cautious, who
aren't sure they have a pipeline to God.

The average investor doesn't have a computer in his kitchen along
side of the automatic dishwasher and the clothes dryer. However,
there are avenues of information readily available to anyone interested in gold shares. Brokerage houses in New York and in London
occasionally issue studies of specific shares. The *Mining Journal
Quarterly Review of South African Gold Shares* is one of the best
ways of studying the market and specific companies. (Publisher: The
Mining Journal, Ltd., 15 Wilson Street, London, EC2M 2TR, England,
£11 per year in Europe, $30 annually air mail to the United States.)
The *Wall Street Journal's* "Heard on the Street" column occasionally
discusses gold stocks. So does the *Journal's* companion publication,
*Barron's*. Investment letters such as the *International Harry Schultz
Letter,* the *Dines Letter,* the *Myers Letter,* Franz Pick's services, and
others follow gold shares closely.

The investing structure in South Africa's mining industry offers
opportunities for spreading the risks, if an investor is so inclined. For
the most cautious investor there are the big mining houses such as
Anglo American Corporation of South Africa, General Mining or
Consolidated Gold Fields. These Groups are involved in platinum,
copper, iron, and other minerals, as well as in South African industry;
Anglo and Consolidated have world-wide interests. Investments are
spread over a wide range, and no one disaster at a particular mine
has much of an effect upon a group.

However, this may be a left-handed way of investing in gold. Anglo, for instance, is the world's largest gold producer; yet in 1973 only
thirty-eight percent of its income came from gold. In that same year,
forty-two percent of General Mining's investment income came
from gold and mining financing.

Some of the groups have established finance subsidiaries which concentrate upon gold mines. This is a way of investing while spreading risks. Anglo American, for instance, has a subsidiary, Anglo American Gold Investment Company, which has its own public share offering. At the end of 1974, it held substantial interests in fourteen mines plus holdings in the Gold Fields of South Africa Group. The latter company is the gold affiliate of Consolidated Goldfields, with eighty-six percent of its assets in gold and uranium properties. Middle Wits is associated with the Anglo-Transvaal Consolidated Group, and has eighty-two percent of its investments in gold and uranium.

Direct purchases of gold are for the pessimist, who is fearful that inflation and chaos may wipe out his savings. In Switzerland, astute financial advisors are telling their clients that fifteen or twenty percent of assets should be in gold coins or bars in troubled times. Yet it is very easy to be rooked when buying gold. Perhaps you might not be like the oft-mentioned hick who buys a bar of gold-gilded lead at gold prices. Still, you probably don't know how to assay a gold bar if one is offered to you.

So, by all means deal with reputable institutions and companies. Look for the appropriate stamp on a bar for ascertaining the quality of the metal. Don't purchase anything under 995 purity, which means 99.5-percent pure gold or better. Remember that anybody can put a stamp on inferior gold, which is why you should be dealing with an established institution which has a reputation to uphold. Remember also that the time to do your checking of the bar is before you make the purchase.

Once you walk away from the establishment, the seller can claim: "But I sold you a 99.5-percent pure bar. Don't come back with another bar of 90 percent purity and claim that it is the same one I sold you."

Obviously, the seller needs some protection, and no seller is going to exchange every bar which is brought back. If he operated that way, very soon unscrupulous operators would be buying 99.5 percent gold, going around the block and returning with 90 percent or 80 percent gold and claiming that they were gypped. This is true of coins, too.

There are advantages to dealing with a bank, or with a company which may hold the gold for you. Gold is not the sort of thing you leave lying around the house. Even if it is insured, and it would have to be for your protection, you do not want to invite robbers to come around. When a reputable institution gives you a receipt for your gold, you can claim exactly what that receipt says at some later time. Of course, if you leave your gold with any such institution, your gold is no safer than is the strength of that bank. If the bank folds, your gold may be tied up until released by the liquidator. And, of course, you collect no interest on your gold. In fact, you may have a small storage charge.

Moreover, you could be charged a steep markup by some gold sellers, especially if you are dealing in small quantities. If you are charged a commission of fifteen or twenty percent for your gold at a time when interest rates are over ten percent annually, you may be out-of-pocket to the extent of a quarter to a third of your investment in the first year.

The very small investor may find coins to be more appropriate to his needs than are the tiny gold bars that are within his price range. Gold may be purchased in half-ounce wafers, in 1-and 5-ounce bars, as well as 400-ounce bars, at the average gold-retailing establishment. In fact, sizes are adapted to almost every purse. But markups rise as the size of the bar gets smaller.

Coins have premiums over their gold content, too. So you should know the weight of the coin, the price of raw gold that particular day, and the average premiums on the particular coin which may interest you. This allows you to estimate the premium on that coin and to see how it compares with the market. Remember that dealer markups for coins sold individually may be anywhere from 25 to 100 percent. In other words, a coin which may be listed in a catalog at $10 may be worth only $5 to $7.50 if you wanted to resell it shortly afterward to a dealer. Gold coins have been appreciating steadily in value over the years, especially in the last three or four years. So, if you are buying coins to hold for a decade or two, chances are they should be worth considerably more at the end of that time than when you purchase them.

Whether or not the value of those coins will rise at the same rate as interest might accumulate in a bank is something else. At least with gold, you should be possessing something which will gain in value through inflation. If Washington shows signs of whipping inflation, then demand for gold should wane. Thus, any purchases you do make, whether of coins or of gold bars, should reflect some thought on your part concerning inflation, the trend of the economy, the level of interest rates, and your own personal financial situation.

Anyone who deals directly in gold soons finds this to be a market which is plagued by rumors, affected by sudden fears, and driven by irrationality as well as by knowledge. Sometimes unscrupulous operators plant rumors for their own ends. For instance, there is the one about "Arabs are buying gold," which sometimes is started to stimulate an upward price movement. Arabs do buy gold regularly, and they may increase or decrease buying as they see fit. When actions are publicized, however, it may be because bankers in Beirut would like to profit by an upward surge in the market.

And there are others who are ready to play gold short, using some trick to confuse the market. For instance, there's the oldie about some mysterious gold hoard which is ready to be released onto the market. In 1973, for instance, the London *Daily Telegraph* and the *New York Times* both fell for this one. The tale which swept through the market was that four-hundred tons of gold bullion belonging to General Juan Peron was to be unloaded. The market for gold is so thin that such a sale might have driven the price downward by a substantial amount.

"This time it's Peron. When Batista of Cuba was alive we used to hear such stories about his gold, or about Trujillo's of the Dominican Republic," says an official of one Big Three Swiss banks.

"Then there's nothing in it," I said.

"Anything is possible. But if you want to sell a large block of gold, you don't try to sell it all at once if you want a good price, and who doesn't?" this banker said. "I haven't seen any of that gold."

Nobody else did, either.

However anyone invests, he will have to follow monetary, economic, and financial developments when managing his portfolio. With central bankers holding over thirty-seven thousand tons of the sixty thousand tons of gold now outstanding, monetary uses of gold are bound to have an effect on its price despite all the claims that gold is being demonetized.

Still, David Lloyd-Jacob, the Consolidated Gold Fields researcher who makes a career of analyzing demand factors in gold, told the 1973 International Monetary Seminar in Montreal that "gold is a good investment even without any change in its monetary price."

Maybe so. But any increase in the monetary price would be a double bonus for the gold-share investor, and that is why investors pay such close attention to monetary developments.

# CHAPTER XIII

# Gold as Money

In October, 1960, a sudden demand for gold from sources through-out Europe and the Middle East burst over the London Gold Market. Buy-orders poured into offices of the five big bullion dealers from Kuwait, from Lebanon, from Zurich, from Brussels, from Paris, and from a host of other places. Telex machines clattered purchase instructions. Telephone lines jammed with calls from eager purchasers.

For years the price of gold had fluctuated within a narrow range, usually between $35.08 to $35.15 an ounce. Rises and falls of an eighth of a cent were duly registered and followed as if these were major price changes. The pennies took care of the insurance, the shipping charges, and a few cents profit for the dealers of gold. The United States was ready to buy or sell gold at $35 an ounce with the huge resources of the Treasury behind it. So nobody believed that the price could fluctuate very far from $35. It never fell under that figure, because the U.S. was ready to buy at $35, so why sell to anybody for $34.95?

Now the price was rising. It edged upward to $35.50, to $36.10, to $37.00. Dealers at Sharps, Pixley & Company, Johnson, Matthey, Mocatta & Goldsmid, Samuel Montagu, and N. M. Rothschild exchanged anxious telephone calls and information. Dealers have a companionable, cozy relationship, like that of old club members among whom competitive instincts are blackballed. The mystique of gold seldom fires them, for the dealer on the London market is handling paper, and seldom even sees a bar of gold, even though he may deal in hundreds of them through a normal day.

"What is happening in the market?" one of the bullion dealers at Sharps, Pixley was asked via telephone.

"There are rumors in the market that the next American administration will raise the monetary price of gold," he answered in the crisp voice which most gold and foreign-exchange dealers develop. They deal in millions of dollars, sometimes closing a transaction literally in seconds, with one following immediately after the other. This is no way to nourish any talent for empty telephone conversation.

"Where did that one start?"

"I don't know. But a lot of buyers seem to believe it. What do you think? Would Nixon or Kennedy increase the price of gold?"

The election campaign in the United States was in its final weeks, with all signs indicating a neck-and-neck race. Nixon was believed to be a sound-money man who might raise the price from $35 an ounce to something higher in order to stem a drain on the United States gold stockpile, which was becoming a hemorrhage. On the other hand, the Democrats had been the last to devalue the dollar by raising the price of gold. They were likely to stress expansionary economic policies, and a radical move such as a dollar-devaluation might be their way of accelerating the economy.

A devaluation of a currency normally stimulates exports because their prices are reduced in foreign-exchange terms. Meanwhile, imports face the opposite reaction; prices rise in foreign-exchange terms, so imports usually tail off. The combination of rising exports plus declining imports improves a nation's balance of payments (the sum total of what it spends and what it earns in foreign markets). So any drain on reserves of gold normally is stemmed, and, hopefully, the nation's financial health improves.

This, of course, doesn't have to be explained to any gold dealer. But I did express my sentiments concerning the philosophies of the Democrats and of the Republicans in America, knowing full well that neither party had more than two or three gold experts who could tell the difference between gold and brass under a bright light.

I had never met this particular gold dealer, but we had reached a cordial level of information exchange. He remained a friendly voice at the other end of the telephone, while I probably was a disembodied but articulate spirit who didn't know much because I was always asking questions. Our unofficial relationship called for me to provide him with any nonsecret information I might possess in return for some of his market knowledge and data about gold dealing.

"What price does thus rumor say the next administration will set?" I asked.

"Forty dollars an ounce."

"That would be a little more than a fourteen percent increase. Do you think that would be enough to stem the U.S. gold drain?"

"I don't know," he said, "but some people believe that if the price is raised once, it might be raised again if the first one isn't enough."

"And if every speculator thinks that, then the speculation in the market might bring it about," I said. "This is one of the arguments used against a gold-price increase. It would only start an enormous speculative wave."

"I know," he said, "but cheerio. I have to get back to work. Orders are pouring in."

They certainly were, as rumors swept the world about that possible gold-price hike. If anyone has inside knowledge about an increase in the price of gold, then a fortune can be made by speculating in the market. Gold may be purchased on margin, so even a fourteen percent increase in the price could spell a substantial profit. Take the investor who buys gold on twenty percent margin with $100,000. He gets $500,000 worth of gold in the deal, though, of course, he ultimately must settle the full account when it comes due. But if gold's price rises by fourteen percent while he is holding that gold (probably in paper form only), its worth rises by $70,000. If he settles the account immediately after the hike, he has $170,000 less interest and small commission, for a gain of nearly seventy percent.

This is the way many of those gold buyers were playing the market, working through Swiss banks. With such profits dangling before their eyes, the gamble seemed worth it. Since gold wasn't going to fall below $35 an ounce, the opportunities for profit seemed to outweigh the chances of loss, at least for those who were early in jumping into this speculative binge.

The price of gold soared to $40 an ounce, an unheard of figure. Then, the bubble burst. The United States Government emphatically denied that any gold-price increase was being considered. Speculators began dumping their gold, and the price collapsed.

But the market had sounded a warning. The United States dollar was headed for trouble, a warning which was to go unheeded. And gold carried the signal, just as it has in other monetary upheavals. Whenever confidence in a currency fades, men rush to gold as a refuge, and demand pushes the price upward.

This is why gold is a monetary metal; it is trusted. When a currency is backed by gold, people transfer that trust to the currency. Still proponents of managed currency keep insisting that gold doesn't matter. Nonsense. In normal times, gold is as good as money. When turmoil threatens, it is better than money.

The United States had emerged from World War I with the largest gold hoard in the world, one which grew even larger in the immediate postwar era. By September, 1949, the total hit a peak of $24.7 billion, and perhaps it is no coincidence that at that time the United

States reached the peak of its power. No other nation on earth could command its resources, its power, its ability to do good or harm. The U.S. dollar was tied to gold, and any American could say with perfect honesty that the dollar was "as good as gold."

With a do-gooding spirit which was sometimes praiseworthy, sometimes naively prodigal, the United States launched massive foreign-aid programs aimed at distributing its wealth about the globe. Its armies took up permanent residence abroad. Its industrial corporations poured cash into factories, facilities, and installations in foreign lands. Its tourists tossed money around from Singapore to Spitzbergen and from Johannesburg to Moscow.

In simple terms, the United States spent much more money abroad than it was earning. As its dollars went abroad, many of them came back through the hands of central bankers who, in effect, told the Treasury: "Please exchange each of these dollars for that one-thirty-fifth of an ounce of gold which you have promised."

As more and more of these dollars came back in this fashion, the United States gold hoard dwindled. What followed is a sad tale which still has many informed people shaking their heads. If you study that tale closely, you find some of the causes of the ills which now beset the United States, of the wild inflation and the declining value of the dollar, of our inability to swing the same punch in international affairs as we did only two decades ago.

"I developed great respect for gold and its essential kingpin role in keeping the international monetary system stable, and for the discipline of the gold standard in eliminating balance of payments problems and of promoting continuously expanding world production and trade," says John Exter, an ex-banker and long-time chrysophilite who has been around long enough not only to know where most of the bodies have been buried but who did the killing, and why.

Sadly, he says: "At the Federal Reserve Bank of New York, I was in charge of twenty-three billion dollars of gold, and in 1958 I had to pay out almost two and a quarter billion dollars worth of it."

That was a drain which continued on and on, at a varying rate, year after year. This was the hemorrhage which prompted gold buyers to believe in 1960 that something had to give. They were right, of course, but their timing was off by more than a decade. The first dollar devaluation didn't come until late 1971, followed by another in February, 1973.

Predicting monetary developments and their effects on gold always has been a risky business. Gold has played a role in the monetary affairs of men ever since Menes, the Egyptian pharaoh, minted his fourteen-gram gold bars more than three thousand years before Christ. Yet few civilizations since have shown any ability to handle monetary affairs in a manner which provided long periods of economic prosperity for citizens.

There are reasons for this, of course. Nearly every ruler or government since time began has found it easier to spend money than to earn or collect it. It costs money to maintain standing armies and to hold subject nations under control. The initial invasion may provide loot. Then sources of income may dry up.

As man progressed up the scale (if what has happened since can be termed progress), citizens began to expect roads, schools, welfare, and other benefits from governments. The more democratic that society became, the more people could clamor for some of these things, and the more necessary was it for governments to oblige if politicians wanted to remain in power. But, even as people expect benefits from governments, they dislike paying taxes. So governments find it much easier to give than to receive, without ever developing any of the moral qualities which this might imply. Quite the reverse. Governments have become like those merry Robin Hoods who used to rob the rich to distribute largess among the poor.

As a sociological exercise, this may seem praiseworthy. But governments reserve for themselves the right to decide who are deserving, who are the rich, and how the wealth distribution is to occur. Often this is done by fiscal and monetary means. Often it is done in such a haphazard way that the biggest sufferers are pensioners and fixed-income people who are least able to afford the government which happens to be in power. Often, too, government measures lead to inflation which erodes the wealth and buying power of everybody, not just the rich.

Even before the time of Christ, emperors and rulers of city-states had learned how to "water" money in a vain attempt to stretch resources. If a pure-gold coin is worth the equivalent of $20, then, by adding fifty percent copper, two coins can be made from one without spending any more than a penny's worth of copper. Presto! A government's financial troubles may be ended. Or so it seemed to many a ruler who opted to follow this route, though usually he was sly enough to move in steps rather than in one big jump.

As soon as the debased coins were recognized in channels of commerce, merchants would raise their prices to compensate for the lesser amounts of gold in them. In effect, debasing of currencies created inflation. This was happening in many Greek city-states long before the time of Christ. It is happening today, though methods of debasing the currency differ since gold and silver coins have almost disappeared from trade. Results still are the same, as inflation around the world today testifies.

Throughout history, however, gold has retained its value, offering holders an opportunity to store their wealth through periods of inflation, turmoil, and wars. This is why it has been used as money, and why central banks still hold thirty thousand tons of it in their vaults. When a gold coin is debased, it isn't the gold which loses its worth, it is the coin itself.

Often, however, gold was too valuable to constitute the bulk of the circulated currency. Silver and bronze usually performed that function while gold was the reserve currency held in treasuries of nations. If a citizen knew that he could exchange a certain number of silver coins for a gold coin, he was willing to accept the silver. The gold backing provided the confidence in the currency which allowed it to function as money in the system.

When gold is the yardstick of a money system, it is said to be the *numeraire*. The value of other currencies is related to it, providing a gauge by which these currencies may be compared. When currencies are not tied to gold, there is no standard for judgment. A dollar might be worth a gallon and a half of gasoline in one place, a dozen eggs somewhere else, and two hamburgers at a corner snack shop. *But the dollar, itself, has no worth at all,* except for its fraction of a cent's worth of paper and ink.

One should carefully distinguish between value and worth if one is to understand why gold has served as money for thousands of years. The value possessed by anything is governed by the demand men have for it. If people want paper dollars, then they do have value. But worth is a factor of intrinsic properties possessed within the item. Gold has worth because of its artistic and industrial uses. If you removed all the ink from a dollar bill, it would have no worth at all. If you melted a gold coin into a blob of yellow metal, that chunk still would have worth. Because this worth is so durable in gold, no other commodity has served as well in the monetary field.

Once in Johannesburg, South Africa, I spent a lively morning discussing gold and money with J. E. Holloway, one of the world's foremost experts on these topics. He occupied a small office in the headquarters building of Union Corporation, one of South Africa's big mining groups, the sort of plain office which sometimes is reserved for aging executives who have such a store of knowledge that the firm hesitates to sever connections. He arose to greet me, a small, gnomelike man with a wisp of gray moustache, rimless glasses, a balding head, and a sharp, clear mind which operates like a well-programmed computer.

I had met him years before, when he had been South Africa's Ambassador to the United States with President Eisenhower in the White House, and he remembered the meeting. After the usual exchange of pleasantries, he said: "In 1916, I decided I wanted to know all there was to know about money."

"And do you?"

"I'm still learning," he said. "But I do know that gold is the most suitable monetary commodity ever found, because gold always has worth. Paper ultimately has no worth at all."

"For nearly a third of a century the world has been experimenting with a currency based on nothing," he continued, warming to his topic.

I nodded. Mr. Holloway, or Dr. Holloway, as he usually is referred to in South Africa, represented his country at the Bretton Woods conference in 1944, which established the monetary system that had existed for twenty-seven years, until President Nixon severed the dollar's connection with gold in 1971. It was this conference, dominated by Britain's John Maynard Keynes and America's Harry Dexter White which created the International Monetary Fund.

"To be efficient, money must be easy to transport, to store, and to subdivide, and it should be easily recognized," said he.

I nodded again. "And it should be difficult to destroy, something that lasts a long time without changing shape." I had read some of his treatises on money.

It was his turn to nod. "And it should be difficult to counterfeit, scarce enough that new supplies won't be pouring onto the market to upset the stability of its value, and of a nature that its worth cannot be readily or quickly changed by arbitrary decrees."

"You are talking about gold."

"Certainly," he said. "Politicians can always order more paper currency to be printed if the treasury is bare because of their spending. They cannot order more gold to be created."

"But if they raise the gold price, they might encourage greater production."

"Not immediately." He shook his head. "After a price increase, mines shift to a lower grade of ore which becomes profitable at the higher price, and production may decline even though a mine's profit rises."

Using a letter-opener as a pointer, he gestured toward a wall map which showed the gold-bearing areas of South Africa. "Over the longer term, of course, the supply of gold is increased by a higher price, but not at such a rate that gold's stability is upset."

The relationship of money and gold may seem almost axiomatic when an economist of Mr. Holloway's stature explains the monetary system. Nevertheless, the topic of money is one of the most complicated which man faces, and this isn't said merely because of the difficulties experienced in acquiring an adequate supply of it. If a nation is to be prosperous, it must have sufficient currency to oil the wheels of commerce and industry. If there isn't enough, a nation may have a depression. If the supply is greater than available goods and services, there may be inflation. How to maintain the correct balance has plagued nearly every government in history.

Through that history gold has remained scarce. It wasn't until the discovery of gold in the New World that Europe had supplies adequate enough to bring gold into nearly every hand, if only for a brief time. For year after year, Spanish galleons sailed from ports of New Spain with cargoes of gold bullion and plate, and as long as the gold flowed Spain was one of the great powers of Europe.

But as Britain gained dominance of the seas, gold flowed through the arteries of commerce into its treasury. Was it the gold which gave Britain power? Or was it British power which attracted the gold? Good questions, for it often seems that a nation reaches the zenith of its political power when its gold supply is at a peak. Still, the questions are like that old conundrum: which came first, the chicken or the egg?

From the sixteenth century onward, gold entered the economic lifestreams of nations as it never had before. Brazil became a producer. Discoveries followed in California, in other western states, in Australia, in South Africa, and in the Klondike. In the nineteenth century alone, more gold was produced than had been mined in the preceding five thousand years, says one report made by the gold producer Union Corporation of Johannesburg, South Africa.

In 1816 legislation was enacted under which Britain, five years later, went on the gold standard, and for nearly a hundred years its pound sterling was backed by the ample gold reserves in the Bank of England.

The gold standard basically is as simple as a cash economy, with none of the complexities of a credit system. Gold coins circulate freely, along with paper money which is convertible into the appropriate coin on demand. Import and export of gold are permitted and gold is used to settle international obligations.

Imports, thus, are paid with gold. But a nation earns gold with its exports. If trade is in balance, the commerce may continue indefinitely, with very little gold moving anywhere, for the debt of one nation may cancel the debt of another.

If a nation spends more abroad than it earns, its gold reserves began to deplete. The country is in the same position as the big spender in a cash economy who is running down his bank account. Like it or not, he will have to reduce his spending as the money runs out. Nations, too, must reduce the outgo in a similar situation under the gold standard.

Imports are reduced. Efforts are made to increase exports to earn more gold, and this may involve layoffs to increase efficiency of plants. In short, nations pull in their belts, through recession. The business downturn ultimately may improve the efficiency of export industries to the point where gold again is earned in greater volume than is spent. Plants rehire workers, and prosperity returns to the land.

With the gold standard, the internal volume of a currency is established by the amount of gold in a nation's treasury. Thus, if the currency has twenty-five percent gold backing, as did the dollar for a considerable period of time, each dollar's worth of gold in the Treasury allows the government to print four paper dollars for circulation. (With a highly leveraged credit system such as exists in the United States, the money expansion could be many times greater.)

It can be seen that, under this system, when a nation's gold reserves start contracting because of overspending, monetary managers must reduce the supply of currency in the country (or change the gold backing). Any reduction in the supply restricts business in general, as manufacturers and commercial establishments find it more difficult to borrow funds at banks. Thus, there is a double action operating toward recession: export industries are trying to become more competitive through layoffs, while all industries experience more trouble in raising money to operate.

The gold standard contains this automatic disciplinary feature which politicians do not like. There is no way that a big spending administration can adhere to the gold standard and freely spend beyond a nation's resources, unless that administration locates some friendly power which is willing to extend credit for the overspending. So, few modern politicians like the gold standard.

In the nineteenth century, the gold standard was supreme as the paramount monetary system for major industrial nations.

World War I saw the suspension of that standard as warring nations sought to conserve vital stocks of gold for purchase of munitions and supplies. Never again was the gold standard to be enshrined on a pedestal, as it was prior to 1914. Britain returned to the gold-bullion standard from 1926 to 1931, then abandoned gold, as did most of the nations of the world through the Great Depression. (The gold-bullion standard is about like the gold standard, except that gold coins do not circulate.)

In 1922, at a conference of international bankers in Genoa, Italy, the gold-exchange standard came into being. Under this system, each nation is free to issue domestic currency not only against its primary reserves of gold, but also against its holdings of key reserve currencies such as the pound sterling, initially, and later the United States dollar, too.

The United States was one of the last countries to depart from the full gold standard, an action prompted by the depression of the early 1930's.

In a message to Congress on January 15, 1934, President Roosevelt asked for a fifty-nine percent devaluation of the U.S. dollar, with the price of gold to be set at $35 an ounce. This became law, shortly, with the United States offering to purchase any gold tendered to it and with the dollar convertible into gold at 1/35th of an ounce. Still, this wasn't the gold standard, for Americans were forbidden to hold gold or to deal in it except with special licenses which proved difficult to obtain. America now was on its own version of the gold-exchange standard, with the dollar to be "as good as gold." The United States couldn't hold its own dollars in its treasury as reserves; but it could do something better. It could print dollars to spend abroad and foreigners were ready to take them just as long as they believed a dollar was "as good as gold." Thus, as long as foreigners continued to behave in that fashion, the United States had an endless source of international credit.

The system was solidified at the Bretton Woods monetary conference of 1944. The United States went to that conference with $20 billion worth of its gold in its treasury, more than enough to provide it with the loudest voice by far at the deliberations. The United States dominated that conference and promoted the addition of something new to the system. From the conference came the International Monetary Fund, an agency which operates as an international bank to promote exchange stability and to encourage monetary cooperation among member nations. Bretton woods also injected another new dimension—the idea of international credit jointly managed by nations.

Credit undoubtedly has stimulated prosperity around the world. Indeed, the post-World War II period saw the expansion of affluence into remote nooks and corners of Europe, and the emergence of Japan as a great new economic power, with exporters who knew how to operate skillfully within that Bretton Woods system. But world money managers in their wisdom (or lack of it), had created a system at Bretton Woods which encouraged the creation of credit without providing any means of controlling that credit.

Here we come to a key factor which divides the goldbug from the antigold fanatic. The former likes cash, while the latter prefers credit. With the gold standard, business is conducted very much as in a cash economy. This is too restrictive, says the antigold man.

Chrysophobes argue that the international credit system must be amplified, with credit replacing gold, just as it has done internally in most countries. All of the plans for reforming the monetary system, with gold being demonetized, call for creation of new credit forms to replace gold.

The gold-haters who advocate this approach claim that there isn't enough gold in the world to perform monetary functions. This ignores the fact that it is just as easy to raise the price of gold as it is to create new credit instruments of thin air. Moreover, the antigold position overlooks the fact that a little bit of gold may go a long way.

If you are a thrifty person with a $25,000 bank account, you are not continually turning over the whole $25,000. Only the upper layer of your account is apt to be touched, a few thousand taken out for something, then more added to raise the total. The bulk of your bank account is never touched, unless you encounter a run of extremely bad luck.

So it is with gold. One London banker mentions how, about ten years ago, a gold shipment of $500,000 was made to a continental bank. Bars were dutifully packed in a wooden box, sealed, and shipped to the particular receiver. No more was heard about that gold, until some years later, when the demands of international commerce called for this continental bank to ship gold back to the London bank. The same gold bars were returned, still in the same wooden boxes, seals unbroken.

The largest repository of gold in the world is the Federal Reserve Bank in New York. There are 12,600 metric tons of gold bars resting deep in vaults beneath the bank's Broad and Wall Street headquarters. About eighty nations have elected to keep some, and in certain cases, nearly all, of their gold there in marked cubicles, with the Bank acting as the custodian.

When Britain makes a gold payment to West Germany or to Switzerland, one of the bank's employees may use a lift truck to transport the bars from Britain's cubicle to that of West Germany or of Switzerland. Accounting tabulations are changed. And life proceeds as before, with the gold still in the vault. Only occasionally does a gold transfer mean the shipment of the metal from the bank to some distant point.

The whole thing might seem ridiculous, and Professor Robert Triffin, the Yale University economist, has noted the incongruity. Said he in one much-quoted remark: "Nobody could ever have conceived of a more absurd waste of human resources than to dig gold in distant corners of the earth for the sole purpose of transporting it and reburying it immediately afterward in other deep holes, especially excavated to receive it, and heavily guarded to protect it."

South Africa's Holloway has an answer to such charges that gold is a "useless metal." He cites the example of Thomas Edison and his experiments with electricity and a vacuum. Nothing, of course, seems more useless than a vacuum, something described by Webster as "a space entirely devoid of matter." Edison found a use for it. After repeated failures at turning electricity into light, he had an inspiration. He put an electrically resistant material into a vacuum and then sent a current through the medium. The light bulb was created.

"People who describe gold as 'this useless metal' should ponder on the parallel between a 'useless vacuum' and so-called 'useless' gold.

The very scarcity of an article frequently gives it an essentiality in the grand design of the universe," says Holloway.

If the antigold clan sometimes views gold almost with vindictiveness, the chrysophilites also sometimes minimize the faults of the gold standard. That standard certainly stabilized exchange rates. It definitely did not stabilize the economic level within a country. Booms and busts sometimes seemed to characterize the system, with millions of people out of work during busts. With the gold standard, money sometimes seems to be more important than human beings.

Antigold folk press such arguments home, as if only they ever have humane sentiments. One of the standard ways of bolstering a thin argument is to ridicule your opponent, and this is especially true if you can maneuver him into defending property while you seem to be unselfishly defending the human rights of all mankind.

The deeper one gets into monetary matters, the more one realizes that the whole argument about gold's monetary role, or its inability to perform it, involves fundamental emotional attitudes toward man and his relationship to his environment.

Not only technical monetary systems are at odds when chrysophilites and chrysophobes argue money. This is cash versus credit. Sound versus easy money. A balanced federal budget versus deficit spending. Rugged free-enterprise versus government economic management. A black-and-gray world meeting utopia. The belief in sinful man meeting the conviction that man is essentially good. The idea that progress comes only through individual gain clashing with the contention that communal efforts spell forward movement. The good guys encountering the bad guys, with each side robing itself in sanctity while professing to see the devil opposite.

Neither side, of course, has angels for companions, because angels have sense enough to avoid the petty quarrels of man. But when sense and nonsense are being evaluated the chrysophobes must explain how come they erred so much in the 1960's when they were denigrating gold and claiming that it was on the way out.

It was in the 1960's and early 1970's that the great monetary battles involving gold and the dollar were fought, with few people in the United States realizing what was happening even after the dollar experienced two devaluations. Briefly, the dollar, which had been "as good as gold" for so long, no longer was as good as a thirty-fifth of an ounce of gold. And many people were discovering this fact.

These people were termed "speculators" through the monetary

cyclones which erupted. Actually, they were ordinary businessmen, bankers and others who had sense enough to protect their assets. In politics, whenever anyone disrupts a pet project of the party in power, it is customary to tack some derogatory term onto the disrupt- ers. The word "speculator" has enough of an unsavory connotation that it appealed to those people in government who saw themselves as "defenders of the dollar," though they couldn't see the easiest method of preserving the whole system—a doubling of the monetary price of gold.

This would have been enough in the 1960's, and perhaps even as late as 1971. Today, the free price has escaped from control of the politicians, and now a much higher price than $70 an ounce would be needed to stabilize gold. When it might have done something about gold, the United States took a stubborn, one can almost say fanatical, position.

Starting right after that particular 1960 flurry of gold demand, the United States sought central banker help to imprison gold at its $35 price. The London Gold Pool was formed to control the gold market, with the Bank of England acting as agent for nations belonging to the pool. American monetary authorities and six European central banks agreed to intervene in the gold market if necessary. If the price started to rise above $35 an ounce, the pool would release gold from their hoards onto the market, driving the price down. Gold held by these nations seemed to be so substantial, about $30 billion worth of the $40 billion in the whole monetary system, that no number of so-called speculators could ever hope to bid up the gold price against such competition. In effect, the situation was like having a millionaire as a participant in a no-limit poker game when the rest of the players share about $20. Nobody could outbid the rich man for any pot, and he would win every hand.

America seemed to be in just that position vis-a-vis gold at that time, or so it seemed to U.S. authorities. America won support of central bankers by implying that it might cut spending to stem the dollar drain. Indeed it did adopt a variety of remedies aimed at choking the outflow, none of which worked, though they did delay the final reckoning.

Cutting spending to end the dollar drain proved impossible. Every politician in Washington is solidly for economy as long as his own pet projects are exempt. In the twenty-five years after World War II, the United States granted, loaned, or advanced to other nations (for nonmilitary purposes) over $105 billion. The Cuban Missile Crisis of 1962 unleashed an arms race which hiked military spending abroad. The Vietnam War bled the country of money and men through more than a decade, and the United States seemed destined to play police-man abroad at a cost of its gold reserves. American tourists insisted on their right to travel (and spend) abroad as they saw fit. U.S. corporations poured billions into plants and facilities in other lands.

And throughout this period, the United States scrupulously adhered to the idea that deficit spending was necessary to stimulate business whenever recessions threatened. The trouble is that some segment of the population always believes a recession is developing, so deficits which might be acceptable periodically become a permanent way of life, as pervasive in their own way as is the miser's inability to spend anything at all. The difference is that the miser may be hurting only himself, whereas deficit spending may hurt everybody through inflation.

The United States gold hoard dwindled from $17.8 billion in 1960 to $16.1 billion in 1962, to $14.1 billion in 1965, and to $11.1 billion in 1970. Put in another way, that U.S. gold hoard, which had amounted to more than 21,775 metric tons in 1949, had fallen to 9,839 metric tons in 1970. (In 1973, it was down to 8,580 tons.)

As the gold supply dwindled, the United States desperately tried those remedies which often were aimed more at the symptoms than at the disease. A system of currency-swap arrangements was established whereby major western nations would hold each others currencies when necessary, to bolster a weak currency. In the 1960's, this meant the U.S. dollar and the British pound. Foreign central banks were encouraged to hold U.S. dollar–bonds rather than have them cash those dollars for gold. Restraints were placed on American investments abroad.

Nothing seemed to help. And confidence in the dollar dwindled when foreign dollar-holders began to realize that it no longer was easy to change a dollar for a thirty-fifth of an ounce of gold. But it was the British pound sterling, suffering also, which cracked first.

On November 19, 1967, the pound was devalued by 14.3 percent, from $2.80 to $2.40. Next to the dollar, the pound was regarded as a second reserve currency, one of the pillars of the whole monetary system established in 1944 at Bretton Woods. Its devaluation shook confidence around the world.

Many foreigners almost instinctively did what they always do in time of monetary crisis. They hurriedly sought to transfer some of their funds from money into gold, and a huge gold-buying wave swept over the gold markets in Zurich and in London. Until that time, the latter market had been the most important of the two. In London, the Bank of England began to pour gold from the Central Bankers Gold Pool into the market.

This tested that American belief that no amount of speculation could break the gold pool which the central bankers and the Federal Reserve Bank of New York had established. America was in a precarious position for the test. By that time, the United States had over $30 billion in foreign obligations abroad due to its heavy overseas spending. Yet gold reserves were less than half that figure.

If every foreign holder of dollars had appeared to claim a thirty-fifth of an ounce of gold for each dollar, there wouldn't have been enough gold at Fort Knox and in the Federal Reserve Bank of New York to maintain the promise that the dollar was "as good as gold." In effect, the United States would have been like some of those Depression Era banks which ran out of cash in 1933 when depositors clamored for their money. Speculators realized that too, and those who were holding dollars figured that they had better transfer those dollars into gold. Since the holders realized they wouldn't get the gold from the United States, they went directly to the gold market to purchase it.

Nicolaas Diederichs, South Africa's minister of finance, was emphatically condemning central-bank attempts to downplay gold. Said he: "Nothing which seeks to discredit gold or to reduce its role as the ultimate unconditionally accepted means of payment can possibly add to confidence and monetary stability." Such advice was ignored in Washington, where Diederichs was regarded as a man perennially grinding his own golden axe. Others listened to him.

Buy-orders poured into the London Gold Market, from Hong Kong, Dubai, Beirut, Zurich, Geneva, Singapore, from everywhere that people were allowed by governments to hold gold. Working through the Bank of England, the Central Bank Gold Pool fed more gold into the market, and more, and more. Where it once had been a good week when eighteen tons of gold were traded on the London Gold Market, orders now reached the point where that much was being traded in a day.

The United States had to contribute the bulk of the gold fed to the market. Market forces proved superior to central banks, an example of how futile it sometimes is for governments to oppose market supply-demand pulls. On March 14, world monetary authorities dissolved the gold pool. There were to be two gold markets, a monetary one with the fixed price of $35 an ounce, and a free market where supply and demand would set the price.

By that time the pool had poured over twenty-five hundred tons of gold worth nearly $3 billion (at $35 an ounce) into the market without being able to satisfy the buying pressure.

The London Gold Market remained closed the rest of the month, stunned by the strength of the gold speculators and hoarders. In Zurich, the Big Three banks recognized an opportunity. Quickly, they formed a gold pool of their own to service the demand, established a source of supply from South Africa and opened for business the following Monday. Bankers set a free-market price in the $43- to $45-an-ounce range, confident that the free-market price would remain above the $35 monetary price. They were right. And their confidence in the market allowed Zurich to seize leadership of gold-marketing. Today, it is Zurich, not London, which calls the shots in gold-merchandising.

As for the American dollar? Events proved that its value had deteriorated, with various monetary gimmicks only delaying its ultimate devaluation in relationship to gold. In Paris, Jacques Rueff, the financial *éminence grise* of General de Gaulle's government, would say: "I told you so." For years he had led an ever-growing claque which insisted that America's monetary policies "could destroy civilization" unless the United States recognized that gold's monetary price must be raised.

I first met M. Rueff in 1969 at his Paris town house on the Left Bank, not far from Les Invalides, to ascertain his views. Alfred Malabre, economic reporter with the *Wall Street Journal*, was along, both of us primed to throw questions at this doyen of a monetary policy which is diametrically opposite to that followed by the United States in the postwar period.

"Every year since 1961, the United States has declared that its deficit was under control and would disappear next year. It hasn't happened," said Rueff after he had led us into his spacious, high-ceilinged living room. The house with its books and works of art had an atmosphere of gracious living, as if it could have fitted just as easily into the eighteenth or nineteenth century, as the twentieth. A garden added a touch of green outside the windows.

Jacques Rueff, a balding man with a fringe of gray around the edges of his head, has the courtly gallantry that you might expect from a member of the French Academy, which he is. He speaks in a firm but thoughtful manner, as if his mind may be racing ahead of his voice.

"The solution? I have been saying for years that a doubling of the price of gold would solve many things," he said.

"Wouldn't that be inflationary?" I asked.

He waved a hand, impatiently. "We already are experiencing inflation with the creation of excess liquidity by the dollar."

During the interview, he took special pains to deride the Special Drawing Rights, or SDR's which were being developed by the International Monetary Fund. These units, sometimes known as "paper gold," are a device for increasing world liquidity. They are accounting units distributed by IMF, in accordance with a nation's reserves, to serve as a means of payment in settling international accounts. The hope is that ultimately these units, or something like them, might replace gold in the monetary sphere, though this hope is by no means universal.

"All past experience, as well as the plainest of common sense, shows that if the paper-gold solution is applied over a period of years, it will lead to general nonconvertibility of currencies, and this could result in inflation, foreign-exchange controls, rationing of imports, and all kinds of economic controls," Rueff warned.

Nobody in Washington paid much attention to what Jacques Rueff had to say. The problems of the dollar increased. In mid-1971, the United States reported a whopping annual deficit of $23.2 billion. For the first time since 1893, imports were outrunning exports. Gold reserves on August 1, 1971, were down to $10 billion, while foreign claims against the dollar had surpassed $48 billion.

On August 15, President Nixon severed the link between gold and the dollar, announced a ten percent import surcharge, cut government spending, and froze wages, prices, and dividends. It was only the first step in a relentless diplomatic march to a momentous monetary conference at the Smithsonian Institution's red-brick building in Washington on December 17 and 18, 1971. The American dollar was devalued for the first time since January, 1934, with the price of gold raised from $35 to $38 an ounce, or 8.57 percent. Other major currencies also were revalued in relationship to the dollar. But the free-market price of gold valued the dollar even less than that figure.

The price consistently held above $42 an ounce, indicating that the market thought that monetary authorities had not gone far enough with the gold hike.

The market was right, as subsequent events proved. By the end of January, the free price was $47 an ounce. At the beginning of May, 1972, it broke the $50 mark, hitting $67 in June, and $70.50 in August.

This was only the prelude for another monetary crisis in late January and early February, 1973, which led to another dollar devaluation, one of ten percent, on February 12. As for gold? In late Spring, 1973, it soared to a record $127-an-ounce price, far above the $42.22 monetary level which had been established with that ten percent dollar devaluation. In early 1974, gold hit $180 an ounce, rising by the year's end to a peak $198 an ounce.

Officially, America had severed that link between its dollar and gold. But gold stubbornly remained the haven to which speculators rushed every time the dollar appeared to weaken. While events indicated that America had failed miserably in trying to hold down the price of gold, the United States does have far more power than any other nation on earth to move gold in the other direction, upward. Americans may know less about gold as a monetary tool than do most peoples of the world, yet they purchase more of it than any other nation.

# CHAPTER XIV

# Americans and Gold

A tousle-haired youth in dungarees cut at the knees bent over the swift-running waters of a creek in California's mother-lode country. His eyes fixed intently on the pan which he rocked back and forth in his hands, allowing some of the water, sand, and gravel to escape over the edge from his miniature whirlpool. The breeze from the mountains in the background stirred the pine branches on forested ridges and brought with it some of the chill of snow that clung to peaks.

The youth stopped his panning, studied the muck on the pan's bottom. There was a pale-yellow glitter in the remaining sands, as if perhaps . . .

He shook his head. "Naw. That's iron pyrites. Fool's gold." With a sigh he dumped the contents of the pan into the creek, then defensively said: "There's gold still around, though. A fellow last week found a nugget as big as your little finger nail. Must have been worth forty dollars, just like that."

The prospector was an English major at the University of California at Berkeley who was spending his vacation panning for gold. Like thousands of other Americans he had been attracted by the lure of gold and the soaring price for it. In 1973 the free-gold price had reached a peak of $127 an ounce, more than three-and-a-half times the price which had been set by Franklin Delano Roosevelt in 1934. Later it was to hit $198 an ounce. A new gold rush was on.

In 1973 and 1974 requests for information about gold mining were running at about a hundred and twenty a month versus only ten a month a year earlier, according to the San Francisco office of the California Division of Mines. One Sacramento store was selling five hundred pans a week for panning gold. The grapevine crackled with the tale of the prospector who had found $200,000 worth of gold in six weeks. Once again El Dorado beckoned many Americans, just as it had in 1849.

Yet few Americans had ever held a gold bar or a nugget in their hands. They have been so brainwashed by the antigold forces in government that they meekly accepted federal policing of gold as part of the system, as if possession not only were illegal but sinful as well.

When Americans think of gold they are apt to conjure pictures of the California Gold Rush of 1849, that first great rush when the ordinary citizen had a chance to stake his own personal El Dorado. But gold was on many minds in America long before that. The first settlers in Virginia really had hopes of striking gold or they probably would not have migrated so far from early seventeenth-century England. Spain had found its El Dorado in Mexico, Colombia, Ecuador, and Peru. So why shouldn't those rich gold fields extend northward into what was to become Virginia?

And those first settlers thought they had discovered just such a field when they found glimmering yellow particles in the creeks of Virginia. Diligently they panned the streams, filled empty powder kegs with gleaming dust, and mentally spent their profits as they worked. It was only when a report came back from metallurgists in England that settlers realized they had collected fool's gold or iron pyrites. Then they turned to tobacco growing and found the golden weed to be much more profitable, than the metal in the brooks.

Gold was discovered in the Carolinas and in Georgia. A mini–gold rush developed in Georgia in the 1830's, and the United States government established a mint at Dahlonega in 1838 to mint coins from the yellow metal. But all the gold found in America prior to 1849 couldn't fill one Spanish caravel. California opened America's golden age.

It was a rainy day in January, 1848, when America's real gold story started. Moisture dripped from pines, and every bush yielded a shower on contact on that day when John Augustus Sutter answered a knock at his rough-hewn door. He was a wealthy Swiss farmer who had migrated to Mexican-controlled California, obtained a huge land grant, and built a feudal agricultural empire. Now he was erecting a small sawmill on the American River, about forty miles from Sacramento, near the site of present day Coloma. James W. Marshall, a New Jersey carpenter, worked as his foreman.

At that time, California had a population of about eighteen-thousand and was in the process of being absorbed into the United States of America through the Treaty of Hidalgo, which was to be signed the next month. Now Sutter opened the door, and saw Marshall standing on the doorstep, rain dripping from his hat.

Surprised, Sutter motioned him inside. Marshall had been down to the post only a few days earlier and wasn't expected to return so soon.

"What brings you here?" Sutter asked, or words to that effect. From all accounts, he usually got to the point quickly for he was a man of authority who could make his own decisions on the spot.

Marshall fidgeted, seemed unsure of himself. "I'd like to see you," he said, softly. He glanced anxiously in the direction of the clerk at the other end of the room, who didn't seem to be paying much attention to either of them. Then he took off his wet coat, hung it on a peg near the door.

"All right. So here I am," said Sutter.

"No. I mean alone. Some place where we can talk."

"Come along." Sutter led the way into one of the rooms used for his living quarters, and shut the door. There weren't many secrets in a small community such as this one at New Helvetia, where everybody knew everyone else for miles, and being inquisitive seemed to be a natural way to spend any idle time.

"Lock the door," Marshall said, emphatically. He reached for something in his pocket, seemed to hesitate.

Sutter glanced sharply at his companion, somewhat uneasy at all this secrecy. "I think you need a drink," said he. "Wait a minute."

He stepped into the anteroom, fumbled in a cupboard, found a bottle, and rejoined Marshall. Inside, he forgot to lock the door as directed. Marshall, eyes intent on the bottle and on the drink which flowed from it, also forgot about that door. Eagerly, he took the glass, downed the fiery whiskey in a gulp, and uttered a grunt of satisfaction.

Now relaxed, he reached into his pocket again. "I want you to look at this," he said. He opened a handkerchief in his hand, revealing several glittering yellow particles in a corner of it. One was the size of a pea.

"What is it?"

"I think I have discovered gold," said Marshall.

"Are you sure?"

Marshall nodded. He took the pea-sized nugget between his calloused fingers, held it up. "I pounded this nugget with a hammer," he said. "It's soft and malleable."

"Just like gold."

"Yes. Because it is gold," said Marshall. He held the small nugget up to the little light which drifted into the room on this drizzling day. That glitter was unmistakable.

At that moment, the door opened and the clerk stuck his head in the door. His eyes widened. The expression on his face suggested that he might have heard that last word "gold." Now he mumbled something about being away from his desk for a little while, then reclosed the door.

"Damn," Marshall said. "We must keep this a secret until we can figure out what to do."

"Yes." Sutter nodded, disturbed at what he had seen. He already was the baron of this whole valley, with several hundred men working for him at harvest time. He didn't need gold to advance his fortune, for he already had nearly everything he wanted. No telling what gold would do to the country when the secret got out, as it eventually would.

The secret already was out, and Sutter lived to regret the fact that he had not locked the door for that private tête-à-tête with Marshall. Within days the word reached San Francisco, then a sleepy port on the Pacific which was popular with whaling-ship crews. Within a week, people all up and down central California were excitedly talking about the discovery, then heading for the American River to strike it rich. Gold-seekers were to dig up Sutter's land, slaughter his cattle, cut down his timber for sluices and firewood, and bring him ruin. About the only thing he got from that gold rush was a ring he made with that first gold, one which was inscribed with the words "The first gold discovered in January, 1848."

That discovery started one of the greatest mass movements of people in history. In San Francisco, Monterey, San Jose, Santa Cruz, and other communities the blacksmith dropped his hammer, the carpenter abandoned his saw, the baker his ovens, the farmer his sickle. Nearly every man who could walk quit his job and headed for the gold country. Soldiers deserted and so did the squads dispatched to arrest them. Incoming ships dropped anchor, then lost entire crews when sailors heard the news. Gold! Lying in nuggets on riverbeds of streams. Anybody's, for the effort of stooping down.

A letter in Washington archives from a Thomas O. Larkin to the secretary of state, James Buchanan, provides an insight into the spirit of the times in the California of 1848. Larkin wrote of the discovery of a "vast tract of land containing gold." Some men were getting $10 to $50 a day working streams for this gold, he said. (This was a lot of money in a time when a man might work ten hours for $1 without feeling underpaid.)

"This town of San Francisco has one half of its tenements empty, locked up with the furniture; the owners, storekeepers, lawyers, mechanics and laborers are all gone to the Sacramento with their families," wrote Larkin.

The *California,* a San Francisco newspaper, ceased publication after the entire staff departed for the gold fields. *The Star,* another publication, continued to appear in desultory fashion, only one man left on the staff to put the paper together.

News of the discovery spread throughout the nation, caught the imagination of people from Boston to the settlements of the Ohio River valley. In December, 1848, outgoing President Polk mentioned the discovery in his farewell message. Newspapers picked up the story, exaggerating it just enough to convince most citizens that fortunes lay on the ground in distant California, waiting for the intrepid to arrive to make claims.

The December 6 issue of the Hartford *Courant,* said: "The California gold fever is approaching its crisis. We are told that the new region that has just become a part of our possessions is El Dorado. . . . By a sudden and accidental discovery the ground is represented to be one vast gold mine. Gold is picked up in pure lumps, twenty-four carats fine."

On the same day, the Washington *Daily National Intelligencer,* wrote: "The accounts of the abundance of gold in that territory are of such an extraordinary character as would scarcely command belief, were they not corroborated by the authentic reports of officers in the public service."

Some men took ship to reach California by rounding the Horn. Others followed the maritime route to Panama for an arduous burro ride across the Isthmus of Panama to the Pacific and another sea journey to San Francisco. Many more whole families took the overland route in wagon trains across the plains and mountains. By 1850 the population of California totaled 92,497. A decade later the Federal Census showed a population of 379,994.

Australians, South Africans, Europeans, Chinese, all swarmed to California. There were so many Frenchmen that they formed ghettos in camps, and became known as "kesquidees," a contraction of what Frenchmen always seemed to be saying: "Qu'est-ce que vous dites?" ("What did you say?")

Boisterous shantytowns scarred the landscape, a series of clapboard shacks here, a row of canvas tents there, joined by rutted tracks which churned dust in summer, then turned into muddy morass all winter. Booted, whiskered men lined banks of streams panning for gold, shoveling gravel into crude cradles, digging into stream sides. At night the lanterns in whiskey shacks glowed until dawn. In other shacks or tents, rows of lanterns brightened card tables where many miners gambled away nuggets and dust which might have taken weeks to accumulate. Angel's Camp. Shinbone Creek. You Bet. Tin Cup Diggings. Hoodoo. Cutthroat Bars. Nigger Slide. Rough and Ready. These were only a few of the California communities which thrived for a brief time as gold fever swept the nation.

Some miners earned fortunes. At Tin Cup Diggings, miners could fill a tin cup with gold every day. At Durgan's Flat, one Frank Anderson and three companions took $12,900 from a pocket with eleven days' work.

But inflation devoured the gold almost as fast as the average miner dug it up. Bread sold for a dollar a slice in hotels. Potatoes also went for a dollar apiece. Whiskey, flour, lumber, everything sold for inflated prices. The real profits of the rush were made by gamblers and saloon keepers, and by shrewd merchants who had capital for inventories which could be sold in gold camps at ten times purchase costs. In Placerville, Philip D. Armour profited enough from a small butcher shop to launch a meat-packing empire. John Studebaker started as a wheelbarrow maker, built an industrial complex, and laid the foundation for an auto company.

Most gold-seekers never did find their El Dorado. They returned to distant homes with glowing adventure tales only. These, with the stories of Bret Harte and Mark Twain, grew into a mythology of the Days of Forty-Nine.

Pieter Jacob Marais, a Cape Towner, joined the Rush at twenty-three, returned to his homeland to become its first gold prospector. Edward Hammon Hargraves, a brash, loud Australian, likewise returned to his native clime after a futile attempt to find fortune in California. He launched the Australian Gold Rush of 1850.

Perhaps to cover his own failure in California, Hargraves boldly declared that he would find gold in Australia in a week. The terrain of Australia was very much like the rock structure of California, he said. So the gold was just lying there in the wilderness waiting to be found.

It was. Within a week of his return from California he discovered gold on a tributary of the Macquarie River not far from Bathurst in New South Wales.

At the time that gold was discovered in California, Russia was the world's leading producer thanks to discoveries in 1774 at Ekaterin-burg (Sverdlovsk) in the Urals and others later in Siberia. In 1848, California produced $250,000 worth of gold; the next year the total jumped to $10 million. In 1852, production jumped to $81 million, and California led the world in output. Soon it was joined by other west-ern states, giving America a gold-production leadership which lasted until the 1890's, when South Africa emerged as the number one producer. California's peak production by weight was about 3.2 mil-lion fine ounces in 1853, about half of the total world output.

America's peak gold production was in 1915 when 4,897,000 fine ounces were produced. Even then South Africa was producing nearly twice as much.

In the United States, gold circulated freely in double eagles ($20 pieces), eagles ($10), and half eagles ($5). In 1873, those coins were minted at the Philadelphia, San Francisco, and Carson City mints of the United States Bureau of the Mint. The Mint was established in 1792 as an arm of government; but it wasn't until 1873 that it became a bureau of the U.S. Treasury.

Gold production and distribution was not controlled in those days of laissez-faire capitalism, a factor which generated one of the most unscrupulous and audacious financial undertakings in United States history, the attempt by the unprincipled Jay Gould to corner the gold market.

In the Civil War era and immediately after, there were few laws affecting free enterprise in the United States. Every man felt he had a right to enlarge his capital, though, unfortunately there wasn't enough of it to reach more than a very few hands. The man with ethics was apt to be someone who didn't possess enough to provide temptation. Gould was just as unscrupulous when he didn't have any money as he was with it. In fact, his youthful deprivations made him even more determined to succeed, which to him meant getting money by any means.

A fortunate marriage helped give him a stake in a small railroad, and he managed that so well that he could sell at a profit. But honest toil bored him. With his capital, he wrangled his way onto the board of the Erie Railroad. There he found a partner of like temperament, Jim Fisk, a financier who felt that the world owed him a living, at $100,000 a year. Together they found it easy to print stock shares to enlarge the Railroad's capital structure. Funds went into the pockets of Gould and his clique. Gould, a prudent man where the law was concerned, bought off the right judges and civic authorities in the graft-ridden New York City of Boss Tweed, thus covering his rear and flanks as he planned his biggest frontal attack, the move to corner gold.

The Gold Board, established on Beaver Street in 1864, then was the largest gold-trading market in the United States. It had a function to perform. During the Civil War, the Union had issued about $400 million worth of "greenbacks," which weren't backed by anything except the government's promise to pay off, eventually. Their value fluctuated against gold, according to the fortunes of the government.

In early 1869, Gould noted that about $20 million-worth of gold comprised the total volume then available to the market. Meanwhile, the government had $75 to $100 million worth of gold in its treasury. If the government could be induced to cling to its gold, a sharp trader might be able to corner that $20 million-worth of gold. Then, he could sell it back to speculators at his own price, always provided, of course, that the government didn't release some of its gold to break the corner.

The more Gould considered this scenario, the more intrigued he became. And in his typical freebooter style, he didn't organize his campaign at a low level. He aimed to enlist none other than the president of the United States, Ulysses Grant, as his ally, though not necessarily as a coconspirator. President Grant, a hard-bitten military man with an acute taste for strong drink, was a naive gentleman who believed well of his fellowmen until events proved otherwise.

Gould had a contact, a lawyer named Abel Rathbone Corbin, who had married President Grant's sister. Corbin seemed enthusiastic about the idea, especially after Gould purchased $1.5 million-worth of gold to Corbin's account, with profits accruing to Corbin. If the price went up, Corbin stood to gain those profits. If the price fell, he lost nothing. And Gould intended to force that price upward, so he didn't figure he would lose any of that $1.5 million, either.

Through Corbin, Gould met Grant, seemed to get along well with him. Jim Fisk's private box at a theatre provided entertainment for the President and Gould. There was a pleasant trip aboard a yacht, with Gould spending most of the time talking about how important it was to the country for gold's price to rise. Gould played the part of a successful financier interested only in maintaining prosperity in the country. This was a goal above criticism, and Grant listened.

Gould had thought of all angles. He hired a noted British economist for what, today, would be called a public-relations job. The economist, who really did believe that gold should be higher priced, wrote some penetrating articles stating why America might benefit from such a development. Articles were passed along to important newspapers and magazines, which published them without question.

As the plot unfolded Gould quietly began to purchase gold contracts on the market, operating alone at first. But there still were some holes to plug. He had to be sure that the government wouldn't spoil the plot by dumping gold at the crucial moment. So now he lobbied through Corbin to have a pliable General Butterfield appointed as assistant treasurer in New York City. The United States government maintained its liaison with the Gold Market through this post. The General got the job that summer of 1869, and he also had $1.5 million-worth of gold placed to his account, the same as for Corbin.

On September 2, 1869, the plot seemed to be coming to a head. Corbin told Gould about a recent conversation with President Grant. The president had been reading some of the stories about the merits of a gold-price hike. He had become convinced that Gould had the right idea, and he had followed his convictions by dispatching a letter to Secretary of the Treasury Boutwell directing that no government gold be sold without presidential authorization.

This was it. Gould plunged heavily into the gold market, began to buy, buy, and buy some more. Jim Fisk and other of his friends sensed that something big was developing. They knew Gould well enough to realize that he wouldn't be risking his money except on a sure thing. So they bought, too. The price of gold started to climb.

Gould had a source of unlimited cash for this venture, the Tenth National Bank, an institution in which he had an interest. Nobody questioned Gould as he wrote check after check for his gold purchases, far exceeding his deposits in the bank.

Now Gould overplayed his hand as he sought to make his coup even more foolproof. The president, for all his naiveté, wasn't one to be bought. But Gould offered $500,000 to the president's private secretary, a man named Porter, with the understanding that Porter would alert Gould concerning any movements of government gold which might be authorized by the president. Porter refused the bribe.

In his office in New York, Gould paced back and forth, nervously chewing on a cigar. This was bad news, indeed. He had started buying gold in June when gold contracts were priced at $130 each. Now the yellow metal was selling at $137. But a substantial short element had developed in the market. Some bankers were convinced that the price had gone too high, and they were betting that the price would drop. A short-trader, of course, makes his profit from a price drop, while a long-trader, as was Gould, benefits from the price rise. That growing volume of shorts made it difficult for the market to rise.

Gould ascertained that short-traders had sold about $50 million-worth of gold for future delivery. With the price at 137, they hoped that, when called upon to deliver, they could buy gold at 130, 125, or even less to make such deliveries. The difference between the 137 and the lower price would be profit. Gould himself had purchased about $100 million-worth of gold at the spot rate, so any climb from the 130–137 range where he had purchased would be his profit. But if gold dropped?

He shuddered at that thought. He could be wiped out. There was only $20 million of gold in the market, so all this activity was in paper, promises to deliver gold on demand or to accept it at a specific time. But the sheer volume of all those contracts hanging over the small supply meant that the market easily could take a violent swing in either direction.

If Gould could only push that price upward slightly, he might catch some of the shorts. Margins might be wiped out, and the shorts would have to purchase gold in the market to cover their contracts. Each successive purchase would help push the price upward, assuring Gould of a fantastic profit.

He briefed Jim Fisk and other cronies concerning the bare facts of the plot, without revealing the whole story. The partners had been buying gold steadily, too, and had private reasons for wanting a price rise. Gould convinced them that if Fisk led a clique to buy every gold contract in sight, the price could be forced up and up. The technical position of the market would create a bandwagon effect.

On Thursday, October 2, 1869, the plot hatched. Fisk strode onto the floor of the Gold Exchange, confidently offered to buy any gold submitted. His friends joined in, creating the impression that a buying upsurge was developing. Gould remained in the background. He had convinced his cohorts that this was for the best.

Fisk bought and bought. In the first two hours he and his group purchased $50 million in gold contracts. Excitement shot through the exchange. Something was in the wind. Traders didn't know what, but others decided to latch onto the bandwagon. They began to buy, too.

In a quiet corner of the exchange, Gould watched the denouement. But he wasn't buying anything. In fact, his agents were quietly selling, and selling. Gold's price went up, hit 145 at the close of the day. It seemed to be riding a strong upward surge. By the end of the day, the Fisk group had $100 million in contracts. Some members thought gold would hit 200 on the next day, providing staggering profits for everyone.

The Gold Market opened on Friday, October 4, 1869, a day which was to be known as Black Friday from then on. At a conference just before the opening, Fisk gave orders to buy and buy some more. Gould, who chose to listen rather than to talk, didn't offer any advice. He told no one that most of his $100 million in contracts had been dumped the previous day, with the rest scheduled to go this morning.

Once more the gold price started climbing upward under the relentless buying pressure of the Fisk group. Short-trader after short-trader was wiped out when forced to buy at 145 or 150 or 160.

Gold was going through the roof, it seemed. Thousands of small investors joined the parade, ordering brokers to buy. Brokers caught the fever, placing orders for their own accounts. Never had the gold market seen anything to match this roaring demand. Gold hit 162.

In the pandemonium, a trader suddenly shouted above the din. "The government is selling gold!"

There were a few seconds of stunned disbelief. It couldn't be true. Was it? Yes. Then, sell. Quickly the word spread. Sell. Sell. Sell. In minutes, the price dropped to 140. It closed at 135.

The day broke the Gold Exchange. Hundreds of firms and thousands of investors went bankrupt. Jim Fisk and other pals of Gould were wiped out. Gould disavowed any connection with Fisk and the others, bribing New York judges when attempts were made to squeeze some of his gold profits from him.

Gould had found his El Dorado, not in the mountains and streams of the West, but in the paper flowing through Wall Street. Today, gold distribution in the United States is so closely controlled by the government that no Jay Gould could ever again hope to corner the nation's supply.

It wasn't many years after Gould's coup that America's biggest gold mine, the Homestake, got its start, at Lead (pronounced Leed), South Dakota. The Black Hills of Dakota Territory were little more than markings on maps when General George A. Custer explored the area with a troop of cavalry in 1874. His party found traces of gold, and that was enough to attract the attention of adventurers.

By 1876 a gold rush in the Black Hills was underway. The Homestake Mining Company was incorporated in 1877 and brought into production in 1878. It was to become the central core around which America's gold-producing industry was to develop. But gold was not a monetary metal that was adopted with wild enthusiasm in America.

In the United States, the second half of the nineteenth century saw fierce battles between proponents of silver and advocates of gold. After major discoveries of silver in the western states, a formidable silver bloc developed within the Democratic Party. Every election found the party pressing for bimetallism—the use of silver as well as gold as a monetary metal.

Farmers in the Middle West and factory workers around the land didn't have enough gold to weight down pockets. They listened eagerly to the glowing oratory of the silver-bloc speakers. It is always easy to be against something, such as gold, if one doesn't have any of it.

In a ringing speech in the U.S. Senate in February, 1878, Senator John J. Ingalls advocated the coinage of silver, while attacking gold. Said he: "Gold is the money of monarchs. Kings covet it. The exchanges of the nation are affected by it. It is the instrument of the gamblers and speculators and the idol of the miser and the thief. No people in a great emergency ever found a faithful ally in gold. It is the most cowardly and treacherous of all metals. It makes no treaty that it does not break. It has no friend whom it does not sooner or later betray."

Strong words! But no stronger than those used in money speeches by William Jennings Bryan, the Democratic politician who lost an epic battle for the presidency to William McKinley in 1896. He charged that America was being "crucified on a cross of gold," a figure of speech which caught the attention of the country even if it didn't win him enough votes to move into the White House. Perhaps Bryan, more than anyone else, is responsible for the familiar characterization of the gold owner—a banker or financier with a pot belly, a perpetual cigar in his mouth, the smoke blowing into someone else's face, and an arrogant manner which becomes more insolent as the size of his gold hoard grows. In truth, the gold-owner is more apt to be a frightened free enterpriser who might have worked hard for his money, so hard that he doesn't want to see his capital devoured by a government-rooted inflation.

In 1900, gold won the political battle in the United States. America went on the gold standard to remain there until April 1933 when the depression dethroned gold, though it remained as a monetary regent if not as an emperor.

Few nations had the same traumatic experiences as did the United States when it went off the gold standard in 1933. By the tail-end of the Hoover administration it was apparent that the country was in the deepest depression of its history. Nobody knew what the incoming Roosevelt administration would do about it, and people with money began to do what they have usually done in periods of great crisis. They turned to gold, withdrawing savings from banks in the form of gold coins or bars. Other people who were not quite so astute financially merely withdrew savings. Banks folded all around the country as people scrambled to withdraw money, with few wanting to make deposits.

One of Roosevelt's first acts was to declare a bank holiday in order to sort things out. The announcement, made without warning, caught the nation by surprise, and short of money. Nonsavers always do greatly outnumber the savers, despite all the clocks, household appliances, and other gifts distributed by deposit-hungry banks. Moreover, at that time, despite the bank panics, many savers had not been fast enough on their feet to withdraw deposits ahead of the closing. So many people didn't have enough change on hand to buy a package of cigarettes. In one New England city where a newspaper made a survey, it found that the average family had $18.23 in cash on hand.

Lack of banking facilities and inability of firms to draw on bank accounts for wages meant that from March 4 to 14, 1933, America had little currency for conducting business. Stamps, phone slugs, and IOU's appeared as "currency." In Clear Lake, Iowa, nearly five hundred farmers sold 12,200 bushels of corn to the local merchants' association at 25 cents a bushel, and the association issued in payment "corn money" to the extent of approximately $3,000 in 25-cent notes. It was stipulated that all the chits had to be spent in local shops by the following night. (One note changed hands twenty-two times within three hours of issue.)

In Tenino, Washington, the local chamber of commerce issued wooden money in denominations of 25 cents, 50 cents, and $1. In all, it issued over twenty-five thousand such pieces for a total value of $6,000. When banks reopened, only $40 of this was returned for redemption, as most people kept the wooden money as souvenirs. Elated, the chamber purchased a building with its profits in order to establish—would you believe it—a bank.

In Wallowa County, Oregon, notes were issued, and stamped on bucksin in denominations of "half buck" and "one buck." In Waterloo, Iowa, the Unemployed Relief Club issued notes in terms of "hours of work." If a carpenter worked for six hours, for instance, he would be given a note good for an equivalent amount in goods, or in the services of some worker he might require, such as a plumber or mason.

This was a salutary lesson in the value of sound money, one which was to leave its impression upon many of the people who lived through the Great Depression.

Banks reopened. The United States officially dropped the gold standard in April, 1933, not daring to risk having a currency convertible into gold on demand. About that time, George F. Warren, a professor at Cornell University, was advancing the thesis that the price of gold determined commodity prices. To raise the general price level, the government needed only to hike the price of gold, he claimed.

Whether or not President Roosevelt got the idea from Professor Warren, this was a thesis which the president adopted. Like most of America's presidents, what Roosevelt knew about gold and monetary movements could have been put in a package of needles. On October 22, 1933, in a fireside chat, he made an announcement which was to have far-reaching consequences, though there is no evidence to indicate that the president realized the scope of his statement when he made it.

Speaking with a hearty ring of confidence, he said that: "I am authorizing the Reconstruction Finance Corporation to buy gold newly mined in the United States of America at prices to be determined from time to time."

The United States was setting out to control the price of gold, with deliberate intention of increasing the price above the $20.67-an-ounce level which had prevailed when Roosevelt took office. This definitely was a move into uncharted waters. The last time that anybody had tinkered with the price of gold was in 1717, when Sir Isaac Newton had studied price levels, international commodity movements, and trade factors, then had established a price of 84 shillings 11½ pence per ounce of gold. It was a price which stuck for two centuries.

But then, Newton was a mathematician who at that time happened to be Britain's Master of the Mint. He specifically sought a price which would be stable, a valuation around which other prices would fluctuate. Roosevelt was seeking to shake a great country from a depression, and he was a man of action who usually did something rather than sit on his hands whenever confronted with a difficult problem. He didn't know much about gold. So what? Raise the price. Let's see what happens. At that particular time it didn't seem as if much worse could possibly happen to stagnant America.

That he had little understanding of gold is indicated by the fact that, initially, the U.S. tried to establish the price only through purchases of domestic gold, an omission soon corrected to include all gold submitted wherever its source. But the price-settings were haphazard, made every morning in the president's bedroom in a meeting of Jesse Jones, head of the RFC, and a presidential aide, Henry Morgenthau, with the President. The only apparent consistency of policy seemed to be that the price should edge upward. Ultimately that price was pushed up to $41.34 an ounce.

But by the end of 1933 it was apparent that a stable base was needed for the currency. A different gold price every day meant that the currency valuation varied every day, and if the price were going steadily in one direction speculators would have a guaranteed profit mechanism for benefiting from the situation.

In January, 1934, President Roosevelt announced that the price of gold would be frozen at $35 an ounce. It was an act which stimulated gold production around the world. In 1929, the total annual output of gold had been 19,673,000 fine ounces. In 1936, after the increase in price had stimulated production, it was 35,254,000 fine ounces.

America's best gold production year was in 1915, when mines produced 4,897,000 ounces (152.3 metric tons), a figure that still was only about fifteen percent of South Africa's peak production. Moreover, United States output has declined drastically from that 1915 record, down to less than a third of that level.

Today America is the world's largest consumer of gold, accounting for around two hundred twenty-five tons of the metal annually for industrial use alone. This covers everything from dental fillings to electronic contracts and from jewelry to building-reflectors.

The world industrial demand showed a marked rise during the affluent 1960's, for with a frozen price of $35 an ounce gold in any form represented a bargain for buyers. When Charter Consolidated, Limited, and Consolidated Gold Fields, Limited, the two London-based mining companies, made their epic studies of gold merchandising and use, that zooming industrial demand was spotlighted. Studies showed that this particular area of demand was rising so fast that in the early 1970's it would take all the new gold produced in the world. The soaring gold price cut that demand in 1974, especially for jewelry. But coin minting more than took up all the slack.

For the goldbugs this was a confirmation of their most optimistic dreams, for it not only told them that they were right, it promised a financial reward for their sagacity. Almost anyone can be right some of the time. Not everybody is paid for being right.

On Friday, February 8, 1974, the *Wall Street Journal* carried a front-page story about goldbugs which must have been as welcome as a tax refund. The story said:

> New York—The "gold bugs" are flying high. Once pesky pariahs on Wall Street for their stubborn insistence that gold rather than cash or the stock market is the only source of true wealth, the gold fanciers suddenly have become respectable. Says Harry Schultz, publisher of a London-based newsletter on gold: "No more are we nut-cases, kooks, antediluvians, weirdoes, crackpots and dreamers."
>
> While all currencies and most securities have taken a drubbing in the past few years, gold and gold-mining stocks have rocketed in price. Now just about everybody seems to be scurrying to get a piece of the action.

Long before this, however, industrial users of gold had learned to appreciate the yellow metal. That relatively cheap price of $35 an ounce which had pertained for nearly forty years had stimulated usage of gold in many ways. With the expansion of electronics and space technology, gold found exotic uses. The metal is such a marvelous reflector that gold-plated spacesuits became the accepted thing. Rocket engines were given gold-coated shields, with only 0.000004 of an inch of the metal helping to protect spacemen from the tremendous heat. And thousands of other uses were found in industry for this versatile metal.

It is gold's characteristics which make it so valuable in industry. The metal is corrosion-resistant. It blocks ninety-eight percent of incident light and other radiation. It has low specific heat. It has excellent electrical-conducting characteristics. And it is an easily workable metal which may be shaped into microscopic thicknesses. Thus, an ultrathin sheet over base metal may do the same job as might a solid-gold component, yet that gold sheet may cost only a comparatively small amount.

The telephone industry is one of the key users of noble metals. Tiny palladium contact points coated with gold often are found in electro-mechanical switchgear. Gold is utilized in the transmitter domes of telephones and for plating transmitter electrodes. Printed circuits for radar, computers, and detection devices sometimes employ gold.

Gold brazing alloys are finding increasing applications in missiles and aircraft. Certain alloys in these fields provide a good resistance to oxidation, and also provide good strength characteristics.

The building and construction industry has found that gold may be used effectively as a building sheath and as a glass facing. Perhaps you may have noticed that some of the new high-rise office buildings have windows that have brown-tinted glass. That tint may be due to an ultrathin layer of gold deposited on the glass through a thermal evaporation process. Vaporized gold is allowed to condense on the surface of the glass being treated. The resulting film is exceedingly fine and even. Varying degrees of transparency and reflectivity can be obtained by carefully regulating the amount of gold actually applied.

The glass appears golden brown from the outside and a gentle blue-green from the inside. The coating cuts down the glare and transmitted heat of the sun by a considerable extent, yet does not reduce the light appreciably. Air-conditioning bills may be reduced in hot weather, an important point in this age of high-cost electricity.

Gold-coated plastic ceiling-lenses channel the light into the elevators of Standard Oil Company of Indiana's new eighty-story headquarters in Chicago. Gold Key Drive-Ins in the United States have gold-shingled roofs which glitter brilliantly in sunshine like the palace of Kubla Khan.

Gold may even be used to face sides of buildings. Gold spandrelite, manufactured by Pittsburgh Plate Glass Company, was installed initially on the Provident Mutual Society Building in Sydney, Australia. Twenty-two-carat gold was applied in a very thin coating to glass, providing the twenty-eight story building with a facing which will never fade.

Such applications may seem very expensive. This isn't necessarily so, for the gold sheaths are of microscopic thicknesses, and a little gold goes a long way. Those shingles on Golden Key Drive-Ins, for example, are of porcelain with a twenty-three-carat-gold coating which is only five-millionth-of-an-inch thick.

Industrial uses for gold are almost endless, as new uses are found for it every year. In 1972, sixty-eight tons of gold went into electronics, space, and defense areas alone in the United States. Another twenty-three tons of gold found places in the mouths of America in the form of gold dental work. Still, jewelry accounts for three-fourths of the yellow metal going into industrial usage, and this corner of industry has been experiencing traumas since the price of gold soared above $100 an ounce then kept climbing.

The Homestake Mine in South Dakota still is a key producer, the country's biggest gold-mining concern, nearly a century after the mine started operations. From its two hundred miles of workings on thirty-four levels about four hundred thousand ounces of gold still are recovered annually.

One might think that the new gold rush into America's golden west would be stimulating a massive upsurge in gold production in this country. This is not so. Established mines are dropping the grade of ore which is brought to the surface, and new mines require a long lead-time before going into production. Higher prices, of course, make it economic for operating mines to handle lower grades of ore which otherwise might have been by-passed. This reduces the gold output but increases ore reserves and so lengthens the lives of mines. And profits may rise because of the better prices.

"I doubt if there will be any significant increase in U.S. gold production over the next several years," says R. J. Stoehr, vice-president of Homestake Mining Company.

Kennecott Copper Company, which produces its gold as a by-product, Newmont Mining Company, and Placer Development, Limited, are other U.S. gold producers of importance. In addition, a couple-of-hundred small companies contribute their bits to the over-all production total, along with thousands of weekend placer miners who live on hope rather than on their output.

So America consumes five times more gold than it produces, depending upon imports, chiefly from South Africa, to fill the gap. That consumption, should rise considerably now that the United States government allows its citizens to hold gold. Even without this support of Americans, demand for gold is at record levels, much to the discomfiture of the chrysophobes who have been saying for years that gold is being phased out of the monetary system.

# CHAPTER XV

# Golden Twilight

On January 2, 1974, gold traders in London returned to their offices after the first New Years to be celebrated in Britain as an official holiday. Britain was facing a three-day workweek because of a slow-down of coal miners. But there wasn't going to be a three-day work-week in the gold market this week, nor for weeks to come.

Buy-orders already cluttered telex machines. The London Market price that day jumped by $5.75 an ounce to $117.50, a sizeable hike when one remembers that the price already had climbed from $65 at the end of 1972 to $111.75 an ounce at the end of 1973. The 1974 start seemed to stimulate more buying. Orders poured in from Switzerland, from industrial users in Britain, from Germany, from Dubai. And in Zurich, where far more of the world's new gold is traded, the activity was just as intense. Everybody wanted to buy. Nobody except the dealers wanted to sell.

Even more hectic trading developed on the London Stock Ex-change and on the Johannesburg Stock Exchange, the world's two key markets for gold-mining shares. Investors around the world seemed to be discovering that gold shares existed and that a soaring gold price meant superprosperity for mines. American industrial shares were languishing as investors feared a recession and possible ill-effects of an oil shortage upon the United States economy. Every-where, inflation eroded currency-values and investors were search-ing desperately for investments which might insure the preservation of capital and perhaps some appreciation. Gold and gold-mining shares seemed to be just the thing for the turbulent times.

The *Financial Times of London* gold-share index had ended 1973 at 207.1, representing more than a doubling of the gold-share average since the end of 1972, when the index had been 95.3. In that first trading day of the new year, the index soared by 14.5 percentage points to 221.6, the biggest one-day rise ever noted in gold-mining shares. By April 3, the index had hit 424.3 while the free-market price of gold hit $180, five times the $35-an-ounce price which the United States had maintained for so long.

Belatedly, American investors were discovering gold shares, too, and were tapping the profits. Fortunes were made overnight, while goldbugs who already had made fortunes with long-held gold-mining shares saw their wealth double again. Few things are as difficult to surrender as is the handle of a slot machine when it is steadily spewing jackpots.

Dramatically, the laws of supply and demand in free markets were showing that gold is far from the dead metal that antigold fanatics claim when they seek to eliminate it from the monetary scene. Six-thousand-year-old instincts in human beings say otherwise. Gold is forever in the minds of many people, one of the few things which holds value in an inflationary age, for you might claim that a gold price rise isn't so much a case of the value of the yellow metal going upward as it is a case of money values falling when compared to stable gold. A gold price of $180 an ounce merely means that it takes $180 to purchase what was worth $35 a few years ago. So your dollar of today is worth only 19 cents when measured against its gold worth of a few years ago. This is what the politicians in Washington have been doing to your dollar.

It was no coincidence that—as the rush to gold and gold shares exploded—two-figure rates of inflation were being noted in the United States, in Britain, in Japan, and in other nations of the world. Everywhere paper currencies seemed to be eroding. Even such stalwart currencies as the Swiss franc and the West German mark declined in value when measured against gold. This was the real reason why gold was becoming so popular.

Some people may like gold because of its glister, its beauty when in a jewel. Others, however, may regard it as an extremely useful monetary metal, one which retains its value no matter what happens to paper currencies. This is something which monetary authorities should recognize. It is about time that international money-men took another look at gold and the place it might play in bringing about monetary stability, instead of ridiculing it and its adherents at every opportunity. It may sound sophisticated for the managed-currency advocate to ridicule the goldbug, for it is far easier to belittle anyone who doesn't agree with the philosophies of easy credit for solving the world's financial problems than it is to make those cheap-money policies work.

When you are noting those high inflationary rates now being experienced, please heed also that it is the antigold forces which have been at the economic controls of nations for the past couple of decades. Gold certainly is not a universal panacea for mankind. But all the dire things of which its opponents accuse gold couldn't be much worse than what they have produced, as they sat beside their computers, controlling the world's economies. High prices. Stagflation. Declining standards of living.

No wonder that there is a rush to gold. The more pessimistic of the goldbugs really do believe that the world is heading for a gigantic crash. They see violence in the streets and a depression which will curl your hair (note that they say "your" hair, for they think they have found their escape in gold).

Hopefully, things won't be that bad. But there is no doubt that the necessity for a sounder currency is acute. People wouldn't be rushing into gold if the dollar were "as good as gold."

People, today, are not only crying for sound money, they are shouting from rooftops for it. The politicians, bureaucrats, and statesmen of this world should heed this rush into gold and should be trying to interpret it insofar as their own skins are concerned. They are to blame for the present state of world currencies, and voters have been making them responsible, too. In America, housewives have staged strikes against high food-costs by shifting to lower-quality items, by skipping meat, and by working harder in the kitchen to reduce home-maintenance bills.

Thus, the goldbug and the housewife now are on the same side of the fence, both passionately wanting sound money to supplant the paper script which floats ethereally from the currency printing presses on both sides of the Atlantic. And they want it badly enough to replace the inept politicians and bureaucrats who have been so interested in pumping paper currency into systems that they don't even seem to hear what people are saying.

Perhaps the world may move ultimately onto a plateau of cooperation, where international economic management becomes possible and where the SDR outmodes gold. It should be evident by now, however, that an interim period of adjustment may be necessary before we reach this monetary utopia, even if one is really convinced that we are headed in that direction. During this period, which might last ten or twenty years, gold could play a very important role in restoring the faith of men in paper currencies, provided that some attempt were made to make those currencies "as good as gold."

At what price? A completely free market might help to determine that. But this should be a free market where central banks buy and sell gold too, not the ultrathin market of today which has speculators and hoarders bidding against each other for the current production of mines. The thirty-seven thousand metric tons held by central banks represents a thirty-year supply at today's production levels, enough to carry some clout in the market, too. But one need not expect any "dumping" of that metal by central banks with banks showing a preference for paper.

Even the mighty United States dollar was found wanting when it was pitted against gold in the monetary battles of 1968–1973. In all man's history, no single paper currency ever has proved to be better than gold, though some, like the post–World War II dollar and the British pound sterling through most of the nineteenth century, did prove to be as good as gold for a long period of time. But inflation has been eroding steadily the values of both the pound sterling and the dollar. Meanwhile, gold holds its value, desired by men, accepted even more avidly by women. Diamonds may be a girl's best friend, but most girls, also, find it easy to be intimate with gold in any form.

In February, 1974, *The Economist* added a postscript to the rush into gold which had started that January 1. *The Economist* is not a publication which gives much space to the merits of gold as an inflationary hedge, but it does have writers who know and understand causes and effects of inflation. In this particular article, the magazine warned that Britain faced an inflationary rate of above fifteen percent in 1974. Then, it said:

> That is an inflation rate which doubles prices in five years, multiplies prices by sixteen in the twenty years of many old people's retirement on fairly fixed incomes, and brings the value of a pound down to 0.006 pence during an average lifetime.

Stop and think that over for a moment. When this was written the pound was worth $2.32 on foreign-exchange markets. So a little arithmetic shows that a fifteen percent inflation repeated year after year over the seventy-year lifetime of an average person would bring the value of the British pound sterling down to *one tenth of a 1974 American cent.* Certainly, one would not expect such an inflationary rate to be repeated year after year without creating some form of political reaction in the hapless country in which it was occurring. But unfortunately, politicians everywhere have been showing little ability to contain inflation.

This was what the gold rush of 1974 was all about. Smart investors were deciding that it was wiser to be holding gold and gold-mining shares than paper currencies in the wild inflations which prevailed, and which promised to prevail for some while.

It is a bit ironic to consider that in that hectic month of January, 1974, the Committee of Twenty met in Rome to consider reform of the world monetary system. The Committee is an international grouping of nations affiliated with the International Monetary Fund. It has been given the task of formulating new rules and procedures to replace the defunct Bretton Woods system which died when the United States severed the link between gold and the dollar in August, 1971.

The Committee meeting was something of an anticlimax, for nobody who showed up for the conference really believed that the world was ready for creation of a new monetary system. Still, participants labored over the question of Special Drawing Rights, the monetary unit created earlier by the IMF as a supplement to gold in monetary affairs.

The SDR is really only a bookkeeping entry in IMF's books that is aimed at increasing world liquidity. It is like a chip in a poker game, a means of extending the money in the game without putting the actual cash on the table. It has no worth except between nations. Because it may be substituted for gold in international settlements, it is sometimes termed "paper gold."

Now, in Rome, the Committee of Twenty decided that the SDR should not be tied to gold but should have a valuation based upon average values in a package of key currencies. It sounds complicated, but it may not make much difference to anybody except those monetary experts who talked as if they really were eliminating gold from the monetary system in favor of this new currency cocktail. Nobody in the free market paid much attention.

Demand for gold soared along with the free-market price. That free market was saying quite convincingly that gold was going to be around for a long while yet as a store of value even if monetary experts did designate some standard of value for world currencies other than gold. If the free market says gold is worth $180 an ounce, then a dollar is worth 1/180th of an ounce of gold no matter what monetary authorities say to the contrary.

In 1974, those authorities were displaying more liking for gold in private than they were in public. When America severed the dollar's link to gold in August, 1971, the Federal Reserve Bank of New York and other central banks had about thirty-seven thousand tons of monetary gold stored in vaults. Even as bankers claimed that gold was finished as a monetary metal, they all clung tightly to their gold holdings.

When settlements had to be made between nations, those central banks first paid dollars or other foreign exchange, then SDRs, and only begrudgingly their gold. So little gold moved between banks that monetary specialists worried about the immobilization of all that liquidity represented by gold. In 1974, those central bankers still hoarded their thirty-seven thousand tons while wild inflation raged in most nations of the world.

Forty years earlier, in an editorial published April 27, 1934, the influential London *Times* had warned:

> As regards the alleged unsoundness of the gold standard system, history has shown that if currencies remain unlinked to gold for prolonged periods, the tendency is inevitable towards a true inflation (with its usual accompaniment of speculation, unmerited gains and losses, and general social injustices), and it is experience or fear of this inflation that has invariably driven countries back to gold after they tried the1 reply tbx to opts alternative path.

The gold standard has its weaknesses, and there are strong reasons why we are unlikely to see a pure gold standard again unless the world slips into fearful chaos. Still, that forty-year-old paragraph is cause for thought. Note the inflation which America has encountered since that fateful August 15, 1971, when President Nixon cut the link between the dollar and gold. In retrospect does that seem to have been a wise move? Wouldn't it have been better to have retained the link between gold and the dollar and to have increased the price of gold? Perhaps it would have been far better if this action had been taken in the mid-1960's long before the overseas claims against the United States dollar exceeded $100 billion.

Today, of course, there are many goldbugs who say monetary authorities should fix a new monetary price for the yellow metal at $150 or $200 or even $400 an ounce. This overlooks the fact that nobody, currently, even knows what the price should be, because there is no universal free market in the metal. Millions of the worlds peoples aren't even allowed to hold gold, and nobody knows how much pent-up demand may be dammed by restrictions.

Obviously, if restrictions everywhere were lifted it would push the gold price upward. How much would depend upon the strength and duration of that buying wave.

"Under a properly functioning gold standard, the official gold price must be higher than the price the current output would fetch if gold were used as only another commodity in industrial and personal use," explains W. J. Busschau, one of South Africa's most renowned authorities on gold.

Goldbugs should note, however, that as gold's price rises, industrial demand for the metal slackens accordingly.

Overall industrial use, after climbing in volume for years, leveled off, then showed a decline. In 1971, total world industrial usage reached 1,410 metric tons, declining to 1,300 tons in 1972, and to an estimated 1,000 tons in 1973. So industrial demand no longer takes all of the new gold being produced. New production (including sales from the Communist Bloc) totaled 1,300 tons in 1973, leaving 300 tons for hoarders and speculators, with minute quantities going into monetary reserves.

That decline in industrial use shows very clearly that the demand-price upsurge of 1974 was based largely upon monetary worries. People wanted a hedge against the fearsome erosion of currencies underway because of world-wide inflation. Gold was proving to be the financial haven which it always has been in difficult times.

Unquestionably, gold and gold-mining shares have proved their worth in recent years. One must beware, however, of thinking that any metal, or anything else for that matter, truly provides security. The only true security is that of the grave, and not many people want that.

But a sound dollar should not be an impossible dream. With such a currency Americans would not be listening to the tunes played on golden pipes.

Sometimes those tunes are funeral dirges for anyone not in gold, according to some investment letters. Buy gold, their song says. Democracy and capitalism are collapsing in the muck of inflation, and only gold offers any hope of financial salvation. There are reasons why gold has allure, but this isn't one of them. If we are sliding into anarchy, then gold-holders will need bazookas and machine-guns to cling to their wealth.

We haven't come to that yet, and gold does have much to offer the investor. Gold has been around for six or seven thousand years, sought by man, traded as a precious commodity. It retains its value

through war, natural disasters, and currency upheavals, often purchasing safety for refugees or food for the near-starving. It shines and
glitters, beckoning men to take possession, offering an illusionary
security to holders who find such illusions far more real than those
engendered by cellulose pulp currencies.

We are all creatures of illusion, victims of the biases and of the
prejudices which have been instilled in us by our experiences in life.
The durability of gold is one of those constants in a world which
increasingly seems to have fewer and fewer anchors amid strange
and violent crosscurrents. Gold is forever because man must have
something durable in this life even as he hopes for eternity in the
next.

Distrust of currencies only enhances the appeal of gold. Most
Americans would prefer a strong dollar to gold, for the American
wraps the flag about his dollars and views them with a patriotic fervor
which fades only when those dollars betray him at the cash register.
So he turns to gold or gold shares with much greater reluctance than
is the case with Europeans, where emotional ties are bound to wealth
and not to any particular currency in which that wealth happens to
be dressed. But the interest of American investors in gold stocks
shows that even he looks to gold after being burned by the fires of
inflation.

"Gold is so firmly entrenched in the thoughts and emotions of
mankind as the ultimate measure of value, and social and religious
traditions for holding gold are so strong in most parts of the world,
that the strong demand for gold to hoard will continue for at least
another generation. The retention of gold as a basic monetary commodity in some form seems equally secure," says J. K. Gustafson,
chairman of Homestake Mining Company.

Only another generation? Perhaps for this current hoarding upsurge. But, then, there may be another crisis and another and another. And gold is likely to be the first material thing millions of
people will think about in any of these crises. For man has never
found anything else which matches gold for retaining its value.

# INDEX

237